7 5.00

Śakti:
The Power in Tantra

A Scholarly Approach

Śakti:
The Power in Tantra

A Scholarly Approach

Pandit Rajmani Tigunait, Ph.D.

The Himalayan Institute Press
Honesdale, Pennsylvania, USA

The Himalayan Institute Press
RR 1, Box 405
Honesdale, PA 18431 USA

9 8 7 6 5 4 3 2 1

Cover design by Robert Aulicino

The paper used in this publication meets the minimum
requirements of the American National Standard for Information
Sciences—Permanence of Paper for Printed Library Materials,
ANSI Z39.48-1984.

Library of Congress Catalog Card Number: 98-70188

ISBN 0-89389-154-1

To my beloved teachers

Dr. Hari Shankar Tripathi
University of Allahabad, India
and
Dr. Wilhelm Halbfass
University of Pennsylvania, USA

CONTENTS

Introduction

IN THE SPRING OF 1982, soon after I completed my doctorate of philosophy from the University of Allahabad in India, my gurudeva, Sri Swami Rama of the Himalayas, began to say, "You should do another Ph.D. at one of the Western universities." At first I thought that he was joking. Later his tone of voice changed—it was no longer a remark but an order. One day he called me and said, "You are too obstinate. Why are you not listening to me?" I asked him why another Ph.D. was necessary. With a smile he said, "Because you have not gone through enough pain. If you do not do your Ph.D. here in America, I will send you to Europe and I will not see you until you have completed your Ph.D. there." Without further argument I joined the Asian Studies department of the University of Pennsylvania, and after completing the course work I began a dissertation on my favorite subject, Tāntrism.

In the process of writing the dissertation I was faced with a struggle between Eastern and Western approaches to research work. I was trained not to criticize previous masters and commentators, but instead to understand them with respect and faith. If their presentation did not make sense, I was trained to doubt my own ability to comprehend the subject and to make further attempts to study it by myself or with the help of learned teachers. I was taught to believe that a commentator represented the tradition of the scripture involved, and that whatever the commentator said was always in conformity with the original text. Since my first dissertation was written at an Indian university, these inherent tendencies did not become obstacles in obtaining my degree.

At the University of Pennsylvania I had to reorient my attitude toward an academic undertaking. I began my research work under the supervision of Professor Wilhelm Halbfass, an unmatched scholar of Indian philosophy. His kindness and wisdom gave me the strength and clarity to cultivate an analytical mind. Professors Ludo Rocher and George Cardona not only opened the door to a comparative study of different branches of philosophy, but also helped me think in a Western way without dismantling my Indian way of thinking. Professor Alexis Sanderson at All Souls' College, Oxford, taught me how to be precise and how to build a thesis on the basis of pure fact, and after spending some time with him I realized I did not need to abandon my faith in the practices described in the scriptures in order to be a scholar. Although I did not enjoy the hairsplitting logic and nitty-gritty details of academic work, I developed great respect for scholars when I realized they are conduits for transmitting knowledge without distortion or biased interpretation. This present work, *Śakti: The Power in Tantra,* is a direct derivative of my dissertation, *The Concept of Śakti in Lakṣmīdhara's Commentary on the Saundaryalaharī in Relation to Abhinavagupta's Tantrāloka.* For its existence I am greatly indebted to my professors at the University of Pennsylvania.

Since early childhood I have been drawn to Tāntric studies, especially to the role of Śakti, the Divine Mother, in the attainment of inner and outer prosperity. My doctoral work at the University of Allahabad and at the University of Pennsylvania gave me an opportunity to study the vast range of Tāntric literature in both the traditional and the Western analytical styles. These academic studies, coupled with experiential knowledge gained from the Tāntric adepts, enabled me to realize that the secret of success, be it worldly or spiritual, lies in the unfoldment of *śakti,* the power that lies dormant in the core of our being. All spiritual traditions, particularly Tantra, aim at awakening *śakti.* Without having an in-depth knowledge of the role of *śakti* in spiritual unfoldment, the study and practice of any spiritual tradition is like farming barren ground. That is why I undertook this endeavor, and that is why I am presenting the findings to serious students of Tantra and kuṇḍalinī yoga.

The liberal use of Sanskrit terms in this text may make it difficult reading for those who are not familiar with the language, but there is no other way to convey the meaning. I am confident that this work will brighten the horizon of Tāntric philosophy and practice and dismantle a number of misunderstandings surrounding Tantra, the worship of Śakti, and the yogic practices related to kuṇḍalinī and the cakras. After reading *Śakti: The Power in Tantra*, a student of Tantra will understand that Tāntric wisdom and practices are far more meaningful and profound than is commonly understood today. This text clarifies how Tāntric philosophy and practice unify the concepts of yantra, maṇḍala, mantra, cakra, kuṇḍalinī, and deities, as well as ritualistic and meditative practices. It explains the relationships between different branches of Tantra and tackles the controversial issues concerning the right- and left-handed Tāntric practices. But even though the subject matter compressed into this work focuses mainly on the concept of *śakti,* it opens the door on a vast range of Tāntric philosophy and practices. Each time I read the manuscript I feel inspired to undertake further Tāntric studies, especially those of a nonacademic nature. I hope all students of Tantra will be similarly inspired.

CHAPTER 1

A Brief Discussion of the Concept of *Śakti*

Parameters of This Study

The school of Śrīvidyā is the most important branch of Śākta Tāntrism because of its well-defined philosophical position, its literary standards, and its coherent doctrines. Historically, it seems to be the first branch of Śāktism to have been systematized. Unlike other branches of Śākta Tāntrism, the adherents of the Śrīvidyā school made an attempt to create a coherent structure of speculative ideas and give a philosophical explanation for the practices outlined in this system.[1]

The concept of *śakti* in Śrīvidyā is essential to the study of Indian religious thought because it elucidates the general problem of causality in Indian philosophy and religion. More specifically, this concept provides deeper insight into Śāktism, Śaivism, and other branches of Tantra. It holds an important place throughout Tāntric literature, especially in Śāktism and Śaivism. *Śakti* also appears in Pāñcarātra Āgama, Vyākaraṇa Āgama, Mīmāṃsā, Vedānta, and even Kāvya Śāstra, although the meaning varies. These sources express a variety of views on this concept; they introduce elaborations and often employ idiosyncratic terminology.

In spite of the key role of the concept of *śakti,* as yet there has been no comparative, philological study of *śakti's* role in two of the most prominent Tāntric systems, Śaivism and Śāktism. Neither has there been a focused study of *śakti* in Kaulācāra-dominated Kashmir Śaivism, in the Samayācāra-dominated Śrīvidyā tradition of Śāktism, nor in the writings of Lakṣmīdhara or Abhinavagupta, the outstanding exponents of Samayācāra and Kaulācāra philosophy, respectively.

Prominent Tāntric texts such as the *Netra Tantra* (hereafter cited as *NT*), *Svacchanda Tantra* (hereafter cited as *SVT*), *Mālinīvijaya Vārttika* (hereafter cited as *MVV*), *Śāradātilaka* (hereafter cited as *ST*), *Nityāṣoḍaśikārṇava* (hereafter cited as *NS*), and *Yoginī Hṛdaya* (hereafter cited as *YH*),[2] offer elaborate but incoherent discussions on the nature and function of *śakti.* All these texts present theories of mantra, yantra, *devatā, mātṛkā,* and *cakras* in the human body, and connect them to *śakti.* However, neither these Sanskrit texts nor modern studies of Tāntrism and Śāktism reveal how the basic concept of *śakti* originated; how the *pratibhā, rasa, dhvani,* and *camatkāra* of Sanskrit poetics, or the *pratibhā, paśyantī,* and *kālaśakti* of Vyākaraṇa Āgama were assimilated into the mainstream of Śāktism; how the mystical doctrines of mantra, *devatā,* yantra, and *mātṛkā,* were integrated into the concept of *śakti*; or whether the concept of *śakti* itself developed in an effort to synthesize these theories. There are elaborate discussions on the concept of *śakti*, but there is no conclusive definition of the term, even in Śāktism itself. Śākta scriptures launch directly into explanations of *śakti's* multilevel role in the attainment of spiritual/mystical experiences, leaving the definition of the term itself vague. Therefore, a study of the concept of *śakti* in Śrīvidyā and an explicit interpretation of the usage of the term in wider Śākta literature, as well as in the literature of Śaivism, Pāñcarātra Āgama, Vyākaraṇa Āgama, and Ṣaḍ Darśana, would be invaluable in illuminating the character of Śāktism in general.

To date, the field suffers from the following difficulties:

1. The historical and literary boundaries of Śāktism are not well defined;[3]

2. The relationship among the principal branches of Tāntric literature within which one can attempt to locate the *śakti*-related materials and pinpoint the precise view of *śakti* in a given tradition or subtradition of Tantra is not well understood;[4]

3. There is a scarcity of critically edited texts and, in most cases, a lack of thematic and comparative studies of available texts;

4. There are no clear and indisputably established criteria to define what characteristic(s) make a text Śākta, and especially what characteristics distinguish Śākta texts from the texts of monistic Śaiva Āgama;[5]

5. There is insufficient historical data about Śākta texts and the exact tradition or subtradition of Śāktism they represent; accurate criteria for distinguishing primary from secondary texts are also lacking;[6] and

6. There is no easy access to the secret oral interpretation, the province of initiates, of which a given text is a part.[7]

Because of these difficulties, the field of the present study is confined to the concept of *śakti* in the Śrīvidyā school. A survey of the literature shows that the most coherent and elaborate discussions of *śakti* occur in texts belonging to the Śrīvidyā, or Tripurā, school of Śāktism.[8] We further confined our study to one specific text—the *Saundaryalaharī*[9] (hereafter cited as *SL*), and again, more precisely, to one of its commentaries, the *Lakṣmīdharā*[10] (hereafter cited as *LD*) by Lakṣmīdhara. We made this selection not only because it enables us to avoid the difficulties enumerated above, but also because *LD* is a brilliant commentary on a well-known Śākta/Śrīvidyā text. The commentator is one of those scholars and staunch adherents of Tāntrism who clearly proclaims his affiliation with the exact branch of Śākta Tāntrism that he practices—the Samayācāra school of Śrīvidyā. To support his view that *SL* belongs to this school, Lakṣmīdhara draws on both Tāntric and Vedic sources. In the process, he outlines the general principles of Śāktism, and highlights what he believes to be the most important factors in the Samayācāra school of Śāktism.

Due to his affiliation with Śaṅkarācārya, which he establishes by writing a commentary on *SL*, a scripture attributed to Śaṅkarācārya, and his devotion to the Vedas, which is apparent in his commentary, Lakṣmīdhara's voice has become influential in the living tradition of Śaṅkarācārya. Although the historical origins of the primary text, *SL*, may be ambiguous, Lakṣmīdhara's influence on the Śrīvidyā tradition, especially the Samayācāra branch of it, is indisputable.

Using *LD* as a basis for this study permits us to concentrate on the general meaning of the term *śakti* in Śākta and non-Śākta traditions and its specific meaning (or the terms that replace it, such as *samayā, sādākhyā*, and *candrakalā*), in the Samayācāra school of the Śrīvidyā tradition. This text-based analysis of the term *śakti,* as well as the concept it conveys, can help us understand *śakti's* precise role, at least in one sect of Śāktism (i.e., Samayācāra), in contrast to the notions of *śakti* that we get from a collection of texts whose sectarian affiliation is often unclear. Furthermore, in recent years, a contemporary scholar, Douglas Renfrew Brooks, has undertaken a thorough study of Bhāskararāya's commentary on the *Tripurā Upaniṣad.* Using this text as a base, he arrives at an understanding of Śrīvidyā in general, and the Kaula aspect in particular. This enables us to focus on Lakṣmīdhara, who propounds Samayācāra, the counterpart of Kaula.

The Concept of Śakti in Early Literature

In order to clarify the notion of *śakti* in Lakṣmīdhara's writings and to place his approach in philological and historical perspective, it is necessary to examine how the word *śakti* has been used in early literature, such as the Vedas, Upaniṣads, and Purāṇas, as well as in later Indian philosophical literature. As Gerald J. Larson observes, the term *śakti* "is used in a bewildering variety of ways ranging from its use as a way of expressing the ultimate creative power of being itself, all the way to its use as a way of expressing the capacity of words to convey meaning *(artha).*"[11] Tracing its origin from the verb root *śak* (or *śakḷ śaktau),* the word *śakti* simply means "the power to produce an effect, capability, efficiency or potency." However, the meaning derived from this etymology is too vague and general to describe the use of the word *śakti* in the wide variety of contexts in which it is employed. According to Sāyaṇa's belief, in the *Ṛgveda* this word occurs in the sense of "capacity";[12] as *vajra*, the thunderbolt; *karma*, the power to act;[13] and as the proper name of a type of weapon.[14] In each of these instances, the term means not a goddess but a force.

It is only when the term *śakti* becomes identified either

directly or by implication with Aditi, Gñā, Sarasvatī, and *vāk* in the Saṃhitās and with Umā Haimavatī, *prakṛti,* and *māyā* in the Upaniṣads, that *śakti* finds a significant place in ancient Indian mythology and philosophy. The earliest clear statement employing the term *śakti* to describe the nature of her relationship to the Absolute Truth appears in *Śvetāśvatara Upaniṣad*: *śakti* is said to be *vividhā*, manifold; *jñāna*, knowledge; *bala*, power; and *kriyā*, the capacity to act; these characteristics are intrinsic to her.[15]

Due to its varied and incoherent subject matter, Paurāṇic literature cannot be treated as a ground for delineating a unified notion of *śakti*, nor can it be entirely disregarded. This is especially true for Purāṇas such as *Mārkaṇḍeya*, *Brahmāṇḍa*, *Brahmavaivarta*, *Nārada*, *Devībhāgavata*, and *Kālikā*, which are extensively Tāntric.[16] For example, in the *Durgā Saptaśatī* (hereafter cited as *DS*), which is a portion of *Mārkaṇḍeya Purāṇa*, Śakti is the intrinsic power not only of *brahman,* the absolute reality, but also of all the gods, i.e., Brahmā, Viṣṇu, Śiva, Indra, Agni, Varuṇa, Yama, etc. Due to her association with these gods, she appears in a variety of forms and thus is given different names.[17] Almost without exception in Paurāṇic literature—for example, in *DS* and "Lalitopākhyāna" of the *Brahmāṇḍa Purāṇa* (hereafter cited as *BP-L*)—Śakti is accompanied by a god, who is her consort, and in that case, her name, form, weapon, and functions correspond to those of the god.[18] Quasi-etymologically, the basic characteristics ascribed to Śakti are *aiśvarya*, lordship, and *parākrama*, valor.[19] In the Purāṇas she is said to be identical to *brahman* ("*brahmamayī*" or "*brahmātmaka rasātmikā*");[20] she is unmanifest, absolute *prakṛti* ("*avyākṛtā paramā prakṛti*"). Śakti, as *prakṛti*, is the cause of the whole universe; in fact, the manifest world is not separate from her.[21] As transcendental Reality ("*parā parāṇāṃ paramā parameśvarī,*"

DS 1:62), she is indescribable ("*unuccāryā*," *DS* 1:55) and unthinkable ("*rūpam acintyam*," *DS* 4:5). At the same time, the entire universe, including its hierarchy of deities, emerges from her and ultimately dissolves into her.[22] It should be noted that in these Paurāṇic sources, *śakti* is treated both as a goddess and as a philosophical category. For example, in many of the *stotras* in *DS*[23] and *BP-L*,[24] she is described as a deity who was born (or at least emerged) in a particular time and place, but at the same time, she is also said to be formless and transcendent.

The Concept of Śakti in Various Philosophical Schools

When we turn our attention to the uses of the term *śakti* in various philosophical schools—such as Mīmāṃsā, Nyāya, Advaita Vedānta, Vyākaraṇa Āgama, and Kāvya Śāstra—we find that one of her roles—that of deity—vanishes. Let us take, for example, references to *śakti* in Mīmāṃsā. Prabhākara's group of Mīmāṃsakas are also referred to as Śaktivādins, those who adhere to the theory of *śakti*. According to the Śaktivādins, everything in the world possesses some sort of *śakti*, which cannot be perceived although it can be inferred. Mīmāṃsakas argue that although fire produces heat, under the influence of certain mantras the same fire fails to produce that effect, although in both cases, the fire as such remains the same. This indicates that there must be something in the presence of which the fire blazes, whereas in its absence it cannot burn:

> To this imperceptible something, Prabhākara gives the name of 'Shakti' or Force. In eternal things, it is eternal, and in transient things it is brought into existence along with them. It differs from 'samskāra' in that this latter is transient in eternal things also.[25]

The concept of *apūrva* as held by Mīmāṃsakas parallels this concept of *śakti*. In the words of Gaṅgānātha Jhā:

> By Kumārila's view the *apūrva* is "a capability in the principal action, or in the agent, which did not exist prior to the performance of the action, and whose existence is proved by the authority of the scriptures." Before the Sacrifices laid down as leading to heaven are performed, there is in the Sacrifices themselves, in the first place, an incapability of leading to heaven, and in the second place, in the agent, that of attaining to heaven. Both these *incapacities* are set aside by the performance of the sacrifice; and this performance creates also a positive force or capacity, by virtue of which heaven is attained; and to this latter force or capability we give the name *apūrva*.[26]

The *Naiyāyikas*, on the other hand, refute *śakti* as a special category of power or causal efficiency.[27] According to Śaṅkarasvāmin:

> The causal efficacy *(Śakti)* which some postulate to explain causation, is nothing more than the collection of causal factors *(sāmagrī)* sufficient to produce the effect. Likewise, lack of causal efficacy *(aśakti)* is merely the absence of one of the necessary conditions for production. However, once an effect is produced, it can remain in existence even though its *sāmagrī-śakti* disappears.[28]

Karl H. Potter summarizes the Naiyāyika opinion about the theory of causality, explaining how Naiyāyikas dismiss the concept of *śakti* as proposed by Śaktivādins (Mīmāṃsakas). However, in his analysis of Udayana's *Nyāyakusumāñjali*, Potter states:

> Udayana becomes very permissive at this point; in fact, he goes so far as to say that if one wants to he *can* admit an additional category of causality *(kāraṇatva)*, and that this new category may be considered to be the old causal efficacy under another name.[29]

On this issue George Chemparathy writes, "The Naiyāyikas, too, admit potency *(śaktiḥ)*, but only in the sense of causality *(kāraṇatvam)*."[30] The main issue in a long chain of debates between the Mīmāṃsakas and the Naiyāyikas is whether *śakti*, the unseen latent potency, alone is the main cause behind an effect or whether several conditions jointly produce the effect. Mīmāṃsakas hold the prior view and the Naiyāyikas, the latter. However, in order to explain how different conditions combine to aid different causes in producing an effect, Naiyāyikas propose the theory of *adṛṣṭa*, which is somewhat similar to the concept of *apūrva* held by the Mīmāṃsakas.[31] Candramati's *Daśapadārtha Śāstra*, an early Vaiśeṣika text dating from A.D. 640, also mentions *śakti* as one of the ten *padārthas.*[32] Here *śakti* means the potentiality that allows things to function.

Śaṅkarācārya, a strict Advaita Vedāntin, proposes Brahma Advaitavāda, the doctrine that there is only one reality *(brahman)*, without a second. However he refers to *śakti* as the sole factor behind the creation or manifestation of the universe. For example, in *Brahmasūtra-Bhāsya* (hereafter cited as *BS-B*) Śaṅkarācārya writes: "Without Her, the creatorship of the great lord Parameśvāra cannot be explained."[33]

In this particular passage, Śaṅkarācārya, commenting on *sūtra*, "*tad-adhīnatvād arthavat*" (1:4.3), attempts to prove that although it is *śakti* through which *parameśvāra* creates the world, she has no existence independent of *parameśvāra, brahman.* In his philosophy, *śakti*—variously known as *māyā, avidyā, prakṛti,* or *jaḍaśakti* is an impenetrable mystery—is responsible for the evolution of the universe, but she, herself, cannot be said to be either existent or nonexistent. As Śaṅkarācārya states:

> Brahman is definitely endowed with all powers, Śaktis. . . . Although Brahman is the only Reality, due to its union with

> unique and numberless powers, multifarious effects (the universe of multiple objects) evolve from Brahman, just as from milk (evolves yogurt, butter, etc.).[34]

In these two passages, as well as in many others,[35] Śaṅkarācārya uses the term *śakti* as well as the concept, but leaves its role and metaphysical status ambiguous in relation to *brahman.*

In these references, however, Śaṅkarācārya is unwilling to accept *śakti* as an entirely independent reality, for he will then have to explain *śakti's* nature as well as its relationship to *brahman.* If he is to explain the existence of the empirical world, he cannot completely deny the existence of *śakti*, but if he is to maintain the integrity of his nondualistic model, he cannot accept it as an independent reality either. To overcome this dilemma, Śaṅkarācārya modifies the basic doctrine of causation—Satkāryavāda, the theory according to which an effect must exist in its cause prior to its manifestation. However, he modifies this theory by claiming that the effect is but an illusory appearance, having its cause in that which already exists. Thus, he still adheres to the theory of Satkāryavāda, although not in the sense of Pariṇāmavāda as held by Sāṅkhya, according to which the actual effect comes from the preexisting actual cause, but rather in the sense of Vivartavāda, the theory of illusory effect appearing from a real cause.[36]

Furthermore, without giving a concrete definition, Śaṅkarācārya uses the term *śakti* interchangeably with *māyāśakti, avidyā*, and occasionally even *prakṛti.* In expounding his main thesis, Brahmādvaitavāda, he devotes more space to discussions of the unreal nature of *śakti*, *māyaśakti*, and other synonymous terms than he does to discussions about *brahman*,[37] a fact which leads adherents of other schools to refer to him as a Māyāvādin rather than a Brahmavādin.

Vyākaraṇa Āgama, on the other hand, not only acknowledges *śakti*, but also assigns it a higher position than do the Vedantins. In Advaita Vedānta, the absolute reality, *brahman*, is devoid of all qualities and distinctions; somehow through a mysterious union with *māyāśakti* (which is substantially neither real nor unreal and is thus simply indescribable), the world of multiplicity evolves.

In Vyākaraṇa Āgama, *śabdabrahman*, the eternal *verbum* is the Supreme Reality. During the evolution of the objective world, *avidyā*, which is one of the powers of *śabdabrahman*, veils the unitary nature of *śabdabrahman* and projects the plurality of the phenomenal world. However, in order to prevent several projections from occurring simultaneously, Bhartṛhari, the foremost philosopher of Vyākaraṇa Āgama, posits the concept of *kālaśakti*. In regard to *kālaśakti*, Gaurinath Sastri states:

> The *kālaśakti* of the grammarian is a Power of the Eternal Verbum by virtue of which the latter is described as the Powerful. It should be noted, however, that though the Eternal Verbum and *kālaśakti* stand in the relation of a substance and an attribute, yet they are essentially identical and not different from each other. In fact the two may be regarded as two moments or aspects of one and the same Reality. The difference between the Eternal Verbum and *kālaśakti* and, for the matter of that, all *Kalās*, is a mere appearance, an intellectual fiction, without a foundation in reality.[38]

There are many other powers of *śabdabrahman* known as *kalās*, but all are controlled *(sarvāḥ paratantrāḥ)* by this unrestricted sovereign power known as *kālaśakti (kālākhyena svātantryeṇa)*. Due to the control of *kālaśakti* over other *śaktis (kalās)*, different projections or transformations occur sequentially rather than simultaneously.[39] *Kālaśakti*, as we will see, plays an important role in the doctrine of Śrīvidyā.

In Indian poetics (Kāvya Śāstra), the term *śakti* is used in an entirely different sense. In his work, *Kāvyaprakāśa*, Mammaṭa defines *śakti* as "unique potential identical to the seed of the essence of a poet, *kavitva bījarūpa saṃskāra viśeṣa*."[40] While considering *dhvani*, suggestion, to be the heart *(ātman)* of Kāvya, Ānandavardhana relates *dhvani* to *pratibhā*, which signifies the supernatural *(alokasāmānya)* intuitive power that enables the word and meaning of the word to flash in the mind of the poet or the reader.[41] In Kāvya Śāstra, the term *pratibhā* refers to *śakti*.[42]

In systems other than Śāktism and Śaivism, the concept of *śakti* was developed in an effort to solve the problem of causality. Within their specific philosophical orientations, these other systems assign *śakti* just enough importance to logically explain causality without compromising the supremacy of their main doctrine (which may be *apūrva, adṛṣṭa, brahman,* or *śabdabrahman).* While in other systems *śakti* remains subservient, in Śāktism the situation is reversed: *śakti* becomes the major theme, the very center or even the only truth, and other concepts are secondary.

In literature that is not devoted exclusively to philosophy, such as the Purāṇas and Tantras, *śakti* assumes various names and forms. According to Paurāṇic and Tāntric sources,[43] she appears in personified form primarily in two circumstances: to reward her devotees or to punish demons. Either before or after her appearance, devotees recite hymns of praise *(stotras)* in her honor, which elucidate both her personified and philosophical/metaphysical nature.[44] Thus, for the sake of study, we can say that there are two facets of *śakti*: the goddess and the philosophical category. In the *stotras*, the two facets are inseparably mixed, forming a single identity. As a goddess, she assumes multiple forms that are beautiful (e.g., Kāmeśvarī or Lalitā), terrifying (e.g., Kālī), heroic (e.g., Durgā or Caṇḍikā), and even inhuman (e.g., Vārāhī and Nārasiṃhī). This facet constitutes the mythological and theological aspect of Śāktism whereas the second facet, i.e., *śakti* as philosophical category, constitutes the speculative aspect of Śāktism.

The Concept of Śakti in Contemporary Works

When we turn our attention to a focused study of *śakti* in the writings of contemporary scholars, we find a number of works and articles addressing general problems of Śāktism. However, they rarely examine the precise meaning or role of *śakti* within a given text or tradition, nor do they compare and contrast this concept in other texts or traditions. Sudhendu Kumar Das, in his work *Śakti or Divine Power,*[45] focuses his discussion on the concept of *śakti* in Kashmir Śaivism and Vīra Śaivism, although he does attempt to trace the origin of *śakti* in the Vedas and Upaniṣads. Although he cites Śaivite texts, his study is neither objective nor analytical from an historical or philosophical standpoint. However, he does conduct a thorough survey of the literature and draws his material from a wealth of textual sources.

Jadunath Sinha's *Shakta Monism*[46] addresses topics such as *śiva, kulakuṇḍalinī, śakti, nāda, bindu,* creation, the individual self, and so on. Unfortunately, he simply gathers and translates quotations from a number of sources (such as the Upaniṣads, Purāṇas, and the texts of Śaiva and Śākta Āgama) without raising any questions and, thus, without stating any points of distinction. Pushpendra Kumar, on the other hand, focuses mainly on the different forms of *śakti* in the Purāṇas in his book *Śakti Cult in Ancient India.* Evaluating the merit of this work, David Kinsley writes that this book, "though lacking in interpretive depth, provides a wealth of textual sources concerned with goddess worship and goddess mythology in the medieval period."[47]

The writings of Gopinath Kaviraj[48] are considered to be some of the most authoritative works not only in the area of Śāktism but also in all of Tāntrism. However, he focuses mainly on philosophy and does not cite his sources. In an attempt to construct the philosophy of Śāktism, Kaviraj apparently fuses ideas that are unique to subschools of Śāktism or Śaivism and presents them as general concepts. Without any serious examination of his assumptions, subsequent Indian writers[49] such as Kailāśa Pati Miśra, Baladeva Upādhyāya, Kamalakar Mishra, and Sangam Lal Pandey used his work as a model and thus produced general works on Śāktism that are duplicative and contain very little original material.

Hindu Tantrism (hereafter cited as *HT*) by Gupta, Hoens, and Goudriaan, and *Hindu Tantric and Śākta Literature* (hereafter cited as *HTS*) by Gupta and Goudriaan, although general works on Śāktism, are of great merit. These studies cover a vast range of Śākta history, philosophy, and religious practices; they also provide literature surveys and scrutinize some important Śākta texts. *Myth, Cult and Symbols in Śākta Hinduism* by Wendell Charles Beane and *The Śāktas: An Introductory and Comparative Study* by Ernest A. Payne are comparative studies that give special attention to the manifestion of Śakti as Kālī and Durgā.[50] Although the historical account of Śāktism given by scholars N. N. Bhattacharyya[51] and D. C Sircar[52] is thorough, their remarks, according to Teun Goudriaan, "are necessarily speculative, not based upon a direct study of Sanskrit sources . . . and the same can be said of the publication by the well-known epigraphist and historian D. C. Sircar."[53]

Other works of great value are those of Douglas Renfrew Brooks, Mark S. G. Dyczkowski, Paul Eduardo Muller-

Ortega, André Padoux, and Jaideva Singh.[54] Except for Brooks, these scholars focus primarily on Śaivism, and it is in that context that they study the nature of *śakti*. The works by Brooks are the only ones that focus exclusively on the Śrīvidyā school of Tāntrism. His doctoral dissertation, "The Śrīvidyā School of Śākta Tāntrism: A Study of the Texts and Contexts of the Living Traditions in South India" (hereafter cited as "Śrīvidyā School"), traces the historical development of Śrīvidyā from the earliest available sources in Sanskrit and Tamil. It also examines the historical and theological materials as they are intrepreted by the followers of Śrīvidyā in South India.

In another work, *The Secret of the Three Cities: An Introduction to Hindu Śākta Tantrism* (hereafter cited as *Three Cities*), Brooks provides a general introduction to Śākta Tāntrism and the tradition of Śrīvidyā; he undertakes a detailed analysis of Śrīvidyā, using Bhāskararāya's commentary on the *Tripurā Upaniṣad* as a basis. Because Bhāskararāya, although a Vedic Brahmin, was a strong proponent of Tāntrism, especially the Kaula branch of Śākta Śrīvidyā Tāntrism, Brooks has ample opportunity to highlight the Kaulācāra school of Śrīvidyā, an opportunity that he uses to full advantage. However, because Bhāskararāya was a prolific writer of independent works as well as a commentator on several Tāntric texts that do not belong exclusively to the Kaula aspect of Śrīvidyā, his writings cover a vast range of materials on Śākta, especially the Śrīvidyā tradition. Thus, while translating and analyzing Bhāskararāya's commentary on *Tripurā Upaniṣad*, Brooks naturally discusses the characteristics of Hindu Tāntrism in general and Śākta Tāntrism in particular, pointing out some of the distinctions between the Kaulācāra and Samayācāra divisions of the Śrīvidyā school. However, like Bhāskararāya, he remains focused on the Kaula school.

In his latest book, *Auspicious Wisdom: The Texts and Traditions of Śrīvidyā Śākta Tantrism in South India* (hereafter cited as *Auspicious Wisdom*), Brooks continues exploring the ideas he presented in *Three Cities*, elaborating on the Kaula aspect of the Śrīvidya tradition. However, this recent work does not focus solely on Bhāskararāya and his commentary on *Tripurā Upaniṣad*, but draws on a wider range of sources, thus providing a more comprehensive view of the history, philosophy, and practice of Śrīvidyā.

Within the confines of the present study, it is neither possible nor relevant to conduct an examination of all these issues; therefore, we have chosen to focus on the concept of *śakti* in the writings of Lakṣmīdhara, a brilliant commentator on the *SL*. Because Kashmir Śaivism is allied to the Śrīvidyā school of Śāktism to which the *SL* belongs, we have elected to include the concept of *śakti* as expounded by Abhinavagupta, the greatest exponent of the Trika school of Kashmir Śaivism. Because Abhinavagupta's writing is more comprehensive than Lakṣmīdhara's, only his *Tantrāloka* (hereafter cited as *TĀ*)[55] has been selected for this study.

The present work, however, is not intended to be a comparative study of Lakṣmīdhara and Abhinavagupta. The purpose of examining Abhinavagupta's *TĀ* alongside Lakṣmīdhara's commentary is to provide a more stable context, a context which makes it possible to examine Lakṣmīdhara's notion of *śakti* with less historical and philosophical ambiguity. Because several relatively satisfactory studies have already been done on Abhinavagupta, relevant historical facts and, to some extent, philosophical doctrines have already been outlined.[56] Thus, the inclusion of *TĀ* helps to establish a boundary within the vast body of Śaiva Āgama, while still permitting the exploration of the historical and philological connections of Lakṣmīdhara's concept of *śakti* in the as-yet-unexplored Śākta literature.

Before we begin our examination of Lakṣmīdhara's view of *śakti*, it is important to establish a general understanding of this concept in the wider context of Śāktism. Only then can we explore its specific implication in the Samayācāra school of Śāktism expounded by Lakṣmīdhara.

CHAPTER 2

Lakṣmīdhara's Commentary in a Wider Context

The Origin and Historical Development of Tantra

The *SL*, which is generally attributed to Śaṅkarācārya, glorifies and exalts Tripurasundarī, a purely Tāntric goddess who is virtually unknown in popular Hinduism. This goddess is worshipped or meditated upon in the Śrīvidyā tradition, a subbranch of Śākta Tāntrism.[1] In the absence of its commentaries, *SL* can hardly be treated as a Tāntric text, as it is basically a *stotra* text, consisting of devotional verses dedicated to the goddess Tripurasundarī. Many other *stotra* texts of this kind, such as *Subhagodaya* (hereafter cited as *SU*), *Tripurasundarī Mahimna Stotra*, *Paraśambhu Mahimna Stava*, *Pañcastavī*, *Saubhāgyasudhodaya*, *Cidvilāsastava*, and *Subhagodayavāsanā,* contain more significant Tāntric materials than does *SL* itself. Beginning with Lakṣmīdhara, the commentaries on *SL* highlight, expound, and stretch the Tāntric elements to such a degree that if the text and the commentaries are treated as an integral work, this becomes one of the most prominent texts of Śākta Tāntrism. It is the weight of these commentaries, along with the popularity of its purported author, that makes *SL* the most influential Tāntric text among scholars and practicing Śrīvidyā adherents alike.

The history of the Śrīvidyā tradition must be studied within the historical context of the origin and development of the main body of Tāntrism. Further, in order to do justice to the study of *SL* and its commentaries, especially Lakṣmīdhara's, we must locate their historical niches within the broad spectrum of the Śrīvidyā school of Śākta Tāntrism. However, the vast and variegated nature of Tāntric literature, as well as the popular beliefs and practices of present-day adherents, make it extremely difficult to accurately define Tantra, which, in turn, makes it difficult to accurately locate the Śrīvidyā tradition within the context of Tāntrism.

One of the main difficulties in defining Tantra, as Padoux observes, arises from the sensational connotations that the term has acquired.[2] In the beginning of the century, Tantra was believed to be a conglomeration of bizarre and unconventional religious disciplines consisting of sorcery, exorcism, and orgiastic practices. According to early scholars, it occupied an obscure niche within the Hindu, Buddhist, and Jaina religions of India. But as research progressed, a broader range of Tāntric material came to light that supported the view that Tantra, far from being an unconventional religious practice limited to a small group, was actually a common element in Hinduism, Buddhism, and Jainism. However, because many Tāntric texts are still in manuscript form and thus have yet to be edited and studied, general assertions about Tāntrism necessarily remain inconclusive. The problem becomes more complex because not every text labeled "Tantra" is actually Tāntric and not every text containing Tāntric materials carries the word "Tantra" in its title. As Padoux writes, "There are so many gaps in this field of research that all definite assertions must be avoided."[3]

Although in the past fifty years many studies have been conducted in the field of Tāntrism, the volume and breadth of Tāntric literature is so enormous and its effect on Indian religion and spirituality so great that this field is still in its infancy. The definitions offered by scholars to date do not give a comprehensive understanding of Tāntrism but rather provide only a general idea of what Tāntrism is about. In Goudriaan's opinion, the word "Tāntrism":

> . . . is mainly used in two meanings. In a wider sense, Tantrism or Tantric stands for a collection of practices and symbols of a ritualistic, sometimes magical character. . . . In a more restricted sense, it denotes a system existing in many variations, of rituals full of symbolism, predominately—but by no means exclusively—Śakta, promulgated along "schools" (saṃpradāya) and lines of succession (paraṃparā) by spiritual adepts or gurus. What they teach is subsumed under the term sādhanā, i.e., the road to spiritual emancipation or to dominance by means of kuṇḍalinī yoga and other psychosomatic experiences.[4]

Even though Tāntrism does not hold the Vedas in high regard, and even frequently condemns them, it still embraces a number of Vedic theories and practices. Ritual worship and meditative techniques associated with numerous deities from the Vedas, Brāhmaṇas, and Purāṇas appear in this literature, although they are presented in a Tāntric manner. While emphasizing the practices related to yantras, *maṇḍalas,* and mantras, Tāntric texts also include discussions on such diverse topics as the nature of absolute reality; the process of evolution, maintenance, and dissolution of the universe; the evolution of sound or word in four progressive states—*parā, paśyantī, madhyamā,* and *vaikharī;* the different centers of consciousness in the human body known as *cakras;* methods of awakening the *kuṇḍalinī śakti,* the primordial force that lies dormant in the human body; practices for propitiating different gods or goddesses at different *cakras;* and *pañca-makāras* and *ṣaṭkarma sādhanā (māraṇa, mohana, vaśī-karaṇa, stambhana, vidveṣaṇa,* and *uccāṭana).*[5] This vast literature even contains instructions on building temples and consecrating images of the deities, as well as information on places of pilgrimage and the exact ritualistic or meditative practices to be performed there. Practices concerning the application of herbs, gems, minerals, and astrology are also brought into the fold of Tāntric spirituality.

In contemporary Indian languages, such as Hindi, Tamil, Marathi, or Bengali, the term "Tantra" connotes black magic, spiritual or religious practices involving sex, and manipulation of psychic powers or evil spirits to seduce women, defeat or injure opponents, or mesmerize others. Even though Tantra usually carries a negative connotation among the masses of India, Brooks observes:

> The word "Tantra" . . . is frequently used to conjure notions of effective black magic, illicit sexuality, and immoral behavior. It is also clear, however, that Tantrics are considered "powerful" people. Recently, a popular movement in modern India links the cure of "sexual problems" experienced by married couples to specialists who openly call themselves "Tantrics." Thus, the terms "Tantra" and "Tantric" gain a more positive set of connotations but retain their popular associations with eroticism, alchemy, and magic. The multiple meanings of the term and its historical uses present a historical set of interpretive problems. There is no way, it seems, we can escape the fact that the term "Tantra" is charged with emotional power and controversy.[6]

That Tantra reached the West shrouded with the same or even more elaborate connotations is evidenced in the writings of Omar V. Garrison, Robert K. Moffet, and Marcus Allen.[7] In fact, these negative implications, as well as those which Brooks calls "positive connotations" are neither new to contemporary communities nor totally baseless. Even the Tāntric texts in Sanskrit, whose chronology remains obscure, are replete with all sorts of practices—positive, negative, socially acceptable or unacceptable, philosophically sound or rooted in superstition.

Here, for the sake of remaining focused and gaining a better understanding of the relationship among the principal branches of Tantra, we need only to identify "a standard Tāntric sādhanā," (if possible). In this context, the term "standard Tāntric sādhanā" means the practices that are described in acclaimed Tāntric texts, such as *Śāradātilaka*, *Kulārṇava Tantra*, *Nityāṣoḍaśikārṇava*, *Yoginīhṛdaya*, *Tantrarāja Tantra*, *Netra Tantra*, and *Tantrāloka*, and which have their basis in philosophy and are upheld by a recognized tradition.

"Standard Tāntric sādhanā,"[8] as Sanjukta Gupta says, "consists of two parts: ritual worship (pūjā) and meditation (yoga)."[9] But these two constituents are also found in almost all existing religions in India today, and the practices of idol worship; occultism; visiting holy shrines; and propitiating god(s) through the means of mantra, yantra, pictures and icons, are found in almost all denominations. Due to these shared characteristics, it is difficult to distinguish Tāntrism from existing popular faiths. In fact, Tāntric elements are found in Jainism, Buddhism, and almost all the offshoots of Hinduism, such as Vaiṣṇavism, Śaivism, Śāktism, and so on.[10] Furthermore, adherents of Tāntrism neither claim to follow Tāntrism as an independent religion, nor renounce the religion in which they were born and raised. Due to the intermingled nature of Tāntric and non-Tāntric traditions, Agehananda Bharati goes so far as to say:

> It is not advisable to try to list here the differences between tantric and non-tantric forms of Hinduism and Buddhism, simply because they are not of a philosophical order. In other words, there is nothing in Buddhist and Hindu tantric philosophy which is not wholly contained in some non-tantric school of either. . . . It is on the ritualistic or contemplatively methodical side that differences arise, and these are indeed fundamental. In a similar fashion the non-tantric monists or Śaivites (Śaṃkarācārya and his school, or the Southern Śiva-Āgama teachers), pronounce and emphasize the oneness of Śiva and Śakti, and so do the Hindu tantric Śākta schools—they do not add any speculative innovation to their non-tantric antecedents—but they do different things and practice different *sādhanā* (contemplative exercises). There is thus no difference between tantric and non-tantric philosophy, a speculative eclecticism is pervasive; there is all the difference in the practical, the *sādhanā*-part of tantrism.[11]

Bharati's claims that "there is nothing in Buddhist and Hindu tantric philosophy which is not wholly contained in some non-tantric school of either" and "there is all the difference in the practical, the *sādhanā*-part of tantrism" seem to be overgeneralized and may be only partially true. If we take into account such texts as *Śāradātilaka*, *Kulārṇava Tantra*, *Nityāṣoḍaśikārṇava*, *Yoginīhṛdaya*, *Tantrarāja Tantra*, *Netra Tantra*, and *Tantrāloka*, which are clearly identified as Tāntric, we cannot agree that the philosophical contents of these texts are contained in non-Tāntric schools and the texts belonging to them. And even the *sādhanā*—whether the contemplative exercises or the rituals—described in these texts have their exact parallels in some non-Tāntric texts.

Furthermore, at present, we have no standard criteria for defining exactly which texts can be called purely Tāntric and which non-Tāntric within a given division or subdivision of Hinduism. Tāntric ideas are scattered throughout non-Tāntric sources. For example, traces of the philosophical ideas and ritual practices found in Śaiva Tāntric texts can be seen in the Vedas, the Brāhmaṇas, and the Upaniṣads. In the Purāṇas, we find many of those ideas further elaborated, but whether the Purāṇas should be treated as texts belonging to the Tāntric or non-Tāntric part of Hinduism is still controversial.

On the other hand, at least for the past millennia, there have been authors and practitioners who claimed that their works or practices are Tāntric, although in most cases without making a sharp distinction between themselves and their non-Tāntric counterparts. Furthermore, a number of praiseworthy studies have been conducted in the field of Tāntrism in the twentieth century although, again, without defining the exact boundary of Tāntrism. Thus, in spite of all these ambiguities, there still seems to be a general, though unspoken, consensus regarding what constitutes Tantra. It is on the basis of this unspoken consensus that scholars commonly use the terms Buddhism or Bauddha Tāntrism (or the more frequently used terms Tāntric Buddhism or Buddhist Tāntrism), Jainism or Jaina Tāntrism, and Hinduism or Hindu Tāntrism.

The question of which philosophical theories and religious or spiritual practices distinguish Tāntrism from other philosophical or religious schools of India remains unanswered. Goudriaan states that "the decision at what point a text or sect begins to be called 'Tāntric' is very difficult. The traditions of the relevant groups sometimes contradict each other."[12] At the very beginning of *HTS*, he defines Tantra as "a systematic quest for salvation or for spiritual excellence by realizing and fostering the bipolar, bisexual divinity within one's own body." According to him, this quest for salvation can be accomplished by such specific means as practicing *kuṇḍalinī* yoga, reciting mantras, worshipping the deity in a yantra, and related practices. He also states that such practices constitute the nature and characteristics of Tāntrism.

Attempting to clarify some of these issues by turning to the origin and history of Tantra only serves to highlight the nature of the problem. N. N. Bhattacharyya[13] and B. Bhattacharya[14] claim an extreme antiquity for Tāntrism on the basis of archaeological findings in the Indus valley that resemble *liṅga, yoni,* and a human in a yogic (sitting) pose, all common elements of Tāntrism. Based on this oversimplification and gross generalization of what constitutes Tāntrism, Śāktism, and Śaivism, they attempt to prove the antiquity and prevalence of Tāntrism not only in India, but also in Asia Minor, Syria, Egypt, and several other countries bordering on the Mediterranean.[15] Goudriaan undercuts these hypotheses[16] and proposes that "the safest way to assess the *terminus ante quem* of the crystallization of Tāntrism into a system is to ascertain the date of the oldest Tāntric texts."[17] However, dating the Tāntric texts is not an easy task; the history of Tāntrism proposed by early scholars is constantly under dispute. For example, Farquhar and Eliade believe that Tantra existed in a well-developed form by the sixth century A.D., but this position is now challenged by Goudriaan.[18] At this stage, we can only agree with Padoux that because of the number and magnitude of the gaps in this field:

> . . . all definite assertions must be avoided. . . . Tantric Hinduism would have emerged progressively through a process of ongoing evolution over an extended period of time, granted, however, that we know nothing as to the nature and modalities of the process, and that we do not know how and when it started.[19]

The history of Tāntrism can safely be established only after determining which portion of the literature (e.g., Pāñcarātra Āgama, Śaiva Āgama, *The Atharvaveda*,[20] *Brahmāṇḍa Purāṇa* and *Mārkaṇḍeya Purāṇa*, and texts from Jaina and Buddhist Tantra) to include within the fold of Tāntrism. If Tantra includes Pāñcarātra Āgama and Śaiva Āgama, then the existence of Tāntric literature can be traced to the fifth century A.D., which is also the time when Buddhist Tāntric texts began to appear.[21] Unfortunately, neither of these sources establish a chronology for the origin and development of Tāntrism. However, the relative antiquity of Tāntrism can be postulated from the fact that Hindu, Jaina, and Buddhist Tāntrism could not have developed separately. All of these divisions of Tāntrism must have had some common source from which they derived their Tāntric elements, modifying them in accordance with their specific religious orientations. Tāntric elements, therefore, must have predated the period in which the Tāntric scriptures were written, and certainly predated the time when Tāntrism, as such, gained independent literary status.[22]

In *Three Cities*, Brooks comments that Tāntric texts gained this independent status around the ninth century, although the concepts and practices set forth therein had their antecedents in ancient wisdom traditions, shamanism, yoga, alchemy, and other folk practices, whose adherents may have involved themselves in religious rituals containing elements of asceticism, eroticism, and goddess worship. Whether these diverse traditions and their "Tāntric" elements were rooted in the Aryan subculture that was flourishing on the Indian subcontinent or had their origins elsewhere, they were eventually assimilated and elaborated by brahmans with close ties to the Vedic tradition and absorbed into the rich Indian culture.

In this work, which is both recent and authoritative, Brooks states that by the eleventh century, the influence of Tāntric concepts and practices on mainstream Hinduism was unmistakable. The evidence for this lies in the frequency with which the concepts and practices of Tāntric Yoga are set forth in the works of non-Tāntric writers, as well as in the involvement of people from all strata of society in a broad spectrum of Tāntric practices for the purposes of achieving goals ranging from the acquisition of supernatural powers, sexual prowess, material goods, and physical immortality to the attainment of liberation while still in the physical body and an experiential realization of God.

Brooks also cites Goudriaan's observation that it would be a mistake to define as Tāntric only those texts that proclaim themselves as such. Tāntric literature is not a homogenous body, rather it assumes a Tāntric identity by setting out a diffuse complex of ideas, tenets, and rituals whose universal and denominational "Tāntric elements" are recognizable in the different religions and schools that embody various forms of Tāntric practices.

This is not to say, as Brooks points out, that Tāntric practices are limited to religious tenets and practices—Tāntrism can be understood only if it is placed in cultural and historical contexts that locate these teachings within a larger belief system. One such "larger belief system" within which Tantra can be located is the Vedic tradition, which is rooted in Sanskrit sources. Brooks calls the Tantrics who have close ties with this tradition "Vaidika Tantrics" because they:

> . . . identify themselves as part of the coherent and continuous legacy of Vedic tradition. They stand in contrast to those Hindu Tantrics who openly disdain Vedic traditions and especially the predominant position of brahmins in the interpretative process. While it is true that influential streams within Hindu Tantrism

are not represented in this typology, the catholic definition presented here does provide a working paradigm for the majority of sects that develop a Sanskrit-based form of Tantric Śāktism.[23]

As stated earlier, Tantra is not confined to Hinduism, but can be found in Buddhism and Jainism, the other principal indigenous faiths of India. Regardless of the different and often contradictory ideologies and doctrinal systems, we can with confidence identify the Tāntric streams in these religions by identifying shared patterns of behavior and belief. One such shared pattern is the concept of *śakti.*

The Development of Śāktism

Śakti holds a significant place in Tāntric Buddhism, Jainism, Hinduism, and subschools of Hinduism, such as Vaiṣṇavism, Śaivism, and Gāṇapatya.[24] Some scholars consider the inclusion of Śakti to be the factor that designates a denomination as Tāntric; as a result, Tāntrism and Śāktism are sometimes considered to be identical. However, Goudriaan, who agrees with Payne, points out that Śāktism and Tāntrism are "two intersecting but not coinciding circles."[25] It is true that branches of Tāntrism such as Vaiṣṇavism, Śaivism, and Buddhism have incorporated Śakti, but she is always accompanied by a male partner, who is thought to be incapable of initiating any action or movement, but nevertheless occupies a higher position than Śakti in all Tāntric sects, with the exception of Śāktism. In Śāktism, Śakti is dominant and the male partner is simply an inactive figurehead. Therefore, goddess worship in branches of Tāntrism, such as Vaiṣṇavism and Śaivism, can be called "dependent Śāktism," according to N. N. Bhattacharyya, whereas the latter form can be called "independent Śāktism." This independent Śāktism, according to Bhattacharyya, "had already made its appearance in Gupta age" and is an entirely female-dominated religion in which the male partners remain subordinate to the goddesses.[26]

Referring to N. N. Bhattacharyya, Goudriaan remarks:

> It makes sense to distinguish an "independent" from a "dependent" variety (Bhattacharyya, *Śākta Religion*, p. 73). In the latter case, the *śakti(s)* is (are) worshipped within the fold of another denomination (like Vaiṣṇavism and Jainism) without constituting the essence of its creed or practice, while in the Śākta sect proper, śakti is the chief divinity.[27]

The origin and early development of Śāktism is still a matter of dispute. Studies to date focus mostly on Śakti as a goddess, and on the myths, symbols, and rituals associated with her. Based on recent archaeological findings at Baghor in Central India, J. Desmond Clark postulates the existence of Śakti worship at numerous sites belonging to the Upper Paleolithic, Neolithic, and early Mesolithic periods. Clark reports:

> These groups use this same style of colorful natural stone with concentric geometric laminations, often in the form of triangles, as a symbol for the female principle or the Mother Goddess. . . . We believe that there is a very strong possibility that this structure and the stone represent a shrine to the Goddess of female principle, Śakti, which was built by the group of Upper Paleolithic hunter-gatherers . . . lies between 9000 and 8000 B.C. If this interpretation and dating prove correct and our identification of the shrine is substantiated, then this antedates by several thousand years the next oldest religious structure of this kind in South Asia, and is evidence of the remarkable continuity of religious beliefs and motifs in the Indian sub-continent.[28]

From the beginning of social evolution, according to N. N. Bhattacharyya, primitive man in agricultural societies worshipped the divine force in female form. Bhattacharyya argues that it is natural to associate creativity, fertility, productivity, and receptivity with women and, therefore, to conceive the invisible, supernatural force(s) as female. Bhattacharyya believes the association of the human generative organs with fertility and productivity is the basis for the tendency to conceptualize the earth, rivers, and many other aspects of nature or natural forces, as feminine and therefore to worship them in the female form. Bhattacharyya classifies the early concepts of the goddess in the following categories: tribal divinities; goddesses of mountains, lakes, and rivers: the destroyers of evil; goddesses of healing; goddesses related to the animal world; community goddesses; protectors of children; earth mothers; and corn mothers.[29]

In early Vedic literature, the worship of the divine in female form holds a less significant place than the worship of male gods. There are references to female divinities such as Aditi, Uṣas, and Sarasvatī, but by no means can the Goddess's status be compared with male deities such as Indra, Varuṇa, Agni, Mitra, and others. In the *Ṛgveda*, a female deity, Aditi, is not only called the mother of all gods, she is also said to be heaven, space, mother, father, and son, as well as all which has existed and all that will exist. Such a statement, however, does not necessarily mean that her position was higher or even equal to the position of male gods, such as Indra, Agni, or Viṣṇu.[30]

Scattered references to the Goddess throughout Vedic literature imply the existence of Śakti worship, but such references are not strong enough to prove the existence of an independent Śākta cult. In his work, *Sakti or Divine Power*, Das gathers references to *śakti* from the Saṃhitās, Purāṇas, and Upaniṣads and tries to show a gradual development of the *śakti* concept in Vedic literature. According to him,[31] all principal gods of the Vedic pantheon have a *śakti* basis; *śaci*, for example, is a Vedic word denoting the divine power of the gods. *Gñās*, wives of the gods, or fertility goddesses, represent the earliest concept of *śakti*. According to Das, these *gñās* finally merge into *vāk*. In the Brāhmaṇas, this *vākśakti* in union with *prajāpati* is said to be the creator of the universe and the Gods. In later Vedic literature, *vāk* is identified with Sarasvatī, the goddess of learning. The concept of *vāk* and Sarasvatī continues to expand in the Upaniṣadic period and can be observed in the *Kena Upaniṣad* and the *Śvetāśvatara Upaniṣad*. In the *Kena Upaniṣad*, she appears as Umā Haimavatī and is described as the highest power, superseding all the gods.[32] In the *Śvetāśvatara Upaniṣad*, she is *parā* (transcendent), and the powers of *jñāna* (knowledge), *bala* (might), and *kriyā* (action) are intrinsic to her.[33]

Another scholar, Kaviraj, divides Śāktism into three major periods: (1) ancient or pre-Buddhistic, going back to prehistoric age; (2) medieval or post-Buddhistic extending to about A.D. 1200; and (3) modern, from A.D. 1300 to the present.[34] Unfortunately, Kaviraj's threefold division of Śākta history does not provide any clue to origin or early development, nor does it designate when the pre-Buddhistic period ends, or the medieval or post-Buddhistic period begins.

In regard to the second period, Goudriaan points out, "perhaps we have to consider this period to be closed with the disappearance of Buddhism as a major religion from India."[35] The second period, the medieval or post-Buddhistic, which according to Kaviraj is the most creative period in the history of Tāntrism, would then cover a period of approximately 600 to 1000 years, ending around A.D. 1200. Although, it is extremely difficult to establish a precise history, this may be the period that Bhattacharyya considers to be "independent" Śāktism. For example, it is in this period that the *Brahmāṇḍa*

Purāṇa and *Mārkaṇḍeya Purāṇa* were produced.[36] Most of the Śākta and Śaiva Āgama texts, and the commentaries on them, belong to this period.[37] As Kaviraj points out, the modern period that covers from A.D. 1300 until the present "too has been productive, but with a few brilliant exceptions most of the works produced in this period are of secondary character and include compilations, practical handbooks and minor tracts dealing with miscellaneous subjects."[38]

The texts composed during the second period not only give a general idea of Śāktism, but also present the subdivisions and the unique characteristics distinguishing them from each other. Tāntric texts such as *Kubjikā Tantra*, *Rudrayāmala*, *Catuṣpīṭha Tantra*, *Jñānārṇava Tantra*, *Devībhāgavata*, and *Kālikā Purāṇa* (and even Buddhist Tāntric texts: *Hevajra Tantra* and *Sādhanamālā*) mention several *pīṭhas,* shrines or centers of *śakti* worship; usually fifty, fifty-one, or one hundred and eight *upapīṭhas* (secondary shrines) and four *mahāpīṭhas* (great shrines) are named.[39] The concept of *upapīṭhas* and *mahāpīṭhas* is most often connected with the story of the death of Satī, Śiva's wife.

According to the legend, Śiva was so stricken with grief at his wife's death that he roamed aimlessly with the corpse on his shoulders. To free him from his attachment to the corpse, Viṣṇu followed him, gradually severing the limbs. The sites where the pieces of Satī's body fell subsequently became *upapīṭhas* or *mahāpīṭhas.* There is no agreement in respect to either the number of these *pīṭhas* or the exact distinction between the *upapīṭhas* and *mahāpīṭhas.*[40]

According to scholars, with the passage of time, some of the local goddesses, which were the presiding deities of these shrines, gained prominence and became major deities in Śāktism known as *mahāvidyās.*[41] They are: Kālī, Tārā, Ṣoḍaśī (or Tripurasundarī), Bhuvaneśvarī, Bhairavī, Chinnamastā, Dhūmāvatī, Vagalāmukhī (Bagalāmukhī or Valgāmukhī), Mātaṅgī, and Kamalā.[42] Describing the characteristics of these *mahāvidyās,* S. Shankaranarayan writes:

> Each Vidya is distinct and distinguishable from the other. Each is a particular Cosmic function and each leads to a special realization of the One Reality. The might of Kali, the sound-force of Tara, the beauty and bliss of Sundari, the vast vision of Bhuvaneshwari, the effulgent charm of Bhairavi, the striking force of Chinnamasta, the silent inertness of Dhumavati, the paralysing power of Bagalamukhi, the expressive play of Matangi and the concord and harmony of Kamalatmika are the various characteristics, the distinct manifestations of the Supreme Consciousness that has made this creation possible.[43]

There is a rich literature related to each of these *mahāvidyās*, especially Kālī, Tārā, and Tripurasundarī. The Tāntric worship of all of the *mahāvidyās* follows a standard format; differences are observed only in the structure of the yantras in which they are worshipped, and in the names and the sequence of the deities subordinate to each *mahāvidyā (āvaraṇa devatās).* From a philosophical perspective, these *mahāvidyās* lack distinguishing features and, with the exception of the terms employed to indicate philosophical categories, all present the same doctrines. Scattered references to them can be found in Paurāṇic literature, but the usage of the term *mahāvidyā* itself, as well as the goddesses belonging to that category, first appear in the Tāntric texts, such as the *Muṇḍamālā Tantra*, *Toḍala Tantra*,[44] *Śaktiśaṅgama*,[45] and *Śākta Pramoda.*[46] Most of these texts, according to the criteria set by Kaviraj, probably belong to the third period of Śāktism. Thus, the rise of *mahāvidyās* cannot be accurately traced, but probably occurred after A.D. 1300.

However, none of these Tāntric texts are exclusively devoted to one particular *mahāvidyā.* To date there has been no serious study delineating the boundaries between the *mahāvidyās* in terms of pinpointing either their distinguishing features in ritual worship or the philosophical principles that permit a particular *vidyā* to stand as an independent school of Śāktism. There is a standard format for worshipping these *mahāvidyās*: all have their corresponding yantras. The central *bindu*, the dot of the yantra, represents the *mahāvidyā*, and the surrounding triangles, petals, circles, and squares are occupied by secondary deities of that particular *mahāvidyā*. Among the schools associated with the ten *mahāvidyās*, it is Śrīvidyā and to some extent the Kālī *mahāvidyā* that have developed an elaborate and sophisticated ideology compatible with other systems of thought, such as Vyākaraṇa Āgama and Kashmir Śaivism.[47]

An Overview of Śrīvidyā

In order to draw a literary boundary for Śrīvidyā, it is important to note the other terms that also refer to the same *mahāvidyā*. *Muṇḍamālā Tantra* uses the term Ṣoḍaśī rather than Śrīvidyā to describe the Goddess of this sect, whereas the most popularly used word for this *mahāvidyā* is Tripurasundarī or Mahātripurasundarī. The words Kāmeśvarī, Rājarājeśvarī, Tripurā (Tripurasundarī or Mahātripurasundarī), Subhagā, Lalitā, Ṣoḍaśī, and Kāmakalā are interchangeably used to denote this *mahāvidyā*, but no one has ever paused to examine whether they refer to identical aspects.

Goudriaan considers Ṣoḍaśī to be "an aspect of *tripurasundarī*,"[48] and Tripurasundarī herself, according to him, is "the most important Tāntric form of Śrī/Lakṣmī."[49] These two statements indicate that Ṣoḍaśī simply refers to an aspect of Tripurasundarī which means Ṣoḍaśī is a subdivision of Tripurasundarī, not representing the entire *mahāvidyā* as such. Tripurasundarī, on the other hand, is a form of Śrī, or Lakṣmī, the goddess of wealth and prosperity, who most often appears as the consort of the god Viṣṇu.[50] The association of Tripurasundarī with Śrī or Lakṣmī compromises her status as an independent *mahāvidyā*. Also, the tenth *mahāvidyā*, Kamalā, or Kamalātmikā, who is also the same as Śrī or Lakṣmī, then becomes indistinguishable from Tripurasundarī.

Goudriaan probably identifies Tripurasundarī with Śrī/Lakṣmī because the usage of the term Śrī in front of *vidyā* may have led him to assume the association of this *mahāvidyā* with Śrī, meaning Lakṣmī. In addition, the followers of Viśiṣṭādvaita Vedānta, worship Śrī or Lakṣmī in the center of *śrīcakra*. The *Māhātmyakhaṇḍa* of *Tripurā Rahasya* (hereafter cited as *TR-M*) gives a mythological explanation of how Lakṣmī and the term *śrī* became associated with Tripurasundarī. When Tripurasundarī appeared in front of Śrī (another name for Lakṣmī) and granted her a boon as a result of her prolonged meditation, Lakṣmī asked for *sāyujyamukti*, a state of liberation that would allow her to become one with Tripurasundarī. Because without Lakṣmī, Viṣṇu will fail to protect and maintain law and order, Tripurasundarī substituted another boon, "From now on, I will be addressed by your name, Śrīvidyā: The city of Śrī, Śrīpura, will be my city; the *cakra* of Śrī, *śrīcakra*, will be my *cakra*; and the *pūjākrama* of Śrī will be my *pūjākrama*. From now on, the *sūktas* of Śrī will be Śrī Ṣoḍaśīvidyā and because of the oneness between us, I will be known as Māhā Lakṣmī."[51] According to Lakṣmīdhara, the *tripurasundarī* mantra, having the *bīja śrīm* as its sixteenth letter, is known as *śrīvidyā*.[52]

These references may indicate the association of

Śrī/Lakṣmī with Tripurā. However, they do not substantiate the claim that Tripurasundarī is an aspect of Lakṣmī or vice versa. Rather, the references may indicate the historical inclusion of Lakṣmī in the Śrīvidyā tradition with Tripurasundarī. In the *Tripurā Rahasya*, Tripurasundarī is also known as Rājarājeśvarī, Kāmeśvarī, and Ṣoḍaśī or Śrīmahā Ṣoḍaśakṣarī.[53]

Among the Purāṇas, *Brahmāṇḍa Purāṇa*, especially the second half, known as "Lalitopākhyāna," is exclusively devoted to the glorification of Tripurasundarī. Interestingly, the second half of this Purāṇa, which focuses on the manifestation of Tripurasundarī and her warfare with Bhaṇḍāsura, is known as "Lalitopākhyāna" (the tale of Lalitā), rather than "Tripuropākhyāna." But, throughout the "Lalitopākhyāna," the word *tripurā* is used more frequently than *lalitā*. For example, in one of the most famous prayers to Tripurasundarī, traditionally known as "Lalitā-Sahasranāma" (the one thousand names of *lalitā*), the words *tripurā, tripureśī, tripurāmbā*, and other similar variations are used frequently, while the word *lalitā* occurs only once. Other famous Tāntric texts also prefer *tripurā* over other terms. For instance, *NS*[54] and *YH*[55] use the term *tripurā* and do not mention the terms *śrīvidyā, rājarājesvarī, subhagā*, or *samayā* at all. *YH* uses the term *kāmakalā* once.[56] Similarly, *Kāmakalā-vilasa* refers to Kāmakalā and Tripurasundarī.[57]

Gandharva Tantra (hereafter cited as *GT*) in *Tantrasaṅgraha, Part III* (hereafter cited as TS-III), which most often refers to this *mahāvidyā* as Tripurasundarī, mentions Lalitā only once but identifies Tripurā with Durgā. According to *GT*, due to her unsurpassed beauty, Durgā is known as Tripurā.[58] Lakṣmīdhara in his commentary on the *SL* also identifies Durgā with Tripurāmahāvidyā.[59] Adherents of Tripurasundarī, such as Lakṣmīdhara, Bhāskararāya, Śivānanda, Amṛtānanda, and recent propagators of the tradition, such as Kaviraj and Swami Hariharananda Saraswati (more popularly known in North India as Swami Karpatri), presume that all these terms refer to the same *mahāvidyā* and therefore they consider any text that propagates the worship of the goddess under any of these terms to be a Śrīvidyā text.

In fact, in its *śrīcakra* schema, Śrīvidyā covers a large number of goddesses that are associated with other *mahāvidyās* as well. This leads to an unresolved hypothesis: did such a schema develop in an attempt to bring all the deities to one fold, or did this system with its intricate theory of *śakti's* multiple manifestations develop independently, with later adoptions of some of the subordinate *śaktis* by the followers of other *mahāvidyās*? If the latter, did some of the subordinate deities of *śrīcakra* rise to the status of independent *mahāvidyās*? For example, Tripurabhairavī, who is simply a *cakra nāyikā* and the leader of the eighth circuit of *śrīcakra*, is also classified as the fifth independent *mahāvidyā*. Bhuvanesvarī, the fourth *mahāvidyā*, on the other hand, is sometimes recognized as Rājarājeśvarī, another name for Tripurasundarī.[60]

According to Sanjukta Gupta's observation, "the famous ten goddesses *(daśa mahāvidyās)* are direct or indirect manifestations of one or the other of these three."[61] By "these three," Gupta means Kālī, Tārā, and Tripurā/Śrī. On the basis of the attributes described in the Tāntric texts, Chinnamastā, Bagalāmukhī, and Dhūmāvatī are closer to Kāṃlī and Tārā, whereas Bhuvaneśvarī, Bhairavī, Mātaṅgī, and Kamalā are closer to Tripurasundarī. In this matter, Shankaranarayan also observes:

> . . . they are distinct and unique, they have among themselves many characteristics in common. Kali, Chinnamasta, Dhumavati and Bagalamukhi have the common characteristics of Power

> and Force, active or dormant. Sundari, Bhuvaneshwari, Bhairavi, Matangi and Kamalatmika share the qualities of Light, Delight and Beauty. Tara has certain characteristics of Kali and certain others of Sundari and is correlated to Bhairavi, Bagalamukhi and Matangi in the aspect of Sound-Force expressed or impeded. Thus the ten Maha Vidyas fall into three broad divisions of discipline. . . .[62]

Furthermore, in the Tāntric texts *Prapacasāra Saṅgraha* (hereafter cited as *PSS*)[63] and *Śrīvidyārṇava Tantra*,[64] the *bīja* mantra of Bhuvaneśvarī, Bhairavī, Mātaṅgī, and Kamalā are added to the main Śrīvidyā mantra, creating variations in the Śrīvidyā mantra and subsuming these *mahāvidyās* under the greater fold of Śrīvidyā.[65] This tendency indicates Śrīvidyā's overpowering influence on other *mahāvidyās.* In this sense it can be stated that of the ten *mahāvidyās*, Kālī, Tārā, and Tripurasundarī are the most prominent.

The Śrīvidyā school built around Tripurasundarī holds a more important place than those schools built around Kālī and Tārā for three reasons: its literary standard, its well-defined and coherent doctrines, and the inclusion of Bhuvaneśvarī, Bhairavī, and Kamalā within its fold.[66] Furthermore, this is the only school in Tāntrism that emphatically claims its association with the Vedas; the adherents of this *mahāvidyā* were and still are Hindus well versed both in the Sanskrit language and in a wide range of philosophical literature. In fact, the latter factor helped the Śrīvidyā branch of Śākta Tāntrism develop a sophisticated philosophy and metaphysics.[67]

Tracing the mythological origin of Śrīvidyā still leaves us with considerable historical ambiguity. However, we can also find references to the Śrīvidyā mantra, Śrīvidyā rituals, and Śrīvidyā theology in the literature that is not particularly related to the Śrīvidyā sect of Śāktism. Traditional adherents of Śrīvidyā—both ancient and modern—in an attempt to demonstrate the Vedic origin of Śrīvidyā repeatedly quote passages from the *Ṛgveda* and the Upaniṣads. The main function of such references is to demonstrate how the Śrīvidyā mantra is derived from the various mantras of the *Ṛgveda*, or more specifically, how the worship of *śrīcakra* and the concepts related to fifteen or sixteen *nityākalās* and the name of the *vidyeśvara* of the Śrīvidyā mantra occur in the Vedic literature.[68] To a nonbeliever, however, this evidence is not convincing because this tendency—i.e., to lend authenticity and antiquity to a doctrine or sect of one's preference by quoting passages from the Vedas and by interpreting them on the basis of one's own etymology or even pseudo-etymology—is common among almost all sectarian commentators and adherents of any given doctrine in India, not only Śrīvidyā. Such references and interpretations do not help to determine the origin of Śrīvidyā-related practices.

So far, the best account of the historical evidence for the Śrīvidyā tradition is given by Brooks.[69] Brooks points out that ritualistic elements of Śrīvidyā, such as the use of mantras, *mudrās*, and *nyāsa*, which are common to all forms of Śāktism were in vogue long before they appeared in written sources of Śrīvidyā texts. Ritualistic and meditative practices that are unique to the Śrīvidyā branch of Śāktism, such as the correlation between Lalitā or Tripurasundarī and *śrīcakra* and Ṣoḍaśī or the *pāñcadasaksari* mantra are first mentioned in *Devī Bhāgavatam*, *Kālikā Purāṇa*, *Linga Purāṇa*, and *Brahmāṇḍa Purāṇa*. These Purāṇas are constantly cited by traditional followers of Śrīvidyā to demonstrate its antiquity, which, considering the nature of the Paurāṇic materials, may not be a valid means of establishing historicity. Even if we accept this traditional viewpoint, it still does not take us beyond the eighth or ninth century.

As Brooks observes, "Evidence that Śrīvidya is plainly visible in literature from before the eighth century is at best suggestive and certainly not conclusive."[70] In Tamil sources, Śrīvidyā worship, and that only in its prototypical form, can be found in approximately the sixth or seventh century A.D. Tamil *siddha* master Tirumūlar, in his *Tirumantiram* makes "explicit reference to the *śrīvidyā* mantra in its fifteen syllables according to the *kādimata* interpretation."[71] He also describes the goddess Tripurā and *tripurā cakra* but does not establish any connection between Tripurā and Śrīvidyā or between *tripurā cakra* and *śrīcakra*.[72] In other sections of *Tirumantiram*, Tirumūlar mentions the *cakra* or a portion of it which is associated with the worship of *Naṭarāja* at Cidambaram.

He goes on to describe the variety of *śiva cakras*, including *sammelanacakra*, which is associated with the secret form of *Naṭarāja*. According to Brooks, this *sammelanacakra* can be linked to *śrīcakra* and *Naṭarāja's* consort and *Śivakāmasundarī* to *Tripurasundarī* or *Śrīvidyā*. If this link is correct, then there is strong evidence of the existence of the presence of Śrīvidyā elements in Śaiva temple worship from at least the sixth century.[73] However, the existence of the Śrīvidyā element within the Śaiva temple cult does not give any indication of whether or not the Kaula aspect of Śrīvidyā had been incorporated in the South Indian Śrīvidyā cult.

So far, all this above-mentioned evidence refers to the period of composition for the *śrikula* aspect of Śrīvidyā, whereas the development of Śrīvidyā elements in the Kashmiri tradition and its association with Kaulism may have already taken place in Kashmir and other parts of North India. Although Brooks does not provide any solid evidence, he believes that:

It had moved south by the time of Tirumūlar and perhaps earlier if the evidence at the Cidambaram temple is conclusive. This would lead us to believe that mantra and yantra development within Śrīvidyā comes from a period before the sixth century. If Kālīkula sources are, as Goudriaan says, well before the Śrīkula then these elements in prototypical or unsystematic forms too must be pushed back to a period before the sixth century. This hypothesis is hardly novel but it is perhaps the first time it has been presented with at least some historical and literary references.[74]

Soon after the sixth or seventh century, Śrīvidyā begins to emerge in written form. Based on Padoux's observations in *Recherches sur la symbolique et l'énergie de al parole dans certains textes tantriques*, Brooks asserts "Śrīvidya, like other Śākta sects, incorporates practically the entire speculative foundation of Kashmiri Śaivism into its theology."[75] The connection between *Vāmakeśvara Tantra (VT)* (of which *NS* and *YH* are the two parts), which is a Śrīvidyā text, and its commentators—Jayaratha (Īśvaraśiva, whom Jayaratha mentions as an early commentator of *VT*), Śivānanda, and Puṇyānanda—clearly shows "that Śrīvidyā had taken a fully mature written form by the twelfth century."[76]

Furthermore, all these commentators belong to Kashmir Śaivism and therefore their association with *VT* reinforces the historical ties, or at least a close interaction between Kashmir Śaivism and the Śrīvidyā branch of Śākta Tāntrism. Exactly when and how Kashmir Śaivism arrived from the North and became popular in South India remains an open question, but according to Brooks' belief, "the process is certainly complete before Bhāskararāya."[77]

Also according to Brooks, evidence of the existence of Śrīvidyā elements can be traced from Tirumūlar's writings, Naṭarāja's temple at Cidambaram, the commentaries of

Jayaratha and other Śaivite scholars on the Śrīvidyā text, *VT*, all the way to Bhāskararāya. Even if he is correct and all this evidence is conclusive, it still does not help fill the gap of approximately seven hundred years between Tirumūlar and Bhāskararāya in the truest sense. However, the assimilation of Śrīvidyā practices in the Śaṅkarācārya order could provide a more precise historical perspective.

Throughout India, contemporary Śrīvidyā adherents, whether or not they officially belong to the Śaṅkarācārya order, frequently mention Śaṅkarācārya and his grand-teacher *(paramaguru)* Gauḍapāda as practitioners of Śrīvidyā. Despite the fact that most historians dismiss authorship of *SL*, the *Prapañcasāra (PS)* and the *Lalitātriśatībhāṣya (LTSB)*, the majority of Śrīvidyā practitioners and swamis of the Śaṅkarācārya order consider these texts to be authentic works of Ādi Śaṅkara. Śrīvidyā adherents hold these texts and Gauḍapāda's *Śrīvidyā Ratna Sūtras* and *Subhagodaya* in high regard.

Evaluating the pros and cons of the arguments regarding Śaṅkarācārya's authorship, Brooks concludes that these texts could have been written by heads of Śaṅkarācārya's *maṭhas* and that *PS* "can be dated no later than the eleventh century, and possibly much earlier."[78] Similarly, Brooks asserts that "LTSB was composed in one of the Śaṅkara maṭhas sometime between the eighth and eleventh centuries."[79] When and how Śrīvidyā practices entered the nondualistic, Vedānta-based Śaṅkarācārya order remains unknown, but that they occupied an important place in the spiritual lives of the followers of Śaṅkarācārya after the eleventh century is an established fact.[80] In all Śaṅkarācārya monasteries, from the twelfth century on, Śrīvidyā practice, in the form of either worshipping an image of Śrīvidyā (under the names Tripurā, Lalitā, or Rājarājeśvarī) or worshipping *śrīcakra*, had become part of the daily service.

In this particular respect, adherents of the Śaṅkarācārya order somehow manage to reconcile their nondualistic Vedānta with nondualistic Śrīvidyā despite the significant differences between the two. Doctrinally, they are Advaita Vedāntins and thus they do not hold devotion *(bhakti)* and worship *(upāsanā)* in high regard. But practically, they take devotion to *Tripurasundarī* and ritual worship of *srīcakra* seriously. This tendency seems to have existed in Śaṅkarācārya's monasteries at least from the time of Vidyāraṇya.[81]

Presently there are a good number of Śrīvidyā practitioners who belong neither to the Śaivite nor Śaṅkarācārya orders in the strict sense, but rather to the broad range of Hinduism. Most are householders and, with few exceptions, highly educated *smārta brāhmins.* As Brooks observes:

> In Śrīvidyā, the majority of historical writers are *smārta* brahmins; that is, they identify with traditions that follow the exoteric rituals of the so-called *smṛtis* (i.e., *gṛhya-*, *śrauta-*, and *dharmasūtras*) and worship the *pañcāyatana devatas*, that is, the five divinities (Sūrya the Sun god, Śiva, Viṣṇu, Ganeśa, and Durgā or Devī). All deities, however, are treated in sectarian terms as manifestations or aspects of the Supreme Deity, whoever that may be.[82]

Occasionally, one may encounter Śrīvidyā practitioners, at least in North India, the northeastern part of the Himalayas, Gujarat, and Maharashtra, who officially belong to the order of Ramānujācārya or to Avadhūta Pantha, which mythically begins with Dattātreya. Baba Ramamagaladasa, a *vaiṣṇava swami* in Ayodhya, was a famous Śrīvidyā teacher. A number of Śrīvidyā practitioners, mostly householders, who studied with Baba Ramamagaladasa, worship Śrī or Gopālasundarī (instead of Tripurasundarī) while using *śrīcakra* as the basis of their practice. In none of these cases do the Śrīvidyā practitioners publicly claim their exclusive identification with the Śrīvidyā cult. Ordained swamis publicly identify themselves with their order, whereas in private they practice and teach Śrīvidyā. Śrīvidyā practitioners who are not swamis are usually householders and practice Śrīvidyā without isolating themselves from their religious background.

Śrīvidyā's interaction with two significant traditions, Śaivism and Advaita Vedānta, helped it develop intricate philosophical theories and gain social acceptance, which were and still are missing in other branches of Śāktism. It is on the ground of Śaiva philosophy and metaphysics that Śrīvidyā writers pulled together Śrīvidyā elements, which were scattered throughout Vedic, Upaniṣadic, and Paurāṇic sources. Using Kashmir Śaivism as a model, Śrīvidyā adherents gave a philosophical interpretation of different facets of Śrīvidyā, such as yantra, mantra, *guru*, *mātṛkā* (letters of the Sanskrit alphabet), the main goddess, Śrīvidyā or Tripurā and subordinate deities *(āvaraṇa devatās)* and tried to demonstrate the oneness among these facets.

Śrīvidyā's association with Śaṅkarācārya's followers, who were staunch supporters of the Vedas, helped it become accepted by those who disdained Tantra and Śāktism as "non-Vedic." However, assimilation of Śaivism, which is purely Āgamic and dominated by Kaula rituals in practice, and the Advaita Vedānta of Śaṅkara, which is purely Vedic/-Upaniṣadic and puritan (i.e., completely opposed to Kaula rituals), gradually prepared the ground in which the two branches of Śrīvidyā grew. One group of Śrīvidyā practitioners upheld Śaiva-based Kaulism or simply embraced it as a part of normal Śrīvidyā practice. The other group totally rejected Kaulism, replacing it with what they called Samayācāra. Thus, the two schools—Kaulācāra Śrīvidyā and Samayācāra Śrīvidyā—came into existence.

Generally, the word "Kaula" or "Kaulism" refers to the mainstream of Tāntrism that consists of the most frequently disputed ritual elements, that is *pañcamakāra—madya* (wine), *māṃsa* (meat), *matsya* (fish), *mudrā* (gesture), and *maithuna* (physical union); *kāmakalādhyāna*, the meditation on, or worship of, the female organ; and the inclusion in rituals of aspirants of both sexes from all castes. From its literary inception until it became associated with the Śaṅkarācārya order, Kaula practices did not seem to be an issue in Śrīvidyā, although we do not exactly know whether or not the Kaula elements existed in Śaiva temples and the early phase of the Śrīvidyā cult before the introduction of Kashmir Śaivism in the south. Furthermore, *pañcamakāra* and *kāmakalā* worship are merely part of the external rituals. Other rituals, such as offering water, flowers, incense; lighting the lamp; and the *bilva patra,* the invocation and the prayers to the main as well as the subordinate deities, are also intrinsic characteristics of Kaulism.

In the early phases of Śrīvidyā, Kaula practices, excluding *pañcamakāra* and *kāmakalā*, may have been adopted by Śrīvidyā practitioners. The inclusion of *pañcamakāra* might have been the result of the gradually increasing influence of Kashmir Śaivism. As this process continued, people from all walks of life may have been attracted to it, some embracing the worship of the goddess Śrīvidyā along with every other aspect of Kaulism and some embracing only those elements of Kaulism which did not include *pañcamakāra*. If *Subhagodaya* and the *Śrīvidyā Ratna Sūtras* are actually the works of Gauḍapāda, and *SL* is the work of Ādi Śaṅkarācārya, then we can safely postulate that in the eighth or ninth century there existed a mild form of Kaula-influenced Śrīvidyāṃ. In his works, Gauḍapāda describes the anthropomorphic form of Śrīvidya, *śrīcakra*, and her worship, which is of course ritualistic, but at the same time, gives a yogic interpretation of all these concepts and proposes a process of internalizing the rituals. It is he who first uses the term *samayā* for *śrīvidyā*, the term *samaya* for the path that leads to her realization, and the term *samayin* for one who follows that path. Obviously, he does not attempt to highlight distinctive features of Samayācāra to distinguish it from the Kaula-dominated Śrīvidyā, which was probably more prevalent at that time.

Śaṅkarācārya takes this issue a step further in *SL*, clearly stating that the sixty-four tantras (Catuḥṣaṣti Tantra), which expound Kaulism, are subordinate to the group of five Tāntric texts (Śubhāgamapañcakam), which he considers to be the only valid Tantra. He calls that Śubhāgamapañcakam Tantra, *Te Tantram*, "your Tantra," implying that those sixty-four Tāntric texts do not expound her essence. He also introduces the concept of *śrīvidyā* under the term *samayā* in a more elaborate manner than do the texts attributed to Gauḍapāda. Śaṅkarācārya places great emphasis on the realization of *śrīvidyā* through yogic means, but he also dedicates the majority of the verses in praise of the external form of the goddess. Such a long, detailed description of the anthropomorphic form of the goddess is a clear indication that her worship was widespread, at least in South India. It is plausible that Kaulism, along with *pañcamakāra* and other similar elements, may not have entered Śaṅkarācārya monasteries due to their Vedic/puritan orientation, but this could not prevent the inclusion of Kaula elements in Śrīvidyā outside the monasteries.

Inclusion or exclusion of Kaula elements in Śrīvidyā did not seem to be an issue of particular importance until the sixteenth century. Before Lakṣmīdhara,[83] even Śrīvidyāṃ adherents of the Śaṅkarācārya order, such as Padmapāda (if he is actually the author of *Vivaraṇa Commentary on Prapañcasāra*), Vidyāraṇya Yati, and the authors of *Kalyāṇavṛṣti Stotra* and *Kanakadhārā Stotra*, all of whom bore the name "Śaṅkarācārya," express no interest in this matter. It is Lakṣmīdhara who first introduces Samayācāra as a totally independent branch of Śrīvidyā and draws a sharp distinction between Kaula and Samaya schools of Śrīvidyā.

According to Lakṣmīdhara, Kaulācāra or Kaulism means taking delight in external *pūjā*, ritual worship.[84] Considering it to be an opponent's view *(pūrvapakṣa)*, Lakṣmīdhara neither accords Kaulācāra any respect nor feels any compulsion to review the literature that expounds Kaulism before condemning it.[85] As will be seen, Lakṣmīdhara's description of Kaulism cannot be taken as an accurate account of Kaulism as a whole; obviously he denigrates it to lend more credence to the Samayācāra he propounds.

The Kaula-Samaya Dispute

Before we undertake any further analysis of Lakṣmīdhara's opinion regarding Kaula and the sharp distinction he draws between it and his self-proclaimed Samaya views, we need to have a general understanding of Kaula-oriented Śrīvidyā discipline. Kaula *sādhakas* draw the *śrīcakra* on a piece of bark or cloth, or inscribe it on a gold, silver, or copper plate, or on a wooden board. During the ritual, they use articles such as water, flowers, incense, rice, yoghurt, honey, fruit, and cooked food. This group believes in the oneness of Śrīvidyā and *kuṇḍalinī*, but does not emphasize experiencing it. Prior to the external *śrīcakra* worship, this group performs *mānasa pūjā* (mental worship); this is especially true of the Vāmacārins, left-hand Kaulas, prevalent mostly in Eastern

India, i.e., in Assam and Bengal. *Mānasa pūjā* consists mainly of *prāṇapratiṣṭhā* (meditating on the presence of the goddess in one's heart),[86] *bhūta śuddhi* (purification of the bodily elements), *nyāsas* (visualizing *mātṛkās*, or letters, and different parts of the yantra, mantra, and the limbs of the deity in the different parts of one's own body),[87] and the performance of *antaryāga* (inner offering).[88]

Through this kind of *mānasa pūjā*, Kaula *sādhakas* aim to establish a state of oneness between the different parts of their bodies and those of the goddess or *śrīyantra*, in which the goddess resides. The prayers recited during this worship remind the *sādhakas* of the oneness of Tripurasundarī and *kuṇḍalinī*. But in actual practice they simply worship *śrīcakra* and the deities residing therein, without attempting to work with *kuṇḍalinī śakti*, which requires yogic disciplines. These elements of *śrīcakra* worship are common to all Kaulas—those who incorporate the five *makāras* and those who do not.[89] Kaula *sādhakas* who incorporate the *pañcamakāras* (popularly known as *vāmācārins*, left-handed tāntrics), in addition to performing the above-mentioned *śrīcakra* worship, also worship the deity in the form of *kuṇḍalinī* in their own bodies. After performing rituals, along with mantra recitations for *tattva śuddhi* and purification of both the elements in their own bodies and the external elements—wine, meat, fish, and cooked food—they offer these external elements into the fire of *kuṇḍalinī*, which, according to them, resides at the base of the spine in the *mūlādhāra cakra*. Of course they consume these articles, just as any ordinary person would. It is their contemplative awareness that makes them feel or believe these items are being offered into the fire of *kuṇḍalinī* at the *mūlādhāra (cidagnikuṇḍa)*.[90]

The Samaya group, on the other hand, of which Lakṣmīdhara is the sole representative, considers the human body to be a *śrīcakra* and, thus, does not need to draw it externally. The Samaya method of Śrīvidyā practice is purely *yogic.* Their main focus is awakening *kuṇḍalinī* and uniting her with *śiva* in *sahasrāra*, the highest *cakra*, which is found in or above the head. According to Lakṣmīdhara, Śrīvidyā practitioners of the Samaya group experience the oneness of *cakra*, mantra, deity, *guru*, and their own *ātma* while leading *kuṇḍalinī* from the lower to the higher *cakras.*[91]

Before attempting to analyze how accurate Lakṣmīdhara's observations are regarding Samayācāra and Kaulācāra and how correctly he places the two within the broader spectrum of Tāntrism, we need to examine his opinions as set forth in his commentary on *SL*. According to Lakṣmīdhara:

1. Kaulācāra is *avaidika*, antinomian to Vedic *dharma*, whereas Samayācāra is purely Vedic.[92]

2. Kaulācāra involves external rituals. These practices require knowledge of the seer, meter, and so on of the mantras employed. The Samayācāra style of worship, on the other hand, is totally internal. It involves the experience of oneness with the goddess and, as such, does not require an aspirant to have the knowledge of either the seer or the meter.[93]

3. In the Kaulācāra branch of Śrīvidyā, the practitioners worship the goddess in the *mūlādhāra*, and the *kuṇḍalinī* residing therein is called Kualinī, whereas the followers of Samayācāra worship *śakti* and *śiva* in the *sahasrāra* and therein they are called Samayā and Samaya, respectively.[94]

4. The adepts of the Kaula path worship Kaulinī, who is identical with the *kuṇḍalinī śakti* in the *mūlādhāra* while she is still asleep. Such a worship is *tāmisra*, full of darkness. The moment *kuṇḍalinī* is awakened, Kaula *sādhakas* attain liberation. Following the path of *vāmācāra*, their worship is accompanied with meat, honey, fish, and many such articles. Some others—*uttara-kaulas*, *kṣapaṇakas*, and *digambaras*—

literally worship the triangular-shaped female organ. According to *Samayācārins*, the worship of the goddess in the six lower *cakras* is not required. Rather, the *sahasrāra* is the only *cakra* in which she can be worshipped. Worshipping her in the *sahasrāra* consists of experiencing the fourfold oneness known as *catur-vidhaikyānusandhāna*.[95]

5. Kaula followers draw *śrīcakra* according to *samhārakrama*, the method of withdrawal. In their system, there are five triangles with the apexes pointing upward and four with their apexes pointing downward. *Samayins* draw a *śrīcakra* according to *sṛṣṭikrama*, the method of creation; in their system, there are four triangles with their apexes pointing upward and five with their apexes pointing downward.[96]

6. Kaulas regard the group of sixty-four Tāntric texts as authoritative, whereas, according to *samayins*, the five Tāntric texts known as *śubhagamapañcaka* are the only authentic texts.[97]

7. According to Kaulas, sixteen *nityakalās* are of primary importance in *Śrīvidyā* practice, whereas in *Samayamārga*, they are of secondary importance.[98]

8. Kaulas propose a ninefold oneness between *bhairava* and *bhairavī* whereas *samayins* propose fourfold or sometimes fivefold oneness between *Samayā* and *Samaya*.[99]

Lakṣmīdhara's claim that Kaulācāra is Avaidika and Samayācāra is purely Vedic seems to be only partially true. To substantiate this claim, he deliberately chooses passages from the Vedas and gives his own commentary on them to support his *samayamata*, ignoring other Vedic passages that support Kaula-oriented ideas.[100] In Upaniṣadic literature, one finds references to meat and sex as part of Vedic rituals.[101] Claiming a particular set of spiritual disciplines to be Vedic or non-Vedic only on the basis of these elements is superficial. Furthermore, Kaulas do not consider themselves to be *avaidika*; rather they adopt many Vedic mantras in their *cakra pūjā*.[102] "Kaula tantrics," as Brooks correctly observes, "who are also 'conservative' Vaidikas admit the Upaniṣads and other Kaula-oriented sources into their canon by interpreting potentially scandalous prescriptions in two ways. They treat them either (1) as nominally acceptable symbolic acts to be performed with 'harmless' substitutes *(pratinidhi)*—such as milk for wine, or a fish-shaped ritual spoon for the offering of fish—or (2) they perform them entirely as internal, purely mental forms of discipline or sacrifice *(antaryāga)*.[103]

The distinction that Lakṣmīdhara draws between Kaulācāra and Samayācāra on the basis of their external and internal modes of worship is not correct either. It is true that Kaulas hold external worship in high regard, but they do not condemn internal worship. On the contrary, in many cases, they acknowledge the value of internal worship. Thus, this particular issue cannot be treated as a distinguishing characteristic.[104] As Brooks clearly states: "In contemporary Śrīvidyā, however, this internal/external distinction along Samaya and Kaula lines is blurred. Self-proclaimed Samayins continue to perform external rituals despite Lakṣmīdhara's protestations, though they continue to reject any of the potentially controversial Kaula elements, such as the *pañcamakāras*."[105]

In order to highlight the importance of the *sahasrāra cakra*, Lakṣmīdhara equates *śrīcakra* with the *sahasrāra cakra* and recommends that *samayins* confine their worship to the goddess who resides there. At the same time, he denigrates the *mūlādhāra cakra* and by assigning the *mūlādhāra cakra* as the center of worship for the Kaulas, he also denigrates them. But the fact is, Kaulas worship *śakti*, not only in the *mūlādhāra*, but also in other *cakras* as well. In fact, quoting

Svacchanda Tantra, a Śaivite text,[106] Bhāskararāya, a Śrīvidyā adept of Kaulamārga, describes the *sahasrāra* as the residence of the goddess. According to the majority of Śaiva and Śākta Tāntric texts, "Kaula" means *śakti* and "Akula" means *śiva* and the union of both is called "Kaula." Bhāskararāya, possibly relying on *Tantrāloka*, indicates that the essence common to both *śakti* and *śiva* is called *kaulinī*.[107]

The issue of which Tāntric texts belong to Kaula and which to Samaya is not pertinent. The five Tāntric texts which Lakṣmīdhara claims are Samaya-oriented are now extinct and other texts, such as *Vāmakeśvara Tantra* and the *Yāmala Tantras*, which he quotes frequently in his commentary, are replete with Kaula-oriented ideas and practices.

The idea of attaining the experience of oneness with the goddess or identifying oneself with the goddess and even the "fourfold oneness" is not unique to *samayins*. Before and after Lakṣmīdhara, all Tāntric adepts—whether following the Samaya or Kaula paths—aspired to union with the *iṣṭa devatā*.[108]

Considering all these facts, it appears that the Samaya-Kaula opposition is primarily concerned with two *ācāras*, systems of conduct and cultural values. One is puritan, the other liberal. One insists on vegetarianism, the other does not. Furthermore, this Samaya-Kaula debate seems to be one-sided: it is Samayācārins, including Lakṣmīdhara, who constantly oppose Kaula without considering what Kaulācārins themselves have to say. Furthermore, it is Lakṣmīdhara and the Samayācārins who follow him who insist on demonstrating the Vedic origin of Samayācāra and making a sharp distinction between the two schools, whereas the more convincing fact is—as Mark S. G. Dyczkowski,[109] Goudriaan,[110] and Brooks observe—that Kaulācāra is an older tradition than Samaya, and that in the early stages of Śākta Tāntrism, there does not seem to be any outstanding or distinguishing characteristics separating Samayācāra from Kaulācāra.[111]

Apparently Lakṣmīdhara considers Kaulācāra to be synonymous with Vāmācāra, and Samayācāra synonymous with Dakṣiṇācāra. But Samayācāra and Dakṣiṇācāra, according to his strict definition, cannot be synonymous, since Dakṣiṇācāra simply refers to a system of conduct which upholds the view of using only Dakṣiṇa, "conventionally right" articles, such as flowers, bilva leaves, and so on, as opposed to the wine, meat, sex, etc., of Vāmācāra. The mere exclusion of the articles of Vāmācāra worship, however, does not make the Kaulācāra style of *śrīcakra* worship identical to that of the Samayācārins. Nevertheless, after Lakṣmīdhara, the terms Samayācāra and Dakṣiṇācāra became synonymous. As a result, devotees performing ritual worship of *śrīcakra* in the monasteries of the Śaṅkarācārya order consider themselves to be Samayācārins/Dakṣiṇācārins, not Kaulācārins. Thus, Lakṣmīdhara's discussion has nothing to do with Samaya and Kaula, but with the difference between the Vāmācāra and Dakṣiṇācāra aspects of Kaula itself.

Goudriaan clarifies this issue beautifully in the following manner:

> The antithesis Vāma-Dakṣina is covered also, and still more specifically, by the terms Samaya and Kaula. Samaya 'Convention' has several meanings, but in the present context Samayācāra, as we say, means the practice of internal worship as advocated by Lakṣmīdhara and his followers while the Kaulas (according to the Samayins) conduct external worship including revolting acts, while contenting themselves with worshiping the internal Kuṇḍalinī only in the Mūlādhāra, the lowest cakra (Kaviraj, *Tāntrika Sāhitya*, 42, 45f.). Not all Samayins lived up to this distinction (Chakravarti, *Tantras,* p. 56). This

opposition mainly obtains in Tripurā worship; in practice, every Samayin seems to be a Tripurā worshipper, but this can by no means be said of every Kaula. Indeed, the term Kaula largely transcends the opposition to Samaya. Within the Kaula school, *samaya* may have quite another meaning, as for instance when the KT (11, 99f.) asserts that one becomes a Kaulika only when being aware of the Samayas, i.e., the secret meanings of mantras and details of conduct.[112]

In summary, we can safely conclude that Lakṣmīdhara's understanding of the distinctive features of Kaula and Samaya appears unclear and is often misleading. He may be simply stating the doctrines he learned from the oral tradition, expressing a regional belief regarding Śrīvidyā[113] or even assigning his own opinion to the kind of Śrīvidyā that was in vogue in the monastic order of Śaṅkarācārya. None of these factors, however, diminish his accomplishment of systematizing the philosophy of Śrīvidyā and providing a philosophical foundation for the practices he advocates.

Most of the philosophical doctrines, theories, and practices that center around yantra, mantra, *cakra*, deity, and *śaktipāta* are found, in rudimentary form, in Vedic and Paurāṇic literature. We also find elaborations of these concepts in Śaiva, Śākta, and Pāñcarātra texts, but until Lakṣmīdhara, no *śakta* adherent had organized these elements into a structurally coherent philosophy. It is the way in which he puts them together, building a philosophy parallel to other schools, that is revolutionary. Later Śrīvidyā adherents, including Bhāskararāya, whether they identify themselves as Samayins or Kaulācārins, agree unanimously with the philosophy of Śrīvidyā, as outlined by Lakṣmīdhara.

As has been said before, all the elements that Lakṣmīdhara discusses are found in earlier literature. Lakṣmīdhara must have studied and made use of such sources, but he cites only those which he considers to be of his tradition. He completely ignores the Śaivite sources, especially those which are classified as Kashmir Śaivism and which bear an enormous similarity to his material. If Lakṣmīdhara comes from South India, where Kashmir Śaivism flourished long before his time, and if he was also the author of *Śaiva Kalpadruma*, a work in which the author states that he is a worshipper of Śiva at Ekāmra (Bhuvaneśvara, Orissa), then his affinity with Śaivism is established. This affinity becomes even more evident when, in his own commentary on *SL*, he clearly identifies *mahāvedha*, the highest kind of Śrīvidyā initiation, as Śaiva.[114]

In the closing remarks of this commentary, Lakṣmīdhara makes a statement which also demonstrates his association with Śaivism: "Śaṅkarācārya is gone. Vīramāheśvara is gone. Who can understand my exertions in the piercing of six cakras!"[115] Vīramāheśvara is not an epithet of Śaṅkarācārya, because this epithet is never applied to Śaṅkarācārya anywhere else. Furthermore, in the introduction to the first verse of *SL*, Lakṣmīdhara gives Śaṅkarācārya the epithet *Śankarabhagavatpūjyapādāḥ*, as was customary among all Advaita Vedānta writers. Therefore, Lakṣmīdhara must be referring to a Śaiva adept, perhaps to Vasava, as this epithet is frequently applied to him.

Because Kaulism and Śaivism are closely associated with each other, Lakṣmīdhara seems to deliberately conceal his connection with Śaivism. But he cannot ignore Śaivite philosophical ideas, because by his time such ideas had become an integral part of Śrīvidyā.[116] Thus, he retains the Śaivite doctrines that had seeped into Śrīvidyā, synthesizing them with the Vedic *ācāra* of the Śaṅkarācārya tradition, calling this synthesis "Śamayācāra." Of course, this synthesis is more complex than the above statement suggests. There are several points of difference between Lakṣmīdhara's Samayācāra Śrīvidyā and the Trika philosophy and *sādhanā* of Kashmir Śaivism. A study of Lakṣmīdhara's commentary on the *SL* is the key to identifying the features distinctive to the concept of *śakti* in the Samayācāra-dominated Śrīvidyā tradition.

The Saundaryalaharī

The *SL*, usually attributed to the strict Advaita-Vedāntin, Śaṅkarācārya is one of the most famous *stotra* texts and a standard literary work. On the basis of its philosophical and religious content, the text belongs to the Śrīvidyā tradition of Śākta Tāntric lore. The religious popularity of this text and the respected place it holds in the Indian community is described accurately by W. Norman Brown:

> This work is one of the most widely used devotional texts of modern Hinduism. Many people employ it daily throughout the year; large numbers know some or all of its stanzas by heart. Manuscripts of it abound in every part of the country—north, south, east, west, central—and it is one of the relatively few works which have been embellished with manuscript paintings. There are numerous lists of magic diagrams (yantra) and mystic seed syllables (bījākṣara) for use with the separate stanzas and prescriptions of accessory paraphernalia and methods of reciting the stanzas. . . .[117]

Many different versions of the *SL* are found throughout India, and disagreement on both the number of verses and their sequence is apparent in the numerous printed editions. The most comprehensive critical edition of the original text is by Brown. This edition outlines some of the basic teachings, such as the concept of the material world, the soul, human self-fulfillment, and the means for attaining the soteriological goal. He does not take the commentaries into consideration, nor is the scope of his study limited to one particular field of scholarship, either literary, philosophical, spiritual, or religious.

The text has been edited and translated into the various provincial languages of India (Hindi, Bengali, and Tamil, etc.), and English as well. But as Brown points out, "All have been made primarily for religious use, only secondarily or not at all for scientific study."[118] Thus, without exception, the translators stretch and distort the contents with a panegyric style, saying that they are explicating that which is esoteric and implied.

The *SL* consists of one hundred (sometimes one hundred and three) verses in the *śikhariṇī* meter. The text is generally divided into two parts. The first part, consisting of the first forty-one verses, is known as "Ānandalaharī," "The Wave of Bliss." However, R. Anantakṛṣṇa Śāstri and Karrā Rāmamūrthi Gāru point out that some commentators consider that Ānandalaharī consists of only thirty or thirty-five verses; others put the number at thirty-five; and still others believe that the Ānandalaharī portion consists only of verses 1, 2, 8-11, 14-21, 26, 27, and 31-41.[119] The title "Saundaryalaharī," however, is widely and popularly used for both the second part and the text as a whole.

As far as the authorship of the *SL* is concerned, Indian tradition almost unanimously ascribes it to Ādi Śaṅkarācārya, the first Śaṅkara.[120] However, after surveying the pros and cons of the various positions held by different scholars, Brown draws the following conclusion:

> . . . The author cannot be identified. Its ascription to Śaṅkara was to win it prestige . . . a speculative theory can here be suggested . . . if the Saundaryalaharī happened to be composed in one of the mutts by one of the heads of the mutt, all of whom

> assume the name Śaṅkara, it would have been relatively easy at some later time for it to gain ascription to the great Śaṅkarācārya Bhāṣyakāra. From one mutt it would have spread to all others and to the Śaiva-Śakti cults generally. This theory, being only a theory, may have small merit, but it is perhaps better than no theory at all.[121]

In spite of the questions raised by contemporary scholars, the traditional view ascribing the text to Ādi Śaṅkara prevails (at least in India), and faithful followers consider it to be his work.[122] While the question of authorship remains open, as far as the *SL*'s status goes, Brown correctly says, "the *Saundaryalaharī*, whoever wrote it, is a great work of religious literature."[123]

Content of the Text

The *SL* is essentially a work of devotional poetry and does not concentrate on developing a new system of thought. The philosophical or metaphysical elements it conveys are incidental, for the author's main intent is to express the depth of his devotion to the goddess Tripurasundarī. It is the commentators who stress the metaphysical subtleties and elaborate on them. In attempting to explicate the underlying philosophical ideas, they connect them with the specific discipline and worldview of Śāktism.

The majority of verses are dedicated to describing Tripurasundarī's physical beauty. This description is visual, but the reader often is reminded, especially by the commentators, to be aware that the individual soul, mantra, yantra, and *kuṇḍalinī* are identical to her. In most of the philosophical verses, the goddess is presented as formless and absolute. Thus Advaitavāda (nondualism) seems to be the main philosophical thrust, and the special focus of this text is to explicitly demonstrate the unity of the above-mentioned concepts.

The author may have had some distinct philosophical ideas in mind during the composition of the *SL*, but their actual presentation in the text is disjointed. Themes are fragmented, forcing commentators to discontinue the thematic flow of the commentary in order to follow the numerical order of the verses.

Commentaries and Translations

Tāntrika Sāhitya, the most recent catalog specializing in Tāntric texts and manuscripts, lists forty-one commentaries on the *SL*. However, this catalog does not specify where these commentaries are to be found; it simply collects information from older catalogs, some of which were prepared almost a hundred years ago. Many of the manuscripts mentioned in those catalogs may no longer exist. It was possible to obtain only thirteen commentaries. Among them, ten are edited and published; three are still in unedited manuscript form.[124]

So far, no study has been done with the intention of explicating the commentaries themselves. Swami Viṣṇutīrtha's *Saundarya-Laharī Kā Hindi Anuvāda* and S. Subrahmanya Shastri and T. R. Srinivasa Ayyangar's *Saundarya-Laharī of Śrī Śaṃkara-Bhagavatpāda* are general works that derive their materials from *LD*, as well as from other commentaries such as Kaivalyāśrama's *Saubhāgyavardhanī* and Kāmeśvarasūri's *Aruṇāmodinī*. The most outstanding of the available commentaries are Lakṣmīdhara's *LD*, Kaivalyāśram's *Saubhāgyavardhanī*, and Kāmeśvarasūri's *Aruṇāmodinī*. Rāmakavi's *ḍiṇḍima* and Ānandagiri's *Ānandagirīyā* also deserve mention because they occasionally present unique interpretations oriented towards Sāṅkhya and mantra *sādhanā*, respectively. Lakṣmīdhara, Kaivalyāśrama, and Kāmeśvarasūri attempt to extract and elaborate upon the meaning of the original text within the limits of Śākta philosophy, while Rāmakavi compromises between Tantra and Sāṅkhya doctrines, identifying *śakti* with *prakṛti* and *śiva* with *puruṣa*. Ānandagiri, on the other hand, attempts to demonstrate how a number of *śrīvidyā* mantras or mantras of secondary Śrīvidyā deities are derived from or represented by the verses of the *SL*.

Because of the depth of knowledge it displays in regard to Samaya philosophy and practice, Lakṣmīdhara's commentary on the *SL* holds a place similar to that of Śaṅkara's commentary on the *Brahma Sūtras* or Vyasa's on the *Yoga Sūtras*. Lakṣmīdhara gives a detailed treatment of the Samaya method of Śrīvidyā *sādhanā* and philosophy. He rejects the views of the Kaula and Miśra groups, considering them to be un-Vedic and unworthy. He draws heavily on the *Subhagodaya* of Gauḍapāda, for which he claims to have written a commentary. The version of *SU* published in the appendix of *NS* cites Śivānanda as its author and mainly focuses on describing an external method for ritualistic worship of *śrīcakra*. This version, consisting of a mixture of *anuṣṭup* meter and prose, contains almost nothing related to Samayācāra. Another version of the *SU*, consisting of fifty-two *śikhariṇī chandas*, is published in the appendix of Shiva Shankar Awasthi Shastri's *Mantra Aur Mātṛkāon kā Rahasya* (hereafter cited as *MMR*),[125] and gives Gauḍapāda as its author. There is a great similarity between the Gauḍapāda *SU* and some of the verses of the *SL*; this is particularly evident in *LD*, not only in the usage of terms but even in the duplication of complete phrases.

However, Lakṣmīdhara, in his commentary on the *SL*, quotes the *SU* which is in *anuṣṭup* meter, not in *śikharaṇī*.[126]

Further, the material that he quotes is not found in Śivānanda's *anuṣṭup chanda* nor in the prose version of *SU*. These contradictions lead us to believe that there must have been another version of *SU* by Gauḍapāda, most probably in *anuṣṭup* meter, which was commented upon by Lakṣmīdhara and quoted in his commentary on the *SL* verses 11, 32, and 41. Whatever the case may be, the present version of *SU* ascribed to Gauḍapāda, published in the appendix of *MMR*, is one of the most significant Samayācāra texts, and it either utilizes Lakṣmīdhara's exposition (if it is later than Lakṣmīdhara's text) or vice versa.

In addition to *SU*, Lakṣmīdhara draws heavily on the *Vāmakeśvara Tantra (Catuḥśatī)*, *Sanatakumārasaṃhitā*, *Aruṇopaniṣad*, *Vaśiṣtha Saṃhitā*, and the texts of Vedic lore, such as *Taittrīyasaṃhitā*, *Taittrīyabrāhmaṇa*, *Taittrīyāraṇyaka*, *Taittrīyopaniṣad*, and *Yogakuṇḍalī Upaniṣad*.[127] As stated earlier, *SL* simply consists of devotional verses dedicated to the goddess Tripurasundarī and contains so little Tāntric material that it hardly qualifies as a Tāntric text.[128] It is Lakṣmīdhara who brings in Tāntric ideas and magnifies them in his commentary on *SL*, especially verses 1, 8-11, 14, 31-32, 34-36, 40-41, 92, and 99. Most of the other verses describe the anthropomorphic form of the goddess and carry little philosophical weight. By selecting only those verses which serve his purpose, Lakṣmīdhara clearly demonstrates that he is a sectarian commentator. His interest lies in expounding the theories related to *śrīcakra*, the *śrīvidyā* mantra, the *cakras* in the human body, *mātṛikā*, the awakening of *kuṇḍalinī*, and attaining the direct experience of the union of *śiva* and *śakti* in the *sahasrāra*. He attempts to pull together all these components and unite them under one main concept, *śakti*. Unlike other Tāntric scriptures, commentators, and writers of independent texts, Lakṣmīdhara insists on using the specific terms *samayā*, *sādhākhyā*, and *candrakalā* with precisely defined meanings. By conducting a philological analysis of these terms, and thus understanding the process through which their general meanings resolved into the specific meanings we encounter in *LD*, we may gain a better insight into the historical and philosophical development of Śākta Tāntrism as a whole.

CHAPTER 3

General and Specific Views of *Śakti*

An Overview of Śakti in Prominent Śrīvidyā Texts

If we are to identify the distinctive characteristics of *śakti* in Lakṣmīdhara's commentary on the *SL*, it is first necessary to have a general view of *śakti* in other texts of the Śrīvidyā tradition. Because it is neither feasible nor desirable to scrutinize all of the Śrīvidyā literature, we have selected the following texts for this present study: *YH*, *NS*, *SU*,[1] *SL*, and the writings of Durvāsas,[2] Kālidāsa,[3] Śīvānanda,[4] Amṛtānanda,[5] Vidyānanda,[6] Puṇyānanda,[7] and Bhāskararāya.[8] Other texts which are useful in tracing the distinctive characteristics of *śakti* or which show a philological or historical progression in the use of the term itself will occasionally be consulted.

In these texts, the names *tripurā (tripurasundarī* or *mahātripurasundarī), saṃvit,* and *citi (parā citi)* are used interchangeably to indicate the highest reality. According to these sources, she is pure, unalloyed consciousness, and the only reality. For example, in *NS* she is described as *saṃvit,* identical to *ātman (ātmasvarūpā);* she is also the same as existence, *satsvarṃupā,* and consciousness and bliss, *cidānandarūpā.* Apart from her, nothing exists.[9] In fact, the word *tripurā* itself, according to *NS*, refers to the state of reality that transcends the entire manifest world.

In an effort to prove *śakti's* transcendental status, *NS* gives an etymological, or more accurately, pseudo-etymological, meaning of the term *tripurā*: she is called *tripurā* because she is the source of, and transcendent to, "three cities," or the symbolic triad of the triple world. She transcends the three *bindus—icchā, jñāna,* and *kriyā* (will, knowledge, and action); the three *śarīras—sthūla, sūkṣma,* and *kāraṇa* (the physical, subtle, and causal bodies); the three *avasthās—jāgrat, svapna,* and *suṣupti* (the waking, dreaming, and sleep states of consciousness); the three *pīṭhas*—the shrines *oḍyāṇa, jālandhara,* and *kāmagiri;* the three *mātṛkās—vaikharī, madhyamā,* and *paśyantī;* the three *mūrtis—brahmā, viṣṇu,* and *śiva;* the three *nāḍīs—suṣumnā, piṅgalā,* and *iḍā;* and the three *puras—manas, buddhi,* and *citta.* With more elaboration and variations, the term *tripurā* has also been interpreted in texts such as *Setubandha, Artharatnāvālī, Cidvallī, Tripurarāraṇava, Kālikā Purāṇa,* and Bhāskararāya's commentary on *Lalitā-Sahasranāman.*[10]

The intention behind the pseudo-etymological interpretations in all these texts is obviously to demonstrate that this term carries considerable philosophical weight and that *tripurā* includes in herself every aspect of this threefold creation while remaining transcendent. Bhāskararāya captures the totality of *tripurā's* diverse forms and characteristics in three different categories: *sthūla, sūkṣma,* and *parā* (gross, subtle, and transcendent).[11] Based mainly on Bhāskararāya's commentary on the *Bhāvanopaniṣat,* Brooks[12] considers the anthropomorphic form of the goddess to be gross, the mantric form to be subtle, and the *śuṣumnā nādī,* or the *kuṇḍalinī śakti* traveling through the *śuṣumnā nāḍī*, to be transcendental. Thus *tripurasundarī* simultaneously exists at three levels—gross, subtle, and transcendent. There are threefold spiritual disciplines *(upāsti)* that correspond to these three levels of existence: *kāyikī, vācikī*, and *mānasī*—physical, verbal, and mental.

According to a majority of Śrīvidyā texts, as well as to all Śaivite texts, there are thirty-six *tattvas* covering the entire range of the unmanifest and manifest world, from the earth element to the subtlest *tattva*, known as *śiva*, pure illumination. There are two doctrines—Ābhāsavāda (or Pratibimba Vāda) and Pariṇāmavāda (more appropriately Śakti Pariṇāmavāda)—which explain the relationship between *saṃvit* or *tripurā* and the world. According to the theory of Ābhāsavāda, which is expounded in most of the Śrīvidyā texts, *saṃvit* is like a mirror and the universe is like a reflection appearing in it. However, unlike a physical mirror that only reflects external objects placed next to it, this mirror contains the whole universe inside herself, and through her intrinsic autonomous power *(svātantryaśakti)* makes them appear as though they are outside her.[13]

According to the *Tripurā Rahasya (Jñāna-khaṇḍṁa)* (hereafter cited as *TR-J*),[14] this system does not tolerate the idea of the universe appearing outside *citi* or *saṃvit*, for such a proposition would contradict the very basis of its nondualistic model. But if the universe is inside rather than outside the mirror, then what is the relationship between *saṃvit* and the world? If the relationship is *aupādhika* (conditioned or accidental), then it necessarily implies the simultaneous existence of more than one principle. The other option is *samavāya* (inherence) *sambandha*—a relationship in which two different things such as *dravya* (substance) and *guṇa* (attribute) appear so unified that they represent one whole.[15] This relationship is also known as *ayutasiddha* or *avinābhāva (sine qua non) sambandha*, i.e., the relationship in which neither can exist without the other. This kind of relationship points to an essential oneness of the universe with *citi* (consciousness).[16]

According to Pariṇāmavāda, as held in the *Varivasyā-Rahasya* (hereafter cited as *VR*),[17] *SL*, *SU*, and *NS*, the universe is a transformation or manifestation of *tripurā*. As *NS* states, "One single, unmanifest *tripurā* remains by herself in bliss and becomes manifest."[18] "Just as before germination, a sprout, stem, leaves, flowers, and fruits substantially *(sadātmanā)* exist in the seed, likewise, before its manifestation, the universe exists in Tripurā."[19] In fact, *tripurā* (the cause), and the phenomenal world (the effect), are two different states of the same truth known as *śaktyavasthā* and *pariṇatāvasthā*.

According to Vrajavallabha Dviveda, the doctrine of Pariṇāmavāda held in these Śrīvidyā texts differs from the Pariṇāmavāda in the Sāṅkhya system. According to the Pariṇāmavāda of Sāṅkhya, the world evolves from *prakṛti*. When the equilibrium of *prakṛti's* three intrinsic characteristics—*sattva, rajas,* and *tamas*—is disturbed, *prakṛti* is transformed into the phenomenal world. In that evolutionary state, *prakṛti* becomes *vikṛti* (distorted or contaminated), and is no longer pristine. According to Pariṇāmavāda as propounded in Śrīvidyā texts, *citi* manifests in the form of the universe without losing her pristine nature *(avikṛtā satī)*. This is accomplished through her own unrestricted power of sovereignty *(sva-svātantryeṇa)*.[20] To make a clear distinction between the Pariṇāmavāda of Sāṅkhya, and the Pariṇāmavāda of the Śrīvidyā school, Vrajavallabha Dviveda calls the former

Prakṛti Pariṇāmavāda and the latter Śakti Pariṇāmavāda.[21]

According to the theories of both Ābhāsavāda and Śakti Pariṇāmavāda, there is only one reality, *śakti*, and the universe is either a mere appearance or an actual transformation of her. In both doctrines, the world does not exist apart from *śakti*: it is either an appearance without a substance of its own or a manifest state of unmanifest *śakti*. It is important to note, however, that although all of the above-mentioned texts begin by referring to the highest reality primarily by the terms *tripurā, saṃvit,* and *citi,* they soon start using the generic term *śakti*, sacrificing precision in the process.

Because these texts use *śakti* loosely and do not fully define it, it remains ambiguous in Śākta doctrine. For example, *NS* considers *tripurā* to be *paramāśakti*, the highest *śakti*. She is also *mātṛkā*, the cause of the triple world.[22] *Tripurā* is also said to be the one within whom all thirty-six *tattvas* exist inseparably.[23] In elaborating the concept, Śivānanda explains that all thirty-six *tattvas* exist in *tripurā*, just as the entire tree in its unmanifest form exists in the seed.[24] According to him, her unmanifest state is called *śaktyavasthā,* and the universe is her manifest state, *prapañcāvasthā* or *pariṇatāvasthā*.[25] According to this statement, *śaktyavasthā* is the highest state, and *pariṇatāvasthā* is the immanent state of one nondual reality, *tripurā*. The obvious conclusion is that except for *tripurā*, who is transcendent, *śakti* cannot be the highest reality because she is one of the *tattvas.*

However, in the following verses, the text suddenly drops the term *tripurā*, replacing it with *śiva* and *śakti*.[26] The commentators Śīvānanda and Vidyānanda follow suit: they replace the term *tripurā* with the terms *śakti* or *vimarśaśakti*. They also introduce the terms *parameśvara* or *śiva*. Thereafter, instead of discussing whether it is *śiva* or *śakti* who actually replaces *tripurā*, and speculating on which of the two is highest, they focus their discussion on proving the oneness of *śakti* and *śiva*. Interestingly, here both Śīvānanda and Vidyānanda, while commenting on *NS*, which is clearly a Śrīvidyā text, use Śaiva terminology and quote from Śaiva texts such as *Īśvarapratyabhijñāvimarśinī*, *Saṅketapaddhati*, *Bodhapañcadaśikā*, *Sarvamañgalāśāstra*, and even *Vākyapadīya*, the Vyākaraṇa Āgama text.[27]

Commentators on Śrīvidyā texts frequently quote from Śaivite texts, which indicates that both traditions rely on a common source for their philosophical inspiration. However, the tendency to refer to the ultimate truth by the term *tripurā*, which according to Śrīvidyā followers embraces all categories including the two highest, *śakti* and *śiva*, and the tendency to keep emphasizing the oneness of *śakti* and *śiva*, may indicate the existence of an analogous dualistic tradition. That tradition, as Professor Sanderson points out, is Śaiva-Siddhānta, a dualistic Śaiva school, still in existence in South India.[28] However, it is to be borne in mind that even Siddhāntins accept the inseparability of *śiva* and *śakti*. Their dualism lies in the distinction of *paśu/pāśa* and *paśupati*. Śrīvidyā and Śaiva texts, even in an attempt to expound a perfectly clear and logically sound nondualistic philosophy, use the terms *tripurā, śrīvidyā, samayā, anuttara,* and *yāmala*. Because the terms *śiva* and *śakti* have a long history and are deeply ingrained in the literature and in the popular faith, these texts retain them, although sometimes these terms carry the notion of oneness and other times the notion of duality. However, to ensure the integrity of their nondualistic model, they repeatedly emphasize the oneness of the two.

Consequently, Śrīvidyā and Kashmir Śaivite texts usually begin the exposition of their doctrines by using the terms *tripurā* and *anuttara*, but soon drop them to focus on proving the oneness of *śakti* and *śiva*. For example, in *NS* 4:4, the term *tripurā* refers to the highest reality, which transcends all thirty-six categories. Later, in *NS* 4:6, *tripurā* is replaced by the term *śakti*, which according to general Śākta and Śaiva doctrine represents the thirty-fifth category of reality. The commentators then go into a detailed explanation of the oneness of *śakti* and *śiva*, constantly repeating the phrase, "without *śakti*, *śiva* cannot create the universe." However, neither the text nor the commentators explain why *śiva* or even his *vimarśaśakti* need to be considered as the ultimate cause of the universe, as they themselves have evolved from *tripurā*. Rather, in *NS* 4:10-12, *tripurā* is said to be *ekaiva* (only one) and *paramā* (absolute) *śakti*; she is *parameśvarī* (the highest lord); she is the same as *brahmā*, *viṣṇu*, and *īśa*, or *jñānaśakti*, *kriyāśakti*, and *icchāśakti*. It is this *tripurā* who creates the universe.[29] This discussion from *NS* and the commentaries *Ṛjuvimarśinī* and *Artharatnāvalī* is typical of Śrīvidyā literature. Similar tendencies and the attendant philosophical problems are found in other texts as well.

In other words, Śaiva and Śrīvidyā texts employ a variety of terms to refer either to the highest reality or to a particular category of reality, but are not consistent in the usage of their terminology. The terms *tripurā*, *saṃvit*, *citi*, *samayā*, and *sādākhyākalā* in Śrīvidyā and *saṅghaṭṭa*, *anuttara*, and *yāmala* in Kashmir Śaivism have exact meanings and are always used precisely. However, other frequently used, though less precise, terms include *śakti*, *vimarśaśakti*, *spandaśakti*, *kāmakalā*, *śiva*, *parameśvara*, or *maheśvara*. Discussions related to these less precise terms are an integral part of Śaiva and Śākta literature.

Śākta texts in the Śrīvidyā school never mention *śakti* without *śiva*; similarly Śaivite texts never mention *śiva* without *śakti*. However, each maintains a distinct position relative to these two terms: Śaivite texts consider *śiva* to be the highest reality but retain *śakti* alongside *śiva*; Śākta texts accept *śakti* as the highest metaphysical truth but recognize *śiva* as her inactive partner. These two approaches are popularly known as Śivapāramyavāda and Śaktipāramyavāda, respectively.[30]

On the other hand, texts such as *Kāmakalā-Vilāsa* (hereafter cited as *KKV*), *VR, SL*, and *SU*[31] adhere to the view that in the manifestation of the universe, both *śakti* and *śiva* play equal roles, and in that sense, neither the supremacy of *śakti* over *śiva* nor of *śiva* over *śakti* can be established. With the exception of *BP-L*, *DS*, *TR-M*, and *TR-J*, all the Śākta texts we have reviewed offer equal status to *śakti* and *śiva*. Śākta texts such as the *SL* and *SU*, whose overall tone seems to advocate the supremacy of *śakti*, also mention the inseparability and equal status of *śakti* and *śiva*. The inclusion of *śiva*, therefore, naturally prompts further analysis into the nature of *śakti*, especially in relation to *śiva*.

In Kashmir Śaivism as well as in Śāktism, *śiva*, or consciousness, is considered to be the highest reality. Unlike the *brahman* of Vedānta, *śiva* is endowed with *vimarśa* (self-awareness) and *sphurattā* (reflective awareness). Both systems consistently deny any difference between consciousness and the self-awareness intrinsic to it. Pure consciousness is referred to as *prakāśa* (pure illumination); its intrinsic self-awareness is termed *vimarśa*. *Prakāśa* and *vimarśa*, illumination and the self-awareness of illumination, are called *śiva* and *śakti*.[32]

In Śaivism, although *śiva* is the highest reality, *śakti* is considered to be the heart of *śiva*, the creative force behind the appearance of the universe *(hṛdayaṃ parameṣṭhinaḥ)*; thus, in essence, they are one.[33] To emphasize this point, Abhinavagupta states that neither is *śakti* dependent on *śak-*

timat (śiva) nor is *śiva* dependent on *śakti.* Commenting on Abhinavagupta's *TĀ*, Jayaratha says that essentially *śiva* and *śakti* are the same. The apparent difference created by the two terms is merely a matter of semantics.[34]

The View of Śakti in Saundaryalaharī and the Lakṣmīdharā

Turning our attention to the *SL*, we notice that this text assigns the highest metaphysical status to *śakti*, but recognizes *śiva* as well. At the outset, the *SL* expounds the supremacy of *śakti* over *śiva*, assigning her the highest metaphysical position. As the text says, "If *śiva* is united with *śakti*, He is able to exert his powers as Lord; if not, the God is not able to stir."[35] Thus, the ability of *śiva* to perform an action depends on his union with *śakti.*

At this stage, the text does not clarify the relationship between *śiva* and *śakti.* However, it clearly indicates that although *śiva* is the *deva* (lord), he is powerless without *śakti.* It gives the impression that *spanda* (the process of stirring), which in Śaivism and Śāktism results in the creation, maintenance, and annihilation of the universe, is the work of *śiva* and that he accomplishes it with the help of *śakti.* In *SL* 24-26, 55, 92, 96, and 97, *śakti* is described as the highest sovereign power and highest reality, while *śiva* is simply a figurehead. In *SL* 34, however, *śiva* is neither a figurehead nor secondary to *śakti;* rather the two are of equal status. But in *SL* 35, the tone changes again, and *śakti* appears to be the sole source of creation, maintenance, and annihilation. The entire manifest world and all its governing forces are manifestations of her. In keeping with this, in *SL* 55, *śakti* is said to be the only source of creation and annihilation; when she closes her eyes, the universe dissolves and the moment she opens them, the universe manifests. However, in *SL* 9, she is described as the wife of *śiva*, although in *SL* 97, she is the wife or queen of the transcendent *brahman* and is endowed with unlimited power.

These simple and fragmented statements regarding *śakti* and her position in relation to *śiva* evoke a series of questions: if *śakti* is superior to *śiva*, then how can they be either identical or hold equal status? If they are one and the same, then why does *SL* use two different terms, *śiva* and *śakti*, instead of just one? Why does it portray *śiva* as inactive and powerless, while portraying *śakti* as a vibrant, active force, thereby implying a distinction between the two? Although *SL* itself does not address these issues, Lakṣmīdhara undertakes the task of expounding a coherent doctrine, thus resolving these apparent contradictions.

Lakṣmīdhara prefers the terms *candrakalā, samayā*, or *sādākhyākalā* to *śakti.* He uses the words *śakti* and *śiva* infrequently and then only to indicate the categories below the transcendent *samayāṃ* or to explain the position of *śakti* in Pūrva Kaula or Uttara Kaula doctrines, which he refutes. In his commentary, Lakṣmīdhara uses the terms *śuddhavidyā* and *sadāśiva* to replace the more common terms *śakti* and *śiva.* He goes on to explain how the term *śuddhavidyā* subsumes the content of all the terms that are directly or indirectly related to the concept of *śakti*, such as *buddhi, prakṛti, māyā*, and *śakti.* Similarly, he explains how *jīva, puruṣa*, and *śiva* are subsumed in one term, *sadāśiva.* Moreover, he uses the terms *samayā, candrakalā,* or *sādākhyā*, which, according to him, transcend even the category of reality covered by the terms *śuddhavidyā* and *sadāśiva.* While expounding the doctrine of Samayācāra, he consistently uses the terms *samayā, candrakalā*, or *sādākhyākalā.*

The terms *candrakalā, sādākhyā,* and particularly *samayā*

are rarely used in most Śrīvidyā texts. Lakṣmīdhara, however, seems to have a special interest in these terms, especially *samayā. Samayā* is *avyaya*, an indeclinable word ordinarily used in the sense of "near."[36] The word *samaya* which is different from *samayā*, according to Monier-Williams, means "conventions, conventional rule or usage, established custom, order, precept, doctrine, occasion, time, season."[37] According to the *Kulārṇava Tantra*, as stated by Teun Goudriaan, *samayas* (plural of *samaya*) means "the secret meanings of mantras and details of conduct."[38] However, Lakṣmīdhara does not use the term *samayā* as an *avyaya* to mean "near," or the term *samaya* to mean "convention or conventional rule," etc. Rather, he uses the term *samayā*, in feminine gender, and *samaya*, in masculine gender, to refer to a transcendental reality, *para tattva* or *sarvatattvātītā.*

In tracing the philological origin of the terms *samaya* and *samayin,* we find they are first used in the sense that Lakṣmīdhara uses them, in Gauḍapāda's *SU.* It is important to note, however, that throughout the fifty-two verses of *SU,* the word *samayā* is not used, the words *samaya* and *samayamārga* are used once, while the word *samayin* occurs eighteen times.[39] In *SU, samayin* does not necessarily mean the worshipper of *samayā;* it may mean the knower of the secret meaning of mantra and an accurate method of worship or meditation related to *subhagā, sādākhyā,* or *candrakalā.*[40] However, the terms *subhagā, sādākhyā,* and *candrakalā* themselves do not express the supremacy and transcendence of *tripurā* upheld by *samayamārga.* Other terms, such as *mahākālātītā, mahākālabhujagī, samayasahitā,* and *kālakalanā,*[41] do express this supremacy and explain the nature of *subhagā* or *sādākhyā.* While using all these different terms for higher *śakti,* there is only one place in *SU* which atates, "along with *samaya (śiva),* You *(śakti)* dwell."[42]

None of the terms so far mentioned, including *subhagā, sādākhyā*, and *candrakalā* can be equated with *samaya* (i.e., *śiva*). However, the nature of the presentation requires a feminine-gender term parallel to the masculine-gender *samaya*, if *samayin* scholars like Śaṅkarācārya or Lakṣmīdhara are to build a sound philosophy based on *SU*. Thus, *SL* and *LD* adopt the terms *samayā* and *samaya* and use them more frequently than other terms to refer to the highest reality, although there is no explicit use of the term *samayā* in *SU*.

One of the most common meanings of *samaya* is "time" in general or the "time-principle" as a philosophical category. Although the words *samaya* and *kāla* are synonymous, for some reason *kāla, mahākāla*, and *akālapuruṣa* are the most commonly used terms in philosophical and religious literature. In older literature, such as *The Atharvaveda*, *kāla* is considered to be the highest reality: the universe evolves from it, exists in it, and finally dissolves in it. *Kāla*, the time principle, is *sarveśvara* (god of all), and the father of *prajāpati* (the creator); *kāla* is *paramo devaḥ*, absolute shining being.[43]

This concept in its fully developed form is the central theme in the Kaulācāra-dominated *kālī mahāvidyā*, the Kālī school of Sāktism.[44] This *kālī* or *kālaśakti* also holds an important place in Śaiva and Vyākaraṇa Āgama. (The connection between *kālī/kālaśakti* and the *samayā* of Lakṣmīdhara will be discussed later.) In order to retain the concept expressed by the terms *kālī* (or *mahākālī*) and *kālaśakti*, and yet maintain a distinct doctrinal identity, authors in the Śrīvidyā school use the term *samayā*. This tendency toward more frequent use of the term *samayā* and a greater emphasis on the importance of *samayā's* transcendence of the "time-principle" is apparent in Śrīvidyā literature. For example, *Tantrarāja Tantra* 36:40-66, gives a brief description of *kāla*, the time principle, as the highest reality.[45] *BP-L* simply mentions *tripurā (lalitā)* as identical with time and its divisions.[46] Without going into detail, *TR-M* mentions the oneness of *tripurā* with fourfold *śabda*, the "word," and states that the "word" is identical to *kāla*, the "time-principle."[47] Thus, although the word *samaya* has not been used, the word *kāla* has entered the mainstream of Śrīvidyā doctrine.

In *SU*, although the term *samayā* is not used, the terms *sādākhyā* and *subhagā* appear along with qualifying words such as *mahākālātītā*, *mahākālabhujagī*, *samayasahitā*, *kālakalanā*, and *kālotpattisthitilayakaraṃ . . . śrīcakram*. These words indicate at least partial assimilation of the concepts of *mahākāla*, *mahākālī*, and *kālaśakti*. The *SL*, on the other hand, which derives much from *SU*, uses the term *samayā* twice (*SL* 39 and 41). Finally, Lakṣmīdhara builds his entire thesis around this term in the *LD*.

Lakṣmīdhara's View of Śakti

While setting forth his philosophy and clarifying the exact meaning of the terms he uses, Lakṣmīdhara presents an overview of Śaivism and Śāktism. He mentions and refutes *Vāyavīya Saṃhitā*, according to which there are fifty-one *tattvas*. He also refutes the Śaivite view, which holds that there are thirty-six *tattvas*. Lakṣmīdhara goes on to explain how both the thirty-six and the fifty-one *tattvas* are subsumed in his scheme of twenty-five *tattvas*. Taking the issue further, he enumerates these thirty-six principles as: the five *bhūtas* (gross elements), five *tanmātras* (subtle elements), ten *indriyas* (senses), *manas*, *ahaṅkāra*, *buddhi*, *prakṛti*, *puruṣa*, *māyā*, the five *kañcukas* (veils of *māyā*), *śuddhavidyā*, *īśvara*, *sadāśiva*, *śakti*, and *śiva*. The fifteen additional principles, which make a total of fifty-one, are: the seven *dhātus*, the five *prāṇas,* and the three *guṇas.* [48]

To arrive at his scheme of twenty-five, Lakṣmīdhara states that the seven *dhātus* (primary constituents of the body) are subsumed in the five *bhūtas* (gross elements); the five *prāṇas* in *vāyu* (air—one of the five gross elements), and the three *guṇas (sattva, rajas,* and *tamas)* in *prakṛti.* Eleven of the thirty-six remaining *tattvas* are further subsumed to reach twenty-five principles. Specifically, *ahaṅkāra* (ego) is subsumed by *manas* (mind); *buddhi* (intellect) by *vidyā kañcuka* (knowledge), which is in turn subsumed by *śuddhavidyā;* the *niyati kañcuka* is subsumed by *śakti* and the *kalā kañcuka* by *śuddhavidyā.* The *kāla kañcuka* is subsumed by both *maheśvara* and *sadāśiva; puruṣa* by *maheśvara*, and finally *śiva tattva* by *sadāśiva tattva.* Even *śakti* is subsumed in *śuddhavidyā.* Thus, the five *bhūtas* (gross elements), five *tanmātras* (subtle elements), ten *indriyas* (senses), *manas* (mind), *māyā, śuddhavidyā, maheśvara,* and *sadāśiva* constitute Lakṣmīdhara's twenty-five principles.[49]

When united with *sadāśiva,* however, *śuddhavidyā* herself is called *sādākhyākalā*: according to Lakṣmīdhara, this *sādākhyākalā* is the twenty-sixth *tattva* and is entirely different from the two that combined to form it. This twenty-sixth *sādākhyākalā* is also *paramātman,* the supreme soul.[50] Despite the fact that in his system *śakti* and *śiva* do not stand as independent *tattvas,* Lakṣmīdhara still states that the combination of *śakti* and *śiva* is the twenty-sixth transcendent *sādākhyākalā* in his commentary on *SL* 9, 11, 41, 91, and 92. Thus, it is clear what he means by *śakti* and *śiva* in these instances: he must be using the terms *śuddhavidyā* and *śakti,* and *sadāśiva* and *śiva*, interchangeably.

In order to study the nature of *samayā* or *sādākhyākalā*, it is first necessary to analyze the nature of *śuddhavidyā* and *sadāśiva* separately, and then to consider the nature of their relationship when they are united. It is also necessary to explore how they jointly can form an entirely different reality if they are truly independent. In that joint state, do they exist as identifiable entities or not? If not, then is this *sādākhyā*, the twenty-sixth *tattva*, completely dissimilar to both? Furthermore, because *śuddhavidyā* and *sadāśiva* also stand for the *tattvas* they subsume, the study of *sādākhyā* naturally involves an examination of those *tattvas* as well.

As mentioned earlier, *prakṛti* includes all three *guṇas*—*sattva, rajas,* and *tamas. Prakṛti* and *niyati* are subsumed in *śakti. Buddhi* is subsumed in *vidyā*, and finally, both *vidyā* and *śakti* are subsumed in *śuddhavidyā*. Thus, *śuddhavidyā* incorporates *sattva, rajas, tamas, buddhi, prakṛti, niyati, vidyā*, and *śakti tattvas*, while *śiva tattva* alone is subsumed by *sadāśiva*. Logically, therefore, *śuddhavidyā* and *sadāśiva* must possess the qualities, characteristics, and powers of all the *tattvas* subsumed by them.[51]

Lakṣmīdhara defines *śuddhavidyā* as *mocakajñānam*, the knowledge that grants freedom. In a broader sense, however, *śuddhavidyā* must also have the capacity to be, to become, or to enact all that is to be accomplished by all the *tattvas* subsumed in her. According to Lakṣmīdhara, *sattva, rajas,* and *tamas* are the forces of light, activity, and darkness. *Prakṛti* is the material cause of the manifest world. *Vidyā* is empirical knowledge gained through the scriptures. *Buddhi* and *niyati (niyāmikā śakti)* are the cognitive and controlling powers. *Śakti* is described as the protective and creative power of *maheśvara* and *sadāśiva*. Thus, *śuddhavidyā* is not merely a releasing power, but rather stands for all the powers and potentials that can be imagined.[52]

The *śiva tattva*, which is included in *sadāśiva*, is *śuddha-buddha-muktasvarūpa* (pure, awakened, and free), whereas *sadāśiva* by himself is the one who carries on the functions of creation and maintenance. Right after clarifying this, Lakṣmīdhara states that the power of *sadāśiva* and *maheśvara*, termed *śakti* (which is subsumed in *śuddhavidyā*), is in fact the protective and creative power *("śaktiḥ maheśvara-sadāśivayoḥ rakṣaṇasarjanaśaktiḥ").* This gives the impression that it is not *sadāśiva* or *maheśvara* who creates and upholds the world, but rather *śakti* who carries on the functions of creation and protection. Whether *śakti* is intrinsic to them or fundamentally separate but temporarily united with them is a different issue, but as far as the creation and maintenance of the universe are concerned, it is *śakti* who is directly responsible for such phenomena, not *maheśvara* or *sadāśiva*.[53]

It seems then that *sadāśiva* is simply a figurehead in this system, whereas *śuddhavidyā* is the main principle, possessing all the power and potential except for that of mere illumination, which is attributed to *śiva*. If this is the case, then such a *sadāśiva* is certainly unable to initiate any sort of activity, including the maintenance of his own self-awareness.

In regard to the relationship between *sadāśiva* and *śuddhavidyā (śiva* and *śakti),* Lakṣmīdhara presents three different views: Pūrva Kaula, Uttara Kaula, and Samayamata. According to Pūrva Kaula doctrine, *śakti* is the body of *śiva*, and *śiva* is the one to whom the body belongs. *Śakti* is *śeṣa* and *śiva* is *śeṣin,* meaning that *śakti* is the complement and *śiva* is the essence. However, since they are intermingled, they reciprocally realize each other as complement and essence. As the text states:

> You are the body of Śambhu with the sun and moon as your pair of breasts, your self I take to be the flawless self of Bhava, O blessed lady; hence, as you reciprocally realize each other as complement and essence, this union exists of you two experiencing supreme bliss with equal savor.[54]

Commenting on this verse, Lakṣmīdhara states that as far as their metaphysical status goes, the two are equal. They share common ground *(ubhayasādhāraṇatā)* and are of equal joy *(samarasa).* However, from two different perspectives—that of the threefold activity of creation, maintenance, and dissolution, and that of the period after annihilation—both *śiva (ānandabhairava)* and *śakti (ānandabhairavī)* can take either a *śeṣin* (principal) or *śeṣa* (secondary) role to each other. Their *śeṣaśeṣibhāva* (relationship of being principal or secondary) is totally conditional; that is to say, whether *śiva* or *śakti* is principal or secondary depends on whether emphasis is placed on the threefold process or on that perfectly still state that follows annihilation. In the context of creation, maintenance, and dissolution, where effort is involved, *śakti (mahābhairavī,* also known as *prakṛti)* is superior *(pradhānatvam* or *śeṣitvam)* to *śiva (ānandabhairava).* But, after the dissolution, when *prakṛti* exists unalloyed and *bhairavī* is withdrawn, then *bhairava* appears to be *śeṣin* (main), and *bhairavī* to be *śeṣa* (complement).[55] However, both *ānandabhairava* and *mahābhairavī* refer to the supreme bliss and are essentially one; in their ninefold manifestation they are perfectly equal.[56] Thus, the *śeṣaśeṣibhāva* relationship is conditional rather than real.[57]

In Uttara Kaula doctrine, *śakti* is known as *pradhāna* and is considered to be the existent reality, which alone is the cause of the universe. *Śiva* does not exist at all.[58] Here, Uttara Kaula adheres to a theory that stands between Pariṇāmavāda and Vivartavāda. According to this theory, Lakṣmīdhara writes, "*Śakti* superimposes the entire objective world *(prapañca)* within herself as an effect while she herself stands as cause."[59] Another commentator, Kāmeśvara, elaborates upon the Uttara Kaula view, stating that *śakti* is the nondual reality, but the moment she resolves to create the manifest world, she chooses, through her own will, to assume two forms, i.e., *śakti* and *śiva*. The dual form of *śakti* and *śiva* is therefore a superimposition onto herself brought about through her own will.[60]

Here one must note that Kāmeśvara does *not* say that the transcendent *śakti* is transformed into *śakti* and *śiva*; rather he clearly states that she assumes two forms, i.e., *śakti* and *śiva*, at will. By stating, *"pariṇāma śabdo 'yaṃ vivartaparaḥ"* and *"icchayaiva sisṛkṣādikāyāṃ śaktiḥ śiva iti rūpadvayam aṅgīkṛtam,"* Kāmeśvara clearly expresses his opinion that she does not transform herself into the *śakti-śiva* pair, but illusively projects the pair onto herself in such a manner that they remain intermingled in every aspect of creation and, thereby, can coexist in the world which manifests from them. It is because she assumes these two forms that the concept of *śakti-śiva*, mother-father, develops; otherwise she alone exists.[61]

In describing which particular *tattva* evolved from *śakti* and which from *śiva*, Lakṣmīdhara states that the five gross elements evolved from *śiva*, and the mind (probably all the senses and the subtle elements) evolved from *śakti*. However, he insists that *śakti*, while superimposing this *prapañca* (world), still stands as the cause. This foundational state of supreme *śakti* is known as *ādhāra kuṇḍalinī*.[62]

Lakṣmīdhara gives a brief description of *śakti* found in the Pūrva Kaula and Uttara Kaula schools only because those views are mentioned in *SL* 34-35. Because Lakṣmīdhara claims that Śaṅkarācārya wrote the *SL* in praise of *samayā* or *candrakalā*,[63] therefore he believes Samayācāra is the main doctrine of *SL*. Throughout his commentary Lakṣmīdhara prefers to use the terms *sadāśiva* and *śuddhavidyā* (rather than *śiva* and *śakti*) to construct Samayācāra doctrine. But in his commentary on *SL* 1, 9, and 11, he also proposes an entirely different category of reality, i.e., *samayā* or *sādā-*

khyākalā, consisting of a combination of *sadāśiva* and *śuddhavidyā*. It is from this combination or union that the processes of creation, maintenance, and dissolution originate, never from *sadāśiva* or *śuddhavidyā* alone.[64] In *LD* 9, he explains more precisely how this twenty-sixth transcendent reality known as *sādākhyākalā* is formed:

> It is Śuddhavidyā herself who, united with Sadāśiva is known as *sādākhyākalā. Ataḥ,* therefore (or after this point), Bhagavatī, Śuddhavidyā, transcending the twenty-four *tattvas,* unites with *sadāśiva,* the twenty-fifth, and becomes the twenty-sixth, known as Paramātman, the Supreme Soul. In other words, when united with the twenty-fifth *tattva (sadāśiva), sādākhyākalā* becomes the twenty-sixth. This union is an entirely different *tattva.*[65]

Here Lakṣmīdhara does not say that the union of both *sadāśiva* and *śuddhavidyā* forms the twenty-sixth *tattva, sādākhyākalā.* Rather, he states that *bhagavatī śuddhavidyā* rises above the first twenty-four *tattvas* (she herself being the twenty-third and *maheśvara* the twenty-fourth) and unites with the twenty-fifth, *sadāśiva.* She is then addressed by the term *sādākhyākalā.* This statement indicates the dominance of *śuddhavidyā* over all the other *tattva*s, including *sadāśiva,* as well as her autonomy from them. Furthermore, Lakṣmīdhara emphatically denies that this union contains any distinguishable remnant of either *sadāśiva* or *śuddhavidyā* (*"na cobhayormelanam ubhayātmakam," LD* 9). He also implies that in the same way that *śuddhavidyā* is free to unite herself with *sadāśiva* and thus become an entirely different, transcendent twenty-sixth *tattva,* she can also separate herself from *sadāśiva,* thus keeping *sadāśiva* as the twenty-fifth, and herself as the twenty-third, *śuddhavidyā.*

However, the concept that *śuddhavidyā* and *sadāśiva,* or *śakti* and *śiva,* are two separate principles is refuted by Lakṣmīdhara. While quoting verses from the *Bhairava*

Yāmala, Lakṣmīdhara explains the inseparability of *śakti* and *śiva*: between them there is *avinābhāva sambandha*, a relationship in which neither can exist without the other.[66] Furthermore, once Lakṣmīdhara proposes the twenty-sixth transcendent *sādākhyākalā*, containing no distinguishable remnants of *sadāśiva* or *śuddhavidyā*, then the question of whether or not they can be separated does not arise. In Lakṣmīdhara's system, the transcendent *sādākhyā*[67] alone is the nondual reality; all other *tattvas* including *sadāśiva* and *śuddhavidyā* evolve from this twenty-sixth *sādākhyākalā* or *samayā*. In a strict sense, therefore, Lakṣmīdhara is proposing not Śakti Advaitavāda, but rather Samayā Advaitavāda or Sādākhyākalā Advaitavāda.

The purpose of proposing this twenty-sixth *tattva* seems to be to emphasize the inseparability and oneness of the two aspects of the single absolute truth. However, in *LD* 41, a discrepancy arises in Lakṣmīdhara's delineation of Samayācāra doctrine. In spite of the twenty-sixth transcendent *sādākhyā* or *samayā* that he proposes in *LD* 1, 9, and 11, here Lakṣmīdhara equates *samayā* with *śakti*, and *samaya* with *śiva*. According to his own interpretation, "One who goes through (or has) fivefold sameness or equivalency, *sāmya*, with *śambhu (śiva)* is *samayā*." *Śiva* is also called *samaya* since he too has a fivefold equivalency with *devī (śakti)*.[68]

That fivefold *sāmya* is *adhiṣṭhāna sāmya, anuṣṭhāna sāmya, avasthāna sāmya, rūpa sāmya,* and *nāma sāmya,* i.e., they equally reside in all *cakras* and equally partake in all activities; in every aspect of creation they assume equal places, and in terms of *rūpa* (personified form) and *nāma* (name), they both are equal.[69] Unlike the twenty-sixth transcendent *samayā* or *sādākhyā* that he proposes in *LD* 1 and 9, Lakṣmīdhara now returns to the usual practice of Śaiva and Śākta writers—using the terms *śakti* and *śiva*, and trying to prove that they are one and the same. He simply replaces *samaya-samayā* with *śiva-śakti.* However, he does not explain how this view differs from the view of Pūrva Kaula as described in *LD* 34.

According to the description in *LD* 41, both *samaya* and *samayā* are of equal importance *("ataḥ ubhayoḥ samaprādhānyenaiva sāmyaṃ vijñeyaṃ"),* which may mean that neither is principal *(pradhāna)* nor secondary *(gauḍa)* to the other. However, the phrase "*ubhayoḥ samaprādhānyenaiva sāmyaṃ vijñeyaṃ,*" i.e., *śiva* and *śakti* are of equal status in all respects, does not necessarily mean that they are essentially one and the same. A similar relationship is found between *ānandabhairava* and *ānandabhairavī* in Pūrva Kaula doctrine. In Pūrva Kaula, *ānandabhairava* and *ānandabhairavī* are alike ("*ubhayasādhāraṇatā*" *SL* 34); they both are of equal bliss or essence ("*samarasa*" *SL* 34). Just as there is a fivefold equivalency between *samaya* and *samayā* in the Samayācāra view, in Pūrva Kaula there is a ninefold oneness between *ānandabhairava* and *ānandabhairavī* ("*navātmatā dvayoḥ samānā*" *LD* 34). Thus, the fivefold equivalency between *samayā* and *samaya* does not clearly explain the distinction between the Samayācāra view of Śakti and the Kaulācāra view, because the Kaulācāra school also adheres to the idea of a ninefold equivalency between *ānandabhairava* and *ānandabhairavī.*

As far as Pūrva Kaula's other distinctive feature, *śeṣaśeṣibhāva*, is concerned (*ānandabhairava* being the essence and *ānandabhairavī* being the complement), Lakṣmīdhara clearly states that *śeṣaśeṣibhāva* is conditional rather than real.[70] Furthermore, in several verses, Lakṣmīdhara uses almost the same words to describe the nature of the relationship between *śakti* and *śiva* in both the Pūrva Kaula and Samayācāra schools. For instance, while describing the oneness of *śiva* and *śakti* from the Samayācāra viewpoint in *LD* 9, Lakṣmīdhara uses the phrase "*śivaśaktyor aikyam ityāhuḥ.*" Similarly, while presenting the Kaula view in *LD* 34, he uses a phrase with the same meaning, i.e., "*parānandaparayoḥ aikyaṃ tasmādityarthaḥ.*" The words "*samarase sāmarasyayukte*" used for *ānandabhairava* and *ānandabhairavī* in Kaulācāra, and the words "*samaprādhānyenaiva sāmyaṃ*" used for *samaya* and *samayā* in Samayācāra convey virtually the same meaning: *ānandabhairava* and *ānandabhairavī* experience supreme bliss equally, and *samaya* and *samayā* are of equal importance.

Thus, on one hand, Lakṣmīdhara discusses the nature of the absolute reality and the position of *śakti* and *śiva* from the standpoint of Pūrva Kaula, Uttara Kaula, and Samayācāra, and identifies himself as Samayācārin, but on the other hand, he does not (or cannot) maintain an airtight distinction between the Kaulācāra and Samayācāra views of *śakti.* This suggests that by the time of Lakṣmīdhara, the Kaulamārga and Samayamārga schools (and even Miśramārga, the Tāntric path which combines both Kaula and Samaya) must have been in existence and had already developed noticeably distinct spiritual practices, although their separate doctrines were not yet fully formalized. This may be the reason why Śāktism and nondualistic Śaivism adopt such terms as *yāmala* or *sādākhyā* to refer to the existence of one, single, nondual reality, but still continue to use the terms *śiva* and *śakti*, even though this forces them to prove that these terms do not refer to anything other than one, single, nondual reality. By describing the nature and function of *śakti* from the perspectives of Pūrva Kaula, Uttara Kaula, and Samayācāra, Lakṣmīdhara not only describes the concept of *śakti* in the *SL*, but also provides a model which can be used to study other Śākta and Śaiva texts. This is important because there is no Śākta text devoted exclusively to either Kaula or Samayācāra doctrine.

Abhinavagupta's View of Śakti

Even texts like *SU* and *SL*, whose overall tone is unquestionably Samayācāra-oriented, describe the nature of *śakti* from the viewpoints of Pūrva Kaula and Uttara Kaula. As mentioned earlier, most Śākta and Śaiva texts begin by pointing to the supremacy of either *śiva* or *śakti* or to the supremacy of their union, but soon change their tone and involve themselves in general Śaiva/Śākta issues, i.e., whether or not *śakti* and *śiva* are inseparable, whether or not they refer to two aspects of the same absolute truth, whether they play equal roles in the manifestation of the universe, etc. For example, just as Lakṣmīdhara uses the terms *sādākhyā* and *samayā* for the transcendental reality, Abhinavagupta uses the terms *yāmala, saṅghaṭṭa*, and *anuttara*.[71] However, at one point, Abhinavagupta becomes deeply involved in explaining the oneness of *śiva* and *śakti*. In the course of his discussion, his description sometimes comes close to that of Pūrva Kaula's as described in *LD* 34.[72] In other places, however, his description of *śakti* and *śiva* is similar to the Uttara Kaula view as described in *LD* 35.[73] The only discernible difference is that according to Lakṣmīdhara, in Uttara Kaula doctrine, *śakti* alone is the existent reality and it is from her that *śiva* and the rest of the world evolve, whereas in Abhinavagupta's *TĀ*, the situation is completely reversed: Abhinavagupta considers *śiva* alone to be the nondual reality and it is from *śiva* that *śakti* or a cluster of *śaktis* and the rest of the world manifest.

Just as Lakṣmīdhara identifies himself as a *samayin,*

Abinavagupta identifies himself as a *kaula.* But unlike Lakṣmīdhara, Abhinavagupta does not connect his differing explanations of *śiva* and *śakti* to particular schools. In the majority of the verses of *TĀ*, he adheres to the concept of ultimate reality indicated by the terms *yāmala*, *saṅghaṭṭa*, or *anuttara*, all of which refer to the union of *śiva* and *śakti.* In spite of his firmly held view of the inseparability of *śiva* and *śakti*, he still occasionally expresses the view that one or the other is supreme.

For example, in some instances Abhinavagupta seems to subordinate *śakti* to *śiva.* As Larson observes:

> Śiva or the absolute is ultimately a mystery, transcending all experience and all knowledge, but Śiva or the absolute has within its nature the potency, power, or capacity of self-expression. This potency or capacity is the *svātantryaśakti* ("power of freedom" or "autonomous power"), which is the origin or source for all other powers and capacities in the manifest world and which is synonymous with the *vimarśa* ("dynamic creativity") of Śiva. The *svātantryaśakti* is also the creative capacity of Śiva as the *parā-vāk*, the Supreme Speech, which unfolds itself successively through the *paśyantī*, the *madhyamā*, and the *vaikharī.* [74]

In regard to *śakti's* position in relation to *śiva,* Larson states:

> By means of his *śakti*, therefore, Śiva or Śiva-tattva has within himself all the possibilities of the manifest and unmanifest world. He transcends his *śakti*, and yet *śakti* is inextricably a part of his own nature. As Śiva comes to express his *śakti* or his creative power, the manifest world slowly emerges into actuality. First, *śakti* herself appears to become independent and holds within herself, within her womb, all manifest reality. . . .[75]
>
> . . . [furthermore,] Abhinavagupta more clearly subordinates the *śakti* of Śiva (the *parā-vāk*) to the notion of *parama-śiva*, the Supreme absolute, which transcends *śakti*. . . .[76]

This conclusion is in conformity with Abhinavagupta's description of *śiva* as found in Chapter 9 of *TĀ*. But elsewhere in the text, Abhinavagupta emphatically rejects the idea that *śiva* and *śakti* are different, or that the former is superior.[77] Furthermore, a critical analysis of *TĀ* shows that Abhinavagupta posits a state that transcends both *śakti* and *śiva*. He employs several terms—*yāmala, anuttara*, and *saṅghaṭṭa*—to refer to that state. *Śiva, śakti*, and the remaining thirty-four *tattvas* evolve from, and ultimately merge into, *yāmala*.[78]

As K. C. Pandey points out,[79] Abhinavagupta's main concern is to expound Trika, the triad of *śiva, śakti*, and their union *(saṅghaṭṭa* or *yāmala)*. As there is nothing beyond this union, Abinavagupta calls it *anuttara*. Describing the nature of *anuttara* as held by Abhinavagupta, K. C. Pandey writes:

> Anuttara is that (i) which is higher than and beyond the thirty-six categories from śiva to earth. The categories have their being in it, and therefore, it is superior to them. It is perfectly self-shining and absolutely independent. . . .[80]
>
> . . . . *anuttara is that state in which* the union of śiva and śakti is fully realized and consequently, all duality disappears. It is a state about which no talk is possible. It is neither immanent nor transcendental. This is the highest state, attainable by the follower of the Kula system. (Paraṁ Kaulam) Abhinavagupta holds this view in the highest regard. . . .[81]

It is important to note that just as *śuddhavidyā* unites herself with *sadāśiva* (according to Lakṣmīdhara) and in that state of union is called *sādākhyākalā*, similarly here, *maheśvara*, the great lord, unites himself with his own *śakti* and, in that state of union, is called *saṅghaṭṭa, yāmala, anuttara*, and *paratrika*. This indicates that it is *maheśvara's* choice to be united with *śakti* and it is he who is now said to be *anuttara*. This description indicates that *śiva* predominates in the *anuttara* state, just as in Lakṣmīdhara's system *śuddhavidyā* predominates in the *sādākhyā* state.

However, we cannot find a clear and consistent answer to the question of whether *śiva* predominates over *śakti* in the *anuttara* state, whether they are equal in their subordinance to *anuttara,* or whether they both completely lose their distinct identities in *anuttara.* Different and often contradictory explanations of the nature of *annuttara, śiva,* and *śakti,* which Abhinavagupta himself and later Kashmiri scholars offer, are perhaps attributable either to personal viewpoints or to their inability to connect specific interpretations with the subschools to which they belong.[82]

A Comparative Analysis of the Two Views

These differing views concerning the nature and status of *śakti* in both Śaivism and Śaktism can be explained by applying the model Lakṣmīdhara used to examine *śakti's* status in the *LD.* According to this model, exclusive supremacy of *śakti* is held by Uttara Kaula, equal importance of *śiva* and *śakti* is held in Pūrva Kaula, and the view that *śakti* and *śiva* are one and the same and that there is a transcendent twenty-sixth principle is held in Samayācāra. Similarly, the passages in *TĀ* that express the supremacy of *śiva* over *śakti* belong to the first category, the passages that describe the equal status of *śakti* and *śiva* belong to the second category, and the passages that express the oneness of *śakti* and *śiva* and propose a transcendent thirty-seventh *tattva* belong to the third category. However, strictly speaking, Lakṣmīdhara's model can only be used to describe *śakti's* nature in Saivite literature. His opinion regarding Uttara Kaula, Pūrva Kaula, and Samayācāra cannot be taken as a standard by which to delineate Śaiva doctrines. Lakṣmīdhara represents only

Śaktism and defines Uttara Kaula, Pūrva Kaula, and Samayācāra within that general background. Therefore, according to him, *śakti* holds exclusive supremacy in Uttara Kaula. But in the case of *TĀ* or other Śaivite texts, the passages that expound the supremacy of *śiva* represent the Uttara Kaula view.

The concept held in Pūrva Kaula that *śakti* and *śiva* are of equal importance remains the same in both Śākta and Śaiva systems, but Lakṣmīdhara's Samayācāra model more aptly describes Abhinavagupta's *anuttara*, which, according to K.C. Pandey, is Abhinavagupta's "main thesis" and is generally believed to be Kaulācāra doctrine. This is not to say that Lakṣmīdhara's definitions of Pūrva Kaula, Uttara Kaula, and Samayācāra and the nature of *śakti* described therein, are necessarily representative of these particular traditions and subtraditions. However, it is certain that the basic concern of earlier Śākta and Śaiva literature is the practice, not the philosophy. Therefore, when these texts make a philosophical remark in passing, they do not explain which particular sect they are drawing from. Lakṣmīdhara at least makes an attempt to create a model for categorizing different Tāntric streams on the basis of Śakti's role and status.

Lakṣmīdhara apparently creates this model on the basis of a blueprint which existed both in Śaiva and Śākta Tāntrism. While explaining the Uttara Kaula view and the role of *śakti* therein, Lakṣmīdhara in *LD* 35 describes a special variation of Pariṇāmavāda. In that particular school, according to him, *śakti* is the sole reality. It is she who, through her sovereign will, superimposes the pair *śiva* and *śakti* on herself, and thereafter the universe evolves from this pair. In chapters 9 and 10 of *TĀ*, which explain the nature of *śiva* as the sole and absolute reality and the source of *śakti* and the rest of the *tattvas*, Abhinavagupta adheres to the doctrine of Pariṇāmavāda, similar to that which Lakṣmīdhara describes in *LD* 35. In this particular section, Abhinavagupta omits his firmly held Ābhāsavāda theory. Here, *śiva* is the only *deva.*[83] Just as a sprout comes from a seed, the whole world evolves from *śiva* and the concept of cause and effect is superimposed by his will.[84] In fact, chapter 9 is replete with passages emphasizing the supremacy of *śiva.*[85] Abhinavagupta relates this discussion to Mataṅgaśāstra or Mataṅgamata.

In chapters 3 and 5 of *TĀ*, Abhinavagupta's tone regarding the roles of *śiva* and *śakti* is quite similar to Lakṣmīdhara's description of Pūrva Kaula. In these chapters, in addition to using the terms *anuttara* and *anuttarā*, he also uses the terms *akula* and *khecara* and, parallel to these two terms, such feminine gender terms as *kaulikī* and *khecarī.* Quoting from Abhinavagupta and Jayaratha, Padoux explains the connection between *anuttara, akula,* and *kaulikī śakti* and their roles in the evolutionary process:

> The Absolute, *anuttara*, divides into Śiva and his energy, denoted by the terms *akula* and *kaulikīśakti.* 'The state of union of these two,' says TĀ, third *āhnika, śloka* 68 (p.81), 'is called unifying friction *(saṃghaṭṭa).* It is known as the energy of bliss *(ānanda),* from which the universe will be emitted.'[86]
>
> 'The supreme energy of this God, *akula*, is *kaulikī*, through which *kula* arises, and from which the Lord cannot be divided.' Commenting on this rather obscure stanza and referring to the *PTV*, pp. 61-62, Jayaratha (*TĀV*, p. 75) states that *a*, the *kaulikī* energy, is that energy of which the self, the essence, is the *akula*, the supreme deity, while belonging to and abiding in *kula*, the manifested universe. *Kula*, he says, is the body *(śarīra)* of the Godhead, and its characteristic is the phoneme *a* *(akāralakṣaṇaṃ kulaṃ śarīram asya [akulasya]. . . .)*[87]

Here it is clear that *kaulikī śakti*, in essence, is identical to *anutara* or *saṅghaṭṭa* and in the evolutionary process when *anuttara* divides into *akula (śiva)* and *kaulikī śakti*, *akula* and *kaulikī śakti* still remain inseparable. Nevertheless, the phrases "*kaulikī śakti* of *akula*"[88] and "his śaktis constitute the whole world"[89] give the impression that *akula* is the principal *(śeṣin)* and his *śakti* is not different from him but is complementary *(śeṣa)*, a point on which Abinavagupta remains silent. However, the commentator Jayaratha explains the relationship between *akula* and *kaulikī*: *kaulikī śakti* is the body and *akula* is the one to whom the body belongs. Here Jayaratha also quotes Vāmakeśvarīmata *(Vāmakeśvara Tantra)*, a Śrīvidyā text frequently quoted by Lakṣmīdhara.[90] By implication, this may be an echo of the Tāntric view that Lakṣmīdhara labels Pūrva Kaula.

The most notable areas of compatibility between these two doctrines is the way in which they explain the transcendence of *samayā* (in *LD*) and *anuttara* (in *TĀ*). Lakṣmīdhara considers *samayā* to be entirely different from and transcendent to *śuddhavidyā* and *sadāśiva*. Thus she is the twenty-sixth *tattva*, and therefore is beyond all the *tattvas* that constitute the empirical world. This transcendent *samayā* is also the source of all other *tattvas* including *śuddhavidyā* and *sadāśiva*. Similarly, according to Abhinavagupta, the union of *śakti* and *śiva* is the highest reality. Furthermore, this state is neither quiet *(śānta)* nor active *(udita)*, but rather is the cause of *śānta* and *udita*. It transcends the empirical world and is simultaneously identical to it.[91]

In order to explain this paradox, Abhinavagupta introduces the idea of *svātantrya śakti*, the autonomous power of the absolute, which is intrinsic to it. Realizing that this may not be a perfectly satisfactory explanation, in his commentary on *TĀ*, Jayaratha explains that an immature student of Āgama, *sukumārahṛdaya āgamika*, might find it illogical to regard the same *tattva* as simultaneously transcendent and immanent.[92] To help such a student grasp the point, Abhinavagupta posits a thirty-seventh *tattva* known as *anuttara* or *paraśiva*. This *tattva* is devoid of all divisions *(sarvāvibhāgātma)*, is autonomous *(svatantra)*.[93] Thus, the same *tattva* that refers to an inseparable, unitary state of *śakti* and *śiva* is, in different succeeding stages of a philosophical analysis *(kramatāratamyayogāt)*, said to be simultaneously transcendent *(śānta)* and manifest *(udita)*.[94]

Moreover, to further clarify how pure knowledge is the highest reality and how it is devoid of all qualities and characteristics *(bodhamātra)*, Abhinavagupta goes on to postulate a thirty-eighth *tattva*, which transcends even *anuttara*.[95] This he does only to stress that the union of *śakti* and *śiva* is completely transcendent, and yet is the source of the manifest world. To explain the existence of the world without compromising the unsullied nature of *śiva*, Abhinavagupta credits *śakti* with creation, maintenance, and annihilation, leaving *śiva* uninvolved. Because *śiva* and *śakti* are inseparable and refer to two aspects of the same reality, a category that transcends both seems to be a logical necessity. However, the categories beyond the thirty-sixth *tattva* are conceptual, not actual. Lakṣmīdhara seems to be making the same point, although he considers the twenty-sixth *tattva* to be completely transcendent and entirely different from *śuddhavidyā* and *sadāśiva*.

The compatibility between Lakṣmīdhara's Samayācāra and Abhinavagupta's Kaulācāra becomes even clearer when we study the nature of the terms *samayā* and *annutarā* in relation to *samaya* and *anuttara*. *Anuttarā* is *parā* (supreme or absolute) and *pratibhā* (intuitive spontaneous flash).[96] Commenting on *TĀ*, Jayaratha explains that *anuttarā* is identical to the *śakti* whose autonomous power, lordship, and indescribable wonder is unsurpassed.[97] In the next verse,

Abhinavagupta introduces the term *kaulikī* which, according to him, is the power of *akula,* the one who is beyond all the *kula tattvas,* the thirty-six principles. This *kaulikī śakti* and *prabhu,* the lord *akula,* are inseparable and it is from this *kaulikī śakti* that all *kula tattvas* evolve.[98]

However, in the following verse, Abhinavagupta states that the universe evolves from "the union of Śiva and Śakti, which is *yāmala* or *saṅgaṭṭa* . . . also known as *ānanda śakti.*"[99] In the preceding verse, he states that the *kaulikī śakti* of *akula* is the source of the entire universe. These three verses, *TĀ* 3:66-68, leave no room for the slightest doubt that the terms "*anuttara* and *anuttarā, akula* and *kaulikī, yāmala* and *saṅghaṭṭa,* and *ānanda śakti*" are identical and refer to the same metaphysical truth. A more interesting hypothesis, which at this stage may not be well substantiated, is that Abhinavagupta has based this particular discussion on doctrines already in vogue and the same source is later used by Lakṣmīdhara when he discusses his Samayācāra view.

In the next two verses, Abhinavagupta says, "That which transcends both the absolute and the immanent is the highest *tattva.* She is known as *devī.* It is the essence and the heart. He is the emission, the absolute, and the lord (Prabhu). In the *śāstra* known as *Devī Yāmala Śāstra,* she is called *kālakarṣiṇī.* In *Mahāḍāmara,* which is a section of *Devī Yāmala,* she is called *śrīparā.*"[100] In this particular section, Abhinavagupta's direct reference to the *Devī Yāmala* and his use of the terms *kalakarṣiṇī* and *śrīparā* offers a valuable clue to earlier sources of the Śaiva form of Kaulācāra and Lakṣmīdhara's brand of Samayācāra. The contribution of the Yāmala Tantras, which are Śākta texts, is also quite significant. Jayaratha, in his commentary on *TĀ* 3:66-252, quotes passages from *Vāmakeśvara Tantra* and uses the terms *tripurā, śṛṅgāṭaka, kāmatattva, agni, soma, sūrya, śabdarāśi, vākśakti,* etc. In Lakṣmīdhara's case, the materials are derived mainly from *SU, Vāmakeśvara Tantra,* and the Yāmala Tantras. But Lakṣmīdhara makes good use of the ideas centered around *mātṛikā* and mantra, which were already well developed in Kashmir Śaivism, although he does not acknowledge his sources. However, Abhinavagupta's reference to the terms *kālakarṣiṇī* and *śrīparā* in this particular section of *TĀ* and the further elaboration by Jayaratha, as well as the occurrence of the same terms in *LD* and *SU* during the discussion on *samayā's* transcendence, may be an indication of an analogous sect that contained the seeds of Śaiva and Śākta doctrines and practices.

Just as the terms *anuttarā, kaulikī śakti,* and *khecarī* stand for the intrinsic power of *anuttara* and *akula*, the term *khecarī* stands for the power of *kha,* Brahman, another term used for *anuttara.* This *khecarī śakti* of *kha* is responsible for the rise of the entire objective world. The objective world is identical to *khecarī,* while on the other hand, *khecarī* is identical to *kha, anuttara.* More clearly, the power which spontaneously and eternally vibrates in and remains identical with *kha-anuttara* is called *khecarī.* Just as the highest spiritual goal in the *LD* is attained by experiencing the fivefold oneness of *samaya* and *samayā,* similarly here *khecarī sāmaya,* experiencing oneness with *khecarī,* brings about the highest spiritual realization. *Khecarī sāmaya* means to experience the oneness of *anuttara* with the various states of mind, emotion, and the world of multiple objects. This *khecarī sāmaya* also refers to the oneness of the individual self with the absolute.[101]

TĀ is replete with the terms *mahāguhā, amā, ṣoḍaśī, kuṇḍalinī, malīnī, mātṛkā,* and *kālakarṣiṇī* synonymously and with the concept of the oneness of *nāda, bindu,* and *kalā,* material which is the main focus of Lakṣmīdhara's commentary. The use of these common terms and the similarities in the concepts lead us to believe that these Kashmir Śaivite and Śrīvidyā Śākta writers shared common sources from which they elaborated their doctrines. In the process, they added their unique interpretations and changed the tone of these materials to suit their purposes.

Śaivites emphasized *śiva* and Śāktas emphasized *śakti*, even when they proposed the terms *annuttara* or *samayā*, thus retaining their distinct identities. This tendency also led both schools to develop distinct notions of *śakti*. For example, no matter how emphatically Abhinavagupta and Lakṣmīdhara proclaim the oneness of *śakti* and *śiva*, a difference in the nature and status of *śakti* is still apparent. Lakṣmīdhara considers *samayā* or *sādākhyā* to be absolutely transcendent; in her there is not even the slightest trace of *sadāśiva* or *śuddhavidyā*. Even when the words *samayā* and *samaya* are used together in *LD* 41, these terms refer to *śakti* and *śiva* and are never equal to *samayā*, the twenty-sixth *tattva*. From that highest perspective, there is only *samayā*; there is no *samaya*.

However, in Abhinavagupta's system, as he himself states, *anuttara*, the thirty-seventh *tattva*, is the highest reality and *anuttarā* is parallel to him. Similarly, while referring to the transcendent *tattva* by using terms such as *akula* and *khecara*, he also constantly uses feminine gender terms such as *kaulikī* and *khecarī*. During the discussions of these terms, although he denies any difference between these feminine gender and masculine gender terms and the concepts contained in them, he continually uses phrases such as "*kaulikī śakti* of *akula*," and "his *śaktis* constitute the whole world." Such references convey his conviction of the supremacy of the masculine aspect. Lakṣmīdhara, on the other hand, never uses the phrase "*samayā* of *samaya*." He occasionally uses the phrase "*śakti* of *śiva,*" but only in those contexts where the meaning of the terms *śakti* and *śiva* is perfectly clear. Thus, calling it a Samayācāra doctrine, he establishes the perfect supremacy of *śakti,* which he terms *samayā, sādākhyā,* and *candrakalā.* Because *SL* itself asserts the identity of *śakti* with *śrīcakra*, the *śrīvidyā* mantra, *kuṇḍalinī,* all the *cakras* in the human body, and the anthropomorphic form of the goddess, Lakṣmīdhara goes on to explain exactly how these concepts can be fully equated with each other, and precisely how these concepts fit into this particular nondualistic model.

CHAPTER 4

Śakti: The Origin of Mantra, Yantra, and Deity

How Lakṣmīdhara Builds His Main Premise

Lakṣmīdhara's main thesis, as described in the preceding chapter, is that *samayā* or *sādākhyā* alone is the ultimate reality. All the *tattvas,* including *sadāśiva* and *śuddhavidyā,* manifest from her. She is simultaneously identical with the world she manifests and transcendent to it. She is both one with, and transcendent to, all elements, mantras, *tattvas, avasthās, devas,* the meaning of the Vedas, words, *śaktis,* and *guṇas.*[1] Thus, all which exists, either in its manifest or unmanifest form, is *samayā* alone. But because Śrīvidyā adherents meditate on the *cakras,* do *japa* of the *śrīvidyā* mantra, worship *śrīcakra* (the personified form of *tripurā*), or both, it becomes essential for Lakṣmīdhara to explain how all these components fit into the concept of nondual, transcendent Samayā.

As a first step, he asserts the firmly established Tāntric belief that mantra, *cakra, guru,* deity, and one's own self are essentially one. He goes on to describe how different *cakras,* aspects of mantra (in this case, the different letters of the *śrīvidyā* mantra), different parts of the deity's body, and the aspirant's own personality correspond to *samayā's* manifest and unmanifest forms. With this point as a central theme, he goes into minute detail. However, his presentation is fragmented because, as a commentator, he is forced to follow the order of the verses of the *SL.* These ideas are expressed in a scattered manner in *SL* itself, and so briefly that without commentarial help they do not form a coherent and complete philosophy.

Lakṣmīdhara chooses only those verses for extensive commentary that contain the materials with which he is concerned. He does not comment on the remaining verses as much as he "translates" them, substituting one Sanskrit word for another. Because *SL* is, in a strict sense, neither a text of philosophy nor a ritual manual, but a literary work of devotional poems, less than a quarter of its verses contains material that Lakṣmīdhara can use. However, as a commentator, he can neither omit verses nor change their order; thus, his discussion has an episodic quality—he is able to pursue his theme only when the text provides the opportunity. The verses that enable Lakṣmīdhara to expound his philosophy are primarily verses 1, 8, 9, 11, 14, 31, 32, 41, 92, 98, and 99.

As the text permits, he describes the transcendent nature of *samayā* and her oneness with *śrīcakra* and the *śrīvidyā* mantra, as well as the significance of the *śrīcakra* and *śakti cakras,* which he believes to be located in the human body. His underlying goal as an expounder of pure Samayācāra is to prove that ultimately *samayā* or *sādākhyā* is absolute, that she can be propitiated or experienced only through internal worship, and that such internal worship, in its truest sense, can only be done in the *sahasrāra*, which, unlike the other *cakras*, does not exist in the physical body. It is in this context that he discusses the Samayācāra brand of *kuṇḍalinī* yoga and explains how the six lower *cakras* exist in the *sahasrāra* and how, at the same time, the *sahasrāra* transcends them all. As part of this discussion, Lakṣmīdhara goes on to stress that the universe and the human body are one and the same, and that the *sahasrāra cakra* is beyond.

In an attempt to substantiate this viewpoint, Lakṣmīdhara quotes extensively from prominent Tāntric texts, such as *NS* and *YH* (which he calls *Vāmakeśvara Tantra* or *Catuḥśatī Tantra*), *SU*, *Bhairava Yāmala*, *Rudrayāmala*, *KKV*, and even the *Yogakuṇḍalī Upaniṣad* (hereafter cited as *YKU*).[2] All of these texts make references to yantra worship and internal meditation. They equate the human body with the universe and hold the highest spiritual achievement to be the realization of the oneness of mantra, yantra, *devatā*, and oneself. Lakṣmīdhara also quotes the Saṃhitās, Brāhmaṇas, Āraṇyakas, and Upaniṣads, but because those sources do not directly support his view, he supplements these references with his own commentarial interpretation. For example, in *LD* 32 in order to substantiate his claim that each of the fifteen days of the fortnight is assigned for the practice of one of the letters of the fifteen-lettered *śrīvidyā* mantra, which are identical to fifteen *nityākalās*, Lakṣmīdhara quotes phrases from the *Taittirīya Brāhmaṇa*. Those phrases may have had an entirely different meaning and ritual application in their original context, but Lakṣmīdhara borrows them and reinterprets them in a manner that supports his thesis.

Although Tāntric and Vedic sources refer to the gate of *brahman (brahmadvāra)*; the oneness of *nāda*, *bindu*, and *kalā;* descriptions of *parā*, *paśyantī*, *madhyamā*, and *vai-*

kharī; and the highest reality's transcendence of the triple world, none expands these concepts into a full-fledged doctrine. With *SL* as a ground, Lakṣmīdhara uses the material in these sources to build a rationale for the esoteric elements of Samayācāra practices. The foundation for asserting the oneness between *samayā* and *kuṇḍalinī śakti* is his basic premise that *piṇḍāṇḍa,* the individual body, and *brahmāṇḍa,* the whole universe, are identical, an assertion he makes in his commentary on verses, 14, 41, and 99.[3]

Although this commentary is much better organized than that of most other Tāntric texts, Lakṣmīdhara's presentation is still choppy and repetitious in places because of the limitations imposed by the order of the verses. It is disproportionately expanded in some places and truncated in others. If we are to get a clear understanding of his hypothesis and to analyze the exact nature of *śakti-samayā* in various contexts, it is necessary to collect the information scattered throughout this commentary and group it by topic. Only then can we study the accuracy and coherence of Lakṣmīdhara's equations between *śakti* and her various forms—such as *kuṇḍalinī/cakras, śrīcakra,* mantra, the deity, and the individual self.

Śakti and the Cakras in the Human Body

Because Lakṣmīdhara holds that the whole universe evolves from *samayā* and that the universe is but the transformed state of *samayā*, everything—including the *cakras, śrīcakra,* the *śrīvidyā* mantra, *mātṛkā,* and each individual human—originates from the same source and shares the same process of evolution. According to Lakṣmīdhara, all the *tattvas* of the manifest world are found in the body. The centers of these *tattvas*, as well as their governing forces, are called *cakras.* In Lakṣmīdhara's system there are six *cakras: mūlādhāra, svādhiṣṭhāna, maṇipūra, anāhata, viśuddhi,* and *ājñā,* which are the centers of earth, water, fire, air, space, and mind, respectively.[4] Each of the first five *cakras* also include *tanmātras,* subtle elements, corresponding to their gross counterparts. Thus, the first five *cakras* are also the centers of smell, taste, form, touch, and sound. Similarly, the sixth *cakra, ājñā,* is the center of the ten senses.[5] These *cakras* correlate with the entire manifest world, whereas the *sahasrāra,* the seventh *cakra,* corresponds to pure, transcendental *samayā.* Just as *samayā* is the source of, and transcendent to, the entire world, *sahasrāra* is the source of, and transcendent to, all the *cakras.* To stress the transcendence of *sahasrāra,* Lakṣmīdhara states that this particular *cakra* is beyond the universe as well as beyond the human body.[6] It is in this *cakra* that *śuddhavidyā* and *sadāśiva* are eternally united. This unitary state is the twenty-sixth *tattva,* known as *samayā* or *sādākhyā.*

Excluding the *sahasrāra* from his *cakra* system, Lakṣmīdhara divides the six *cakras* into three parts, each containing a pair. These three divisions are known as *āgneyakhaṇḍa* (the fiery division), *saurakhaṇḍa* (the solar division), and *somakhaṇḍa* (the lunar division). These three divisions are centered in three *granthis,* knots—namely *rudragranthi, viṣṇugranthi,* and *brahmagranthi.*[7] Quoting *Rudrayāmala*, Lakṣmīdhara states, "The whole universe consists of fire, the sun, and the moon."[8] "The moon, sun, and fire pervade individual bodies as well as the universe."[9] He again reminds the reader that the *sahasrāra* is beyond both the human body and the universe.[10] Then Lakṣmīdhara begins a discussion equating *samayā* and *sahasrāra*, the twenty-four evolutes and the lower *cakras,* but before reaching a conclusion, abruptly begins discussing *śrīyantra* and its connection with the *cakras.* Apparently he assumes that the reader is already familiar with the concept of the oneness of the *cakras* and *śrīcakra* because it is not until his commentary on verse 41 that he explicitly states that the *cakras, śrīcakra, śrīvidyā* mantra, the deity, and one's own self are identical. Furthermore, many of the details that establish the precise equation and substantiate the oneness of these components are not described until verses 92 and 98.

Perhaps Lakṣmīdhara's main reason for adopting this particular style is his desire to continually affirm that there is little or no place for an external *śrīcakra* in the Samayācāra school of Śrīvidyā. However, because in the majority of Śrīvidyā texts, including *SL*, the greater part of the philosophy and practices center around *śrīcakra* and the personified form of the deity, thereby supporting Kaulism, he must find a way to place such ideas within the framework of Samayācāra. From the standpoint of the metaphysics of the Samayācāra school, *samayā* or *sādākhyā* is absolute, existing in everything everywhere, yet is still beyond. From the standpoint of one's personal spiritual *sādhanā,* she is the transcendental *śakti* residing in the *sahasrāra* and is to be experienced directly. Thus, to gear the discussion towards Samayācāra, every component of philosophy or practice—be it mantra, yantra, deity, *guru,* disciple, etc.—must ultimately be connected to the *sahasrāra* and the *sahasrāra* to *samayā* or *sādākhyā.*

As shown in Chapter 3, Lakṣmīdhara proposes the theory of twenty-five *tattvas* as opposed to the fifty-one *tattvas* of *Vāyavīya Saṃṁhitā,* which includes the thirty-six *tattvas* of the Śaiva Āgama. The five lower *cakras* cover the realm of the five gross elements and the five subtle elements. The sixth, the *ājña cakra*, covers the ten senses and the mind. Beyond this sixth *cakra* is the *sahasrāra*, which is the residence of, or is identical to, the transcendental *sādākhyā*. Thus, the six lower *cakras* cover only twenty-one *tattvas*. In Lakṣmīdhara's scheme, the remaining four *tattvas,* i.e., *māyā, śuddhavidyā, maheśvara,* and *sadāśiva,* find their place neither in the six lower *cakras* nor in the seventh. Rather, he assigns them to the *brahmagranthi*, which is also known as *brahmadvāra* or *brahmanāḍī*.[11] According to Lakṣmīdhara, unlike the other twenty-one *tattvas* from earth to mind, these four *tattvas* are not part of the manifest world, yet because they evolve from *samayā* and are involved in the process of creation, maintenance, and annihilation, they are not totally transcendent either. Neither are they part of the empirical world because they are the governing and directing forces of all worldly phenomena. Similarly, *brahmagranthi* or *brahmanāḍī* belongs neither to the realm of the six lower *cakras* nor is it an integral part of the *sahasrāra*. Rather, according to Lakṣmīdhara and the sources he cites in his commentary, it is located above the *ājñā cakra* and below the *sahasrāra*.[12] The question then arises: if it is not part of *sahasrāra*, is it still beyond the universe?

Lakṣmīdhara undertakes the task of clarifying this paradox by returning to the topic of the four *tattvas* when he explains the personified form of the goddess Tripurasundarī. In the grand imagery of the goddess, as described in *SL* itself, there is a special island consisting of gems and surrounded by the ocean of ambrosia. Her mansion, made of wish-fulfilling gems, is situated in the center of a *nīpa* grove. She sits on her royal couch in the innermost chamber of this mansion. She herself is *sādākhyā* and the four *tattvas* are the couch. Because of their extreme proximity to the transcendent *samayā*, they are still above the world and thus above the six *cakras*.[13] It is important to note that these four *tattvas* are similar to the concept of *pañcabrahman* or *brahmapañcaka*, the five *brah-*

mans of Kashmir Śaivism. In Kashmir Śaivism, these five *brahmans* are neither part of the manifest world nor are they considered to be transcendent.[14]

Remaining true to his basic premise that the universe and the human body are one, Lakṣmīdhara explains how the various esoteric planes of existence are equated with the different *cakras.* According to him, the *mūlādhāra* is the plane of *andhatāmiśra,* the plane of blind darkness; *svādhiṣṭhāna* and *maṇipūra* are *miśraloka,* the plane that is a mixture of light and darkness; *anāhata* is *jyotirloka,* the plane of light; *viśuddhi* is *candraloka,* the plane of the moon, and *ājñā* is *sudhāloka,* the plane of nectar. The thousand-petaled lotus, *sahasrāra,* is *jyotsnāmayaloka,* the plane identical to the light that is *sādākhyākalā,* the eternal plane transcending all twenty-five *tattvas.*[15] This twenty-sixth transcendent *sādākhyākalā* is also known by the terms *saraghā, śrīcakra,* and *sudhāsindhu.*[16]

Śakti (Samayā) and Kālaśakti

The next and the most intriguing of the concepts that Lakṣmīdhara expounds are the relationship between *kālaśakti* and *samayā* and how *kālaśakti* fits into *cakra* theory. According to Lakṣmīdhara, this universe is created by the 360 rays of *kālaśakti.* These rays refer to the 360 days of the year. Both are called *kalās.* In fact, the concept of 360 *kalās* is based on the solar calendar, whereas the concept of dividing the time into fifteen *kalās* (a fortnight) is based on the lunar calendar. Here, because Lakṣmīdhara considers time as an entity for the sake of his *advaita vāda,* he must demonstrate where *kāla* or *kālaśakti* fits in the scheme of manifestation that he posits. *Kālaśakti* is identical to *saṃvatsara* (year) and *prajāpati* (the lord of created beings).[17]

Demonstrating the relationship between *kālaśakti* and *samayā*, Lakṣmīdhara states that from the *samayā*, which resides in the transcendent *candrakalācakra* (i.e., *sahasrāra cakra* or *bindu*), numberless rays emanate. The sun, moon, and fire collect 360 of these rays, from which they create and illuminate the entire universe. *Samayā* resides above the rays that constitute this universe and the human body.[18] This statement clearly indicates that the *kālaśakti*, which is identical to *saṃvatsara* and *prajāpati*, is lower in status than *samayā*; *kālaśakti* refers to only 360 rays out of an infinite number which emanate from *samayā*. *Kālaśakti*, with its 360 rays, covers only twenty-one elements, from earth to mind, thus remaining below *samayā* and the four remaining higher *tattvas*, which exist in the *brahma nāḍī* above the *ājñā cakra*.

Lakṣmīdhara further elaborates this concept by dividing and distributing these 360 rays among the various *cakras*, thereby reconfirming the equivalency of the universe and the human body. First, he divides all the rays into three categories: *saura*, *āgneya*, and *soma*. One hundred eight *kalās* belong to *āgneyakhaṇḍa*, 116 to *saurakhaṇḍa*, and 136 to *somakhaṇḍa*. More specifically, 56 *kalās* correspond to the *mūlādhāra*, the center of the *pṛthivī tattva* (earth element) and *gandha tanmātra* (smell); 52 correspond to the *maṇipūra*, the center of the *jala tattva* (water element) and *rasa tanmātra* (taste); 62 correspond to the *svādhiṣṭhāna*, the center of the *agni tattva* (fire element) and *rūpa tanmātra* (form); 54 correspond to the *anāhata*, the center of *vayu tattva* (air) and *sparśa tanmātra* (touch); 72 correspond to the *viśuddhi*, the center of *ākāśa tattva* (space) and *śabda tanmātra* (sound); and 64 correspond to the *ājñā*, the center of *manas tattva* (the mind and the senses). Four *tattvas*—that is *māyā*, *śuddhavidyā*, *maheśvara*, and *sadāśiva*—as well as the twenty-sixth, *samayā*, remain above these 360 *kalās*.[19]

Just as Lakṣmīdhara tries to equate all possible Tāntric concepts with *samayā* and the *tattvas* that evolve from her, he also tries to create the same equation between those Tāntric concepts and *kālaśakti.* For instance, according to him the fifty letters of the Sanskrit alphabet correspond to the 360 *kalās* of *kālaśakti.*[20] Interestingly, in this context, Lakṣmīdhara uses the terms *kālaśakti* and the masculine gender term *mahākāla* interchangeably, clearly stating that 360 *kalās* are identical to *mahākāla.* He also establishes an equation between the 360 *kalās* (corresponding to the solar calendar) and the fifteen *kalās* that refer to the fifteen days and nights of the fortnight. All these Tāntric concepts (i.e., the fifty letters, the 360 *kalās,* and the fifteen *kalās* that are identical to each other) belong to the immanent aspect of reality, whereas *sādākhyā* or *śrīvidyā* transcends them all.[21] In the course of this discussion, Lakṣmīdhara introduces the concepts of *nāda, bindu,* and *kalā.* According to him, *parā, paśyantī, madhyamā,* and *vaikharī* collectively are called *nāda; bindu* refers to the six *cakras,* and *kalā* means the fifty letters or the 360 days of the year.[22]

As discussed in the preceding chapter, *SU,* which is one of Lakṣmīdhara's main sources, does not use the term *samayā* at all, and the words *samaya* and *samayamārga* are each used only once. In *SL,* the term *samayā* occurs only twice, but Lakṣmīdhara favors it over all other terms that are synonymous with *tripurā* or *śrīvidyā.* He may prefer this because it is his intention to assimilate the concept centered around *kāla, mahākāla, kālī,* and *mahākālī* without associating himself with the schools in which these particular concepts are prominent, be they the *kālī mahāvidyā* of Śāktism, the *krama* school of Śaivism, or the Vyākaraṇa Āgama.

It is unlikely that Lakṣmīdhara, whose knowledge of Tantra is evidently quite profound, would have been unfamiliar with the Tāntric texts on the subjects he is treating in such depth. For instance, according to *ST*, *kuṇḍalinī śakti* is the same as *śabdabrahman* and identical to the fifty letters that manifest from *śabdabrahman*. This *kuṇḍalinī śakti* is also the source of the whole universe.[23] Similar descriptions regarding *kuṇḍalinī* and *śabdabrahman* are found in *Bhūtaśuddhi Tantra* in *Tantrasaṅgraha, Part III* (hereafter referred to as TS-III).[24] Just as Lakṣmīdhara explains the concepts of *sahasrāra*, the fire, sun, and moon, and the process of manifestation and dissolution, connecting them all with *samayā*, the *Nirvāṇa Tantra* in *TS-II* connect these same concepts with *kālī*.[25] Similar discussions also occur in *Vātulaśuddhākhya Tantra*, *Anubhavasūtra*, *Virūpākṣapañcāśika*, and *Tripurāsundarīmahimnastotra* in *TS-I*; *Toḍalatantra* and *Kāmadhenu Tantra* in *TS-II*; *Laghustuti*; *Carcāstuti*; *Ambāstuti*; *Sakalajananīstava*; *Tripurasundarīdaṇḍaka*; *Saubhāgyahṛdayastotra*; *Saubhāgyasudhodaya*; *NS*; *YH*; *KKV*; and *VR*.[26]

In Vyākaraṇa Āgama, the *kālaśakti* of *śabdabrahman* plays a significant role in the manifestation of the world. According to the observations of Gaurinath Shastri, *śabdabrahman* and *kālaśakti* are two aspects of the same reality. It is through *kālaśakti*, which is the power of *śabdabrahman*, that the twofold but simultaneous process of manifestation occurs. Through *kālaśakti*, *śabdabrahman* manifests into *paśyantī*, *madhyamā*, and *vaikharī* and simultaneously, corresponding to these three, the objective world manifests.[27] In Lakṣmīdhara's system, however, *parā* (a step beyond the *paśyantī* of Vyākaraṇa Āgama), *paśyantī*, *madhyamā*, and *vaikharī* refer to the immanent world. The combination of these fourfold stages of *vāk* is called *nāda*.[28] Tripurasundarī is beyond this fourfold *nāda*.[29] Thus, according to Lakṣmīdhara, *śabdabrahman*, which is the highest reality in

Vyākaraṇa Āgama and *kālaśakti,* which is the intrinsic power of *śabdabrahman* and consists of 360 *kalās,* is only a fraction of the infinite *kalās* that emanate from *samayā.* Clearly, by considering *kāla* or *mahākāla* to be identical to the 360 rays of *kālaśakti* and insisting at the same time that *samayā* is the source of *kālaśakti,* Lakṣmīdhara assimilates these ideas while still maintaining the supremacy of his philosophy.[30]

Śakti and Śrīcakra

The most complex and intricate topic that Lakṣmīdhara undertakes is *śrīcakra* and its systematic equation with the *cakras* in the human body. In general, *śrīcakra* is used as a map for explaining the multilevel universe and the process through which it evolves. Because the places and roles of the group of *śaktis* are described along the visual patterns of *śrīcakra,* it is also a geometrical representation of Śrīvidyā mythology. While adhering to the doctrine of Samayācāra, Lakṣmīdhara faces the challenge of accommodating the complex *śrīcakra* system in his *cakra* theory and of providing an interpretation for all the mythological elements contained in it. Faithful followers of *śrīvidyā* consider *śrīcakra* not just as a locus for worshipping Tripurasundarī and other secondary deities, but also as an emblem of Tripurasundarī. Thus, according to them, *śrīcakra* is not simply a map of creation nor a symbol of the goddess and cluster of goddesses, but actually *is* the goddess. Therefore to make *śrīcakra* fit perfectly into the *cakra* theory, Lakṣmīdhara is obliged to explain exactly which part of *śrīcakra* is the transcendental *samayā* and which parts can be equated with the remaining *tattvas.* He also must explain how *śuddhavidyā* and *sadāśiva* are united in the *śrīcakra* and how, from their unitary state, the universe/*śrīcakra* itself evolves. Furthermore, he must explain how this complex process fits in the *sahasrāra* and his scheme of six *cakras.*

Realizing that this is the most essential aspect of his presentation, Lakṣmīdhara launches into this discussion in his commentary on the first verse of *SL*: *śiva* means the four triangles of *śrīcakra* (with the apex pointing up) and *śakti* means the remaining five triangles (with the apex pointing down).[31] The combination of these two sets of *cakras* forms the *śrīcakra*, and it is from the *śrīcakra* that the process of manifestation, maintenance, and dissolution begins.[32] According to Lakṣmīdhara, this is neither a symbolic nor a figurative statement—worldly existence is actually derived from *śrīcakra*.[33] This terse and seemingly incomprehensible hypothesis is explained further in the rest of the text and commentary.

The structure of *śrīcakra* can be described in the following manner:[34] in the center is the *bindu,* a dot, surrounded by *trikoṇa,* a triangle. *Vasukoṇa,* a group of eight triangles surrounds the central triangle. This group of eight triangles is in turn surrounded by *daśārayugma,* two sets of ten triangles. These two sets of ten triangles are surrounded by *manvasra,* a group of fourteen triangles. The fourteen triangles are surrounded by *nāgadala,* a circle of eight petals, which is then surrounded by *ṣoḍaśāra,* a circle of sixteen petals. Then comes *vṛttatraya,* three circles, surrounded by *sadanatraya* or *bhūpura,* three squares with four gates facing the four directions.[35] Thus, *śrīcakra* consists of nine layers or circuits, with a *bindu* in the center transcending all the layers.

Lakṣmīdhara says that *trikoṇa*, *vasukoṇa*, *daśārayugma*, and *manvasra* are the *śakti cakras. Aṣṭadala*, *ṣoḍaśadala*, *vṛttatraya*, and *bhūpuratraya* are the *śiva cakras.*[36] According to this description, the four *śiva* cakras of *śrīcakra* are outside

Śrīcakra

the *śakti cakras.* In Lakṣmīdhara's own words, "The *śiva cakras* are extracted *(ākṛṣya)* and placed *(sthāpitāni)* inside the *śakti cakras* in the form of the *bindu.* Here, one may recall the Uttara Kaula view, which holds that *śiva* is subsumed in *śakti.* Lakṣmīdhara explains this view by subsuming the *śiva cakras* in the *śakti cakras.* This expresses the supremacy of *śakti,* as held in Uttara Kaula.[37]

Lakṣmīdhara elaborates on the oneness of *śakti* and *śiva* further by identifying and pairing each of the specific *śiva cakras* with a *śakti cakra.* He explains that there is oneness between *bindu (śiva cakra)* and the central triangle *trikoṇa (śakti cakra)*; between *aṣṭakona,* the group of eight triangles, and *aṣṭadalāmbuja,* the group of eight petals; between *daśārayugma,* the two sets of ten triangles, and *ṣoḍaśa-dalāmbuja,* the group of sixteen petals; and finally between *caturdaśāra,* the group of fourteen triangles, and *bhūpura,* the outer square.[38]

Later in his commentary, Lakṣmīdhara traces the exact correspondence between each *cakra* of *śrīcakra* and the *cakras* in the human body. According to him, *trikoṇa* (the central triangle) corresponds to *mūlādhāra; aṣṭakoṇa* (the group of eight triangles) corresponds to *svādhiṣṭhāna; daśāra* (the first set of ten triangles) corresponds to *maṇipūra; dvitīyadaśāra* (the second set of ten triangles) corresponds to *anāhata; caturdaśāra* (the group of fourteen triangles) corresponds to *viśuddhi; śivacakracatuṣṭaya* (the group of four *śiva cakras*) corresponds to *ājñā;* and the *bindu* corresponds to the *sahasrāra.*[39]

As is immediately apparent, this sequence and its correlation with the *cakras* in the human body is not logical. There are nine *cakras* in *śrīcakra*, but according to both *SL* and Lakṣmīdhara, there are only seven *cakras* in the body. This undermines the strength of his model, especially when according to other Tāntric texts, such as *YH* and its commentaries (i.e., *Dīpikā* and *Setubandha*) and *Gautamīya Tantra*, there are two additional *cakras* located between *ājñā* and *sahasrāra*. These two *cakras* are variously known as: *akula cakra* and *indu cakra*, *viṣu cakra* and *tālu cakra*, or *kailāsa* and *rodhinī*.[40] By including the two additional *cakras*, these texts build a more convincing case for the oneness of the *cakras* in *śrīcakra* and those in the human body.

After equating the *cakras* of *śrīcakra* with the *cakras* in the human body, Lakṣmīdhara establishes the oneness between *śrīcakra* and the body itself. In this respect, he divides the human body in *āyurvedic* fashion, according to which the body has nine basic *dhātus* (constituents): *tvak* (skin), *asṛk* (blood), *māṃsa* (flesh), *medas* (fat), *asthi* (bone), *majjā* (marrow), *śukra* (white, i.e., semen), *prāṇa* (vital force), and *jīvadhātu* (individual self). According to him, the first five are the *śakti cakras* and the last four are the *śiva cakras.* The tenth is *paramāśakti,* the highest *śakti* and is identical to the *bindu* of *śrīcakra*. She is *īśvarī,* the ruling lady of the body.[41]

Lakṣmīdhara also explains how the deities residing in the various circuits of *śrīcakra* symbolize different aspects of the human being and what they mean in his Samayācāra system. Each of the nine *cakras* has one presiding goddess, subordinate goddesses, their corresponding male counterparts, *mudrās, śaktis,* and *yoginīs.* These nine *cakras* are made of triangles, petals, squares, or circles, each of which is presided over by a *śakti* or a group of *śaktis.* All nine *cakras* have specific names. The meaning of the names is indicative of the power of that *cakra* and the function it performs. The nine *cakras,* the goddesses, and the different aspects of the human personality corresponding to them, are as follows:[42]

First *Cakra: Trailokyamohana,* Enchanter of the Triple World

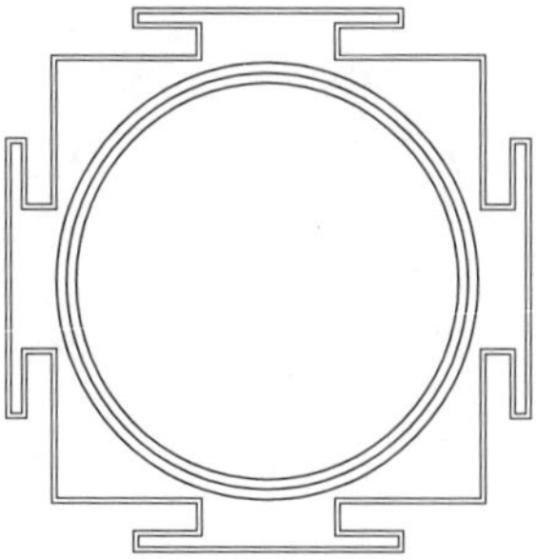

Name of Goddess	*The Human Aspect Corresponding to the Goddess*
Aṇimāsiddhi	*niyati,* past motivation
Laghimāsiddhi	*sṛṅgāra,* love
Mahimāsiddhi	*karuṇā,* pity
Īśitvasiddhi	*raudra,* fury
Vaśitvasiddhi	*bībhatsa,* disgust
Prākāmyasiddhi	*hāsya,* mirth
Bhuktisiddhi	*vātsalya,* parental love
Icchāsiddhi	*vīra,* heroism
Prāptisiddhi	*adbhuta,* wonder
Sarvakāmasiddhi	*śānta,* tranquility
Brāhmī	*kāma,* worldly desire
Māheśvarī	*krodha,* anger
Kaumārī	*lobha,* greed
Vaiṣṇavī	*moha,* delusion
Vārāhī	*mada,* pride
Indrāṇī	*mātsarya,* jealousy
Cāmuṇḍā	*puṇya,* virtues
Mahālakṣmī	*pāpa,* nonvirtues
Sarvasaṅkṣobhiṇī	*mūlādhāra*
Sarvavidrāviṇī	*svādhiṣṭhāna*
Sarvākarṣiṇī	*maṇipūra*
Sarvonmādinī	*anāhata*
Sarvamahāṅkuśā	*viśuddhi*
Sarvakhecarī	*ājñā*
Sarvabījā and Sarvayonī	two *lambikāgras*
Sarvatrikhaṇḍā	combination of all *cakras*

Second *Cakra: Sarvāśāparipūraka,* Fulfiller of All Expectations

Name of Goddess	*The Human Aspect Corresponding to the Goddess*
Kāmākarṣiṇī	*pṛthivī,* earth
Buddhyākarṣinī	*jala,* water
Ahaṅkārākarṣiṇī	*tejas,* fire
Śabdākarṣiṇī	*vāyu,* air
Sparśākarṣiṇī	*ākāśa,* space
Rūpākarṣiṇī	*śrotra,* ears
Rasākarṣiṇī	*tvak,* skin
Gandhākarṣiṇī	*cakṣu,* eyes
Cittākarṣiṇī	*jihvā,* tongue
Dhairyākarṣiṇī	*ghrāṇa,* nostrils
Smṛtyākarṣiṇī	*vāk,* speech
Nāmākarṣiṇī	*pāda,* feet
Bījākarṣiṇī	*pāṇi,* hands
Ātmākarṣiṇī	*pāyu,* organ of excretion
Amṛtākarṣiṇī	*upastha,* generative organ
Śarīrākarṣiṇī	*manovikāra,* modifications of mind

Third *Cakra: Sarvasaṅkṣakaṇa,* Agitator of All

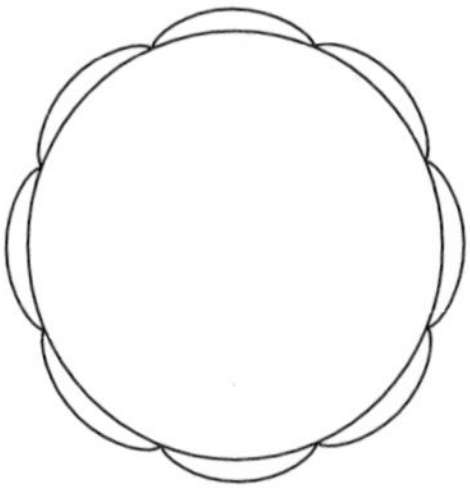

Name of Goddess	*The Human Aspect Corresponding to the Goddess*
Anaṅgakusumā	*vacana,* speech
Anaṅgamekhalā	*ādāna,* grasping
Anaṅgamadanā	*gamana,* locomotion
Anaṅgamadanāturā	*visarga,* evacuation
Anaṅgarekhā	*ānanda,* enjoyment
Anaṅgaveginī	*hāna,* renouncing
Anaṅgāṅkuśā	*upādāna,* receiving
Anaṅgamālinī	*upekṣā,* indifference

Fourth *Cakra: Sarvasaubhāgyadāyaka,* Provider of All Auspiciousness

Name of Goddess	*The Human Aspect Corresponding to the Goddess*
Sarvasaṅkṣobhiṇī	*alambusā*
Sarvavidrāviṇī	*kuhū*
Sarvākarṣiṇī	*viśvodarā*
Sarvāhlādinī	*varuṇā*
Sarvasammohinī	*hastijihvā*
Sarvastambhinī	*yaśovatī*
Sarvajambhinī	*payasvinī*
Sarvavaśaṅkarī	*gāndhārī*
Sarvarañjinī	*pūṣā*
Sarvonmādinī	*śaṇkhinī*
Sarvārthasādhinī	*sarasvatī*
Sarvasampattipūriṇī	*iḍā*
Sarvamantramayī	*piṅgalā*
Sarvadvandvakṣayaṅkarī	*suṣumnā*

Fifth *Cakra: Sarvārthasādhaka*, Accomplisher of All Purposes

Name of Goddess	*The Human Aspect Corresponding to the Goddess*
Sarvasiddhipradā	*prāṇa*
Sarvasampatpradā	*apāna*
Sarvapriyaṅkarī	*samāna*
Sarvamaṅgalakāriṇī	*udāna*
Sarvakāmapradā	*vyāna*
Sarvaduḥkhavimocinī	*nāga*
Sarvavighnanirvāriṇī	*kūrma*
Sarvamṛtyupraśaminī	*kṛkala*
Sarvasarvāṅgasundarī	*devadatta*
Sarvasaubhāgyadāyinī	*dhanañjaya*

Sixth *Cakra: Sarvarakṣakara, Protector of All*

Name of Goddess	*The Human Aspect Corresponding to the Goddess*
Sarvajñā	*recaka*
Sarvaśaktimayī	*pācaka*
Sarvaiśvaryapradā	*śoṣaka*
Sarvajñānamayī	*dāhaka*
Sarvavyādhivināśinī	*plāvaka*
Sarvādhārasvarūpiṇī	*kṣāraka*
Sarvapāpaharā	*udgāraka*
Sarvānandamayī	*kṣobhaka*
Sarvarakṣāsvarūpiṇī	*jṛmbhaka*
Sarvepsitaphalapradā	*mohaka*

Seventh *Cakra: Sarvarogahara,* Remover of All Illness

Name of Goddess	*The Human Aspect Corresponding to the Goddess*
Vaśinī	*śīta,* cold
Kāmeśvarī	*uṣṇa,* heat
Modinī	*sukha,* pleasure
Vimalā	*duḥkha,* pain
Aruṇā	*icchā,* desire
Jayinī	*sattva*
Sarveśvarī	*rajas*
Kaulinī	*tamas*

Eighth *Cakra: Sarvasiddhiprada,* Giver of All Accomplishments

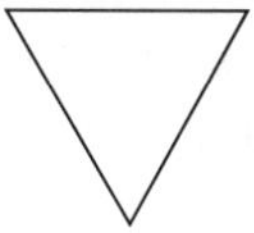

Name of Goddess	*The Human Aspect Corresponding to the Goddess*
Kāmeśvarī	*prakṛti*
Vajreśvarī	*mahat*
Kaulinī or Bhagamālinī	*ahaṅkāra*

Ninth *Cakra: Sarvānandamaya,* Identical to All/Perfect Bliss

●

Name of Goddess	*The Human Aspect Corresponding to the Goddess*
Saṃvit or Lalitā or Sādākhyākalā or Kāmeśvara	Ātman

During this lengthy discussion on the oneness of *śrīcakra* and the human body, Lakṣmīdhara also brings up the equation between the sixteen *nityākalās,* which, according to him, are located in the *bindu* and the square that surrounds the *bindu* and the *ājñā cakra.*[43] During this discussion, he also equates these sixteen *nityākalās* with the sixteen letters of the *śrīvidyā* mantra.

Then, in order to demonstrate that all the *mātṛkās,* the phonemes of the Sanskrit language, are subsumed in the *śrīvidyā* mantra, he opens a whole new discussion. He goes on to describe which Sanskrit letters correspond to which letter of the *śrīvidyā* mantra, which particular aspect of the *śrīvidyā* mantra is equivalent to each of the *nityākalās,* and which *nityākalās* correspond to which particular day of the fortnight. He explains how the 360 *kalās* described previously fit into the theory of the 16 *kalās* corresponding to different aspects of the external moon and the esoteric moon. Finally, he explains the equivalency between all these concepts and the *cakras* in the human body.

Śakti and the Śrīvidyā Mantra

There are many variations of the *śrīvidyā* mantra, depending on which letter the mantra begins with, who first practiced the mantra, and how many syllables the mantra contains.[44] The variation that Lakṣmīdhara gives in his commentary on *SL* 32 is called *kādividyā* and originally consisted of fifteen syllables. He completes the mantra by adding the syllable *śrīṃ* and calls it *ṣoḍaśī* or *śrīvidyā*.[45] The first fifteen syllables refer to the immanent world, which manifests from *samayā*, and the sixteenth refers to *samayā* itself. The fifteen syllables are further divided into three *kūṭas* (parts):

Ka e ī la hrīṃ
ha sa ka ha la hrīṃ
sa ka la hrīṃ
śrīṃ

Equating this mantra with the *cakras* in the body, Lakṣmīdhara states that the first *kūṭa*, from *ka* to the first *hrī*, corresponds to *āgneyakhaṇḍa*, the two lowest *cakras;* the second *kūṭa*, from *ha* to the second *hrī*, corresponds to *saurakhaṇḍa*, the two middle *cakras;* and the third *kūṭa*, from *sa* to the third *hrī*, corresponds to *somakhaṇḍa*.[46] The last syllable, *śrī*, which constitutes the fourth part of the mantra, corresponds to *candrakalākhaṇḍa*.[47]

According to Lakṣmīdhara, the *śrīvidyā* mantra in general, and this version in particular, encapsulates the entire range of *mātṛkās*. The Sanskrit alphabet has fifty, fifty-one, or sometimes only forty-eight syllables and, according to Lakṣmīdhara, each syllable coincides with a syllable of the fifteen-syllable *śrīvidyā* mantra.[48] Lakṣmīdhara begins this discussion with the statement that there are fifty letters in the Sanskrit alphabet, all of which are subsumed in the fifteen syllables of the mantra.[49] But, while giving details and explaining exactly how they are subsumed, he reduces the number to forty-eight, thus creating three equal sets of sixteen. The two extra letters are *ha* and *kṣa.* According to his interpretation, *ha,* the seed syllable of space, is subsumed in the space of the *bindu,* and *kṣa,* which is a combination of *ka* and *ṣa,* does not need to be treated separately.[50] The first set includes the sixteen vowels; the second set, the sixteen consonants from *ka* to *ta;* and the third set, the remaining sixteen consonants from *tha* to *sa.* Lakṣmīdhara also presents a terse and inventive discussion to support his thesis that all the syllables from *a* to *kṣa* are included in the *śrīvidyā* mantra. He does this by proving the existence of the *pratyāhāra "akṣa"* in the *śrīvidyā* mantra. According to him, the first *ka* of the *śrīvidyā* mantra implies that it is preceded by sixteen vowels, which begin with *a,* whereas *ka* itself, being a component of the syllable *kṣa,* represents *kṣa* as well. Thus, in the first letter of the *śrīvidyā* mantra, i.e., *ka,* the *pratyāhāra "akṣa"* is found. Thus the *pratyāhāra "akṣa"* represents all the Sanskrit syllables from *a* to *kṣa.*[51]

In an attempt to prove that all Sanskrit phonemes are present in the *śrīvidyā* mantra, Lakṣmīdhara gives another interpretation of the mantra. According to him, in the third division of the *śrīvidyā* mantra (i.e. *sa, ka, la, hrīṃ),* the syllables *ka* and *la* stand for the word *kalā.* The word *kalā* itself stands for all the phonemes. Thus, all the *mātṛkās* are included in the *śrīvidyā* mantra.[52] In Lakṣmīdhara's own words:

> Thus, the sixteen *nityās* are identical to the sixteen syllables found in the mantra; sixteen syllables are identical to fifty syllables, and fifty syllables are identical to the *kalās* of sun, moon, and fire. On the basis of their association with sun, moon, and fire they are threefold.[53]

Lakṣmīdhara also equates various syllables of the *śrīvidyā* mantra with *śrīcakra*. For example, the three *hrīṃs* and the last syllable, *śrīṃ*, are subsumed in *bindu* (which represents the four *śiva cakras*). All the *mātṛkās* are also included in the various parts of *śrīcakra*, such as the four *antasthas (ya, ra, la,* and *va)* and four *ūṣmṇas (śa, ṣa, sa,* and *ha)*. Together, these eight syllables are identical to *aṣṭakoṇa*, the eight-triangled *cakra* of *śrīcakra*. With the exception of every fifth syllable of each group *(varga)*, all the twenty syllables from *ka* to *ma* are included in the *daśārayugama* (the two sets of ten triangles). The fifth syllable of each group (i.e., *ṅa, ña, ṇa, na,* and *ma)* are nasal sounds and are included in the *bindu.* With the exception of *anusvāra* and *visarga,* the remaining fourteen vowels are included in *caturdaśāra,* the fourteen-triangled *cakra* of *śrīcakra. Anusvāra* and *visarga* are included in the *bindu.*[54] Thus, all Sanskrit syllables are included in the *śrīvidyā* mantra and *śrīcakra,* and, thereby, in the *cakras* in the human body.

In the context of the *śrīvidyā* mantra, the lunar month, which has two fortnights, each consisting of fifteen days, is considered to be the standard measurement of time. Each day and night of the fortnight is considered to be one *kalā,* known as *tithi,* in the lunar calendar. These fifteen *kalās* or *tithis* are represented by and worshipped in *ṣoḍaśāra*, the circle of sixteen petals, corresponding to the *viśuddhi cakra.*[55] The names of these fifteen *kalās* or *tithis* and their corresponding deities are as listed on the following page.[56]

The first five *kalās* correspond to the *āgneyakhaṇḍa*, the second five to *saurakhaṇḍa,* and the third five to the *soma-khaṇḍa.*[57]

Equating the *kalās* with different *tattvas,* Lakṣmīdhara states that the first *kalā, darśā*, is identical to *śiva tattva,*

Kalā or Tithi	*Presiding Deity*
Darśā	Tripurasundarī
Dṛṣṭā	Kāmeśvarī
Darśatā	Bhagamālinī
Viśvarūpā	Nityaklinnā
Sudarśanā	Bheruṇḍā
Āpyāyamānā	Vahnivāsinī
Āpyāyamānā (?)	Mahāvidyeśvarī or Mahāvajreśvarī
Āpyāyā	Raudrī
Sūnṛtā	Tvaritā
Irā	Kulasundarī
Āpūryamāṇā	Nīlapatākā
Āpūryamāṇā (?)	Vijayā
Pūrayantī	Sarvamaṅgalā
Pūrṇā	Jvālā
Paurṇamāsī	Mālinī
[Cidrūpā Ṣoḍaśī	Cidrūpā or Ṣoḍaśī]

dṛṣṭā to *śakti tattva, darśatā* to *māyāṃtattva, viśvarūpā* to *śuddhavidyā,* and *sudarśanā* to *jala tattva* (the water element). All five of these *tattvas* correspond to *āgneyakhaṇḍa*, the two lowest *cakras* in the body; *āgni,* fire, is the presiding deity. The next six *kalās—āpyāyamānā, āpyāyamānā, āpyāyā, sūnṛtā, irā,* and *āpūryamāṇā* —correspond to fire, air, mind, earth, space, and *vidyā tattva,* respectively, and constitute the *saurakhaṇḍa,* the three middle *cakras.* Here, *sūrya*, the sun, is the presiding deity. The remaining four *kalās—āpūryamāṇā, pūrayantī, pūrṇā,* and *paurṇamāsī*— which are identical to *maheśvaratattva, paratattva, ātmatattva,* and *sadāśivatattva,* respectively, form the *somakhaṇḍa*, the two highest *cakras.* The presiding deity of this *khaṇḍa* is the moon. The presiding deities of all fifteen *kalās*, their corresponding *tattvas,* deities, and *khaṇḍas* of the *cakras* are collectively *Kāmadeva* and *Kāmeśvarī.* The sixteenth *kalā, ṣoḍaśī* or *sādākhyā,* is not identical to any *tattva* other than itself.[58]

In his commentary on *SL* 32, Lakṣmīdhara makes two contradictory statements within one paragraph. First, he distributes these fifteen *kalās* into three equal divisions. Later, he assigns five *kalās* to the *āgneyakhaṇḍa*, six to the *saurakhaṇḍa*, and only four to the *somakhaṇḍa*. Lakṣmīdhara attempts to resolve this problem by stating:

> . . . *Āpūryamāṇākalā* (the eleventh) although situated in the *somakhaṇḍa* is subsumed in the *saurakhaṇḍa.* Since *āpūryamāṇākalā* is a sub-branch of *irākalā,* there is oneness between the *irā* (the tenth *kalā*) and *āpūryamāṇā.*[59]

However, this does not provide a reasonable explanation for why the *āpūryamāṇā kalā*, which belongs to the lunar division, should be subsumed in the solar division, nor why the *āpūryamāṇā kalā* is a branch of *irā kalā.* A better reason may be his intention to identify each of the *kalās* with each syllable of the *śrīvidyā* mantra, which is divided into three parts, each consisting of five, six, and four syllables.

Regardless of his reason for distributing the *kalās* unequally, two more problems remain: first, as stated earlier, in order to demonstrate equivalency between the fifteen syllables of the *śrīvidyā* mantra and the fifteen days of the fortnight, Lakṣmīdhara equates the 316 *kalās* with the 15 *kalās* of the moon (a fortnight). By dividing 360 *kalās* by fifteen, each day of the fortnight, or each letter of the *śrīvidyā* mantra will be equal to 24 *kalās*, rays, or days of the lunar calendar. Because the first *kūṭa* of the *śrīvidyā* mantra consists of five letters, it will share 120 *kalās;* the second *kūṭa*, which consists of six syllables, will share 144 *kalās;* and the third *kūṭa,* which consists of four syllables, will share only 96 *kalās* of the solar calendar. Meanwhile, Lakṣmīdhara also equates these three *kūṭas* with the three *khaṇḍas* of the *cakras.* During the discussion on the *cakras* cited earlier, he clearly stated that 108 *kalās,* or rays of *kālaśakti,* pervade *āgneyakhaṇḍa*; 116 pervade the *saurakhaṇḍa;* and 136 pervade the *somakhaṇḍa.* Lakṣmīdhara also states that there is oneness between the first *kūṭa* of *śrīvidyā* and the *āgneyakhaṇḍa*, the second *kūṭa* and the *saurakhaṇḍa*, and the third *kūṭa* and the *somakhaṇḍa*. Therefore, the number of *kalās* assigned to the *kūṭas* of the *śrīvidyā* mantra and the *khaṇḍas* of the *cakras* must match. But in Lakṣmīdhara's presentation, they do not. For example, if Lakṣmīdhara assigns five *kalās* each of the three *kūṭas*, then each *kūṭa*, and therefore their corresponding *cakras*, will consist of 120 *kalās*, which contradicts the number of *kalās* Lakṣmīdhara has assigned to the three *khaṇḍas.* In order to match the number of letters in each *kūṭa*, he assigns the *kalās* unequally, i.e., five *kalās* to the first *kūṭas*, six to the second, and four to the third, yet he still fails to make a perfect equation between the *śrīvidyā* mantra and the *cakras* on the basis of the *kalās*.

The second problem lies in Lakṣmīdhara's statement that fifteen *kalās* rotate around *ṣoḍaśāra,* the sixteen-petalled *cakra* of *śrīcakra,* which corresponds to the *viśuddhi cakra* in the human body.[60] This contradicts his statement that these same fifteen *kalās* are also distributed among all six *cakras.*[61] Moreover, in considering these fifteen *kalās* to be at the *viśuddhi cakra,* Lakṣmīdhara also contradicts his earlier statement that the moon at the *ājñā cakra* has fifteen *kalās.*[62]

In spite of these contradictions, Lakṣmīdhara preserves *samayā's* transcendence by keeping the sixteenth syllable, *śrīṃ,* above the first fifteen syllables and their threefold divisions.[63] When the light of the eternal sixteenth *kalā* "flashes forth" and manifests as fifteen *kalās* either at *viśuddhi* or at *ājñā cakra,* she remains transcendent, serving as the source of evolution for those fifteen *kalās.* Lakṣmīdhara makes a point of explaining the process of the evolution of the universe from *samayā* at the levels of both the microcosm and the macrocosm. Throughout his lengthy discussion on *kuṇḍalinī*, *cakras*, *śrīcakra*, and *śrīvidyā* mantra, he tries to prove his main premise, which he stated at the outset of his commentary: the universe actually evolves from *śrīcakra*, and that *śrīcakra* is but a combination of the four *śiva cakras,* the five *śakti cakras,* and the innermost *bindu*, representing *samayā*, the transcendent *sādākhyākalā.* From this unitary dyad of *śuddhavidyā* and *sadāśiva,* represented by the *bindu,* the pattern of triangles, petals, circles, and squares that constitute *śrīcakra* evolves. By equating the different components of *śrīcakra*, their presiding deities, and their mantras with the cosmos and the human being, Lakṣmīdhara demonstrates the oneness of all.

Śakti and the Personified Form of the Goddess

Although Lakṣmīdhara condemns external worship, he comments on those verses of the *SL* that are exclusively concerned with the description of the physical beauty of the goddess, Tripurasundarī. In order to justify the Samayācāra viewpoint, Lakṣmīdhara explains how this personified form of the goddess fits into theory of the *cakras* in the human body or the *cakras* of *śrīckara,* and how they are identical to each other. He describes the personified form of *śrīvidyā* and its philosophical implications in *LD* 7, 8, 92, and 97. From these verses and his commentary on them, the following description emerges.

In the center of the ocean of nectar, there is an island of

gems bordered by groves of heavenly trees. On this island, in a grove of *nīpa* trees is a mansion. In that mansion, the goddess, *Śrīvidyā*, as a wave of consciousness and bliss, reposes on a couch, which itself is made of four gods. *Paramaśiva* serves as the mattress. The goddess has four arms and three eyes and is most beautiful. She is as radiant as thousands of rising suns. In her four hands she holds a bow, arrows, a noose, and a goad.

According to Lakṣmīdhara, the ocean of nectar is the *bindu* of *śrīcakra*, comparable to *sahasrāra*. The heavenly trees are the five downward-facing triangles in *śrīcakra*. In the center is the *devī's* mansion made of wish-yielding gems. The four gods who make up the couch are *brahmā, viṣṇu, rudra*, and *īśvara*. *Sadāśiva* himself is the mattress on which the *devī* sits.[64] Quoting from *Vāmakeśvara Tantra*, Lakṣmīdhara describes the meaning of the different weapons of the goddess: "*pāśa* (noose) and *aṅkuśa* (trident) are identical to *rāga* (attachment) and *dveṣa* (aversion). Her bow and arrows are the mind and the five *tanmātras*. She resides in the *cakra* made of *karaṇendriya* (the active senses), and she herself is identical to *saṃvit*, pure consciousness."[65] Demonstrating the oneness of the goddess with *kuṇḍalinī śakti*, Lakṣmīdhara quotes from *Bhairava Yāmala*: "After penetrating the circle of *śiva*, the sun, in *sahasrāra*, she, the *kuṇḍalinī śakti* makes the circle of the moon melt or drip. Inebriated with the supreme bliss dripping from the nectar produced by that (union), the wife of *kula (kuṇḍalinī)*, leaves the *kula, suṣumnā nāḍī* (or all *kulatattvas*) and comes to the highest shower, i.e., enjoys the highest bliss."[66] Similar imagery is found in *SL* 10:

> With streams of nectar flowing from between your feet sprinkling the universe, [recreating] through the power of reciting the sacred text that produces the six [cakras which had been dis-

> solved when Devī regressed to the sahasrāra by the kula path], again you reach your own abode and into the form of a serpent, in three and a half coils, you convert yourself and sleep in the kulakuṇḍa hollow.[67]

The commentators Kāmeśvarasūri, Narasiṃhasvāmin, and Gaurīkānta elaborate slightly on the symbolism of the personified form of the goddess. For instance, according to Kāmeśvara, the *bindu,* which is located above the four *śiva cakras* and below the five *śakti cakras,* is the ocean of nectar. In the center is a garden of celestial trees: *kalpa, santāna, haricandana, mandāra,* and *pārijāta.* He also names the nine gems that are used in the *devī's* mansion. By interpreting the words *sura, dvīpa,* and *nīpa,* he brings the visual imagery closer to the theory of the *cakras.* For instance, he states:

> *Jīva,* the individual soul, perfectly or beautifully shines and therefore is called *sura.* Since *jīva* exists in the body from toe to head, and in its absence the body cannot survive, *jīva* is called *viṭapin,* the garden [the ground where different kinds of plants of life can grow]. Furthermore, by virtue of being the abode of gods, *mūlādhāra,* etc. *chakras* are like isalnds which are made of gems or shine like gems. . . .
>
> Due to their function of going out and coming in, the five main prāṇas—*prāṇa, apāna, vyāna, udāna,* and *samāna*—and the five secondary prāṇas—*nāga, kūrma, kṛkara, devadatta,* and *dhanañjaya*—carry a body; therefore (these *pranas* are called) *nīpa.* Or the aforesaid presiding gods of the senses are called *nīpa* because (they) nuture or protect the body.[68]

Narasiṃhasvāmin[69] compares *śrīcakra,* which he calls *sṛṣṭi cakra,* with the ocean of nectar; *saubhāgya (saubhāgya-dāyaka cakra,* the fourteen-triangled *cakra* of *śrīcakra)* with the celestial garden, and *daśārayugala,* the two sets of ten triangles with the island of gems and garden of *nīpa* trees, respectively. *Aṣṭāra,* the eight-triangled *cakra* of *śrīcakra,* is identical to *cintāmaṇigṛha,* the mansion made of wish-yielding gems; *trikoṇa,* the central triangle is identical to the couch, and the *bindu* is identical to *sadāśiva.*

Asserting that *brahmā, viṣṇu, rudra, īśvara,* and *sadāśiva* are the different parts of the *devī's* couch, Gaurīkānta says that since they are *pretas,* i.e., they have attained unsurpassed closeness with the body of the *devī,* they are viewed as part of the *devī's* couch. This imagery indicates both their supremacy over all *tattvas* and the *devī's* supremacy over them.[70]

Lakṣmīdhara is obviously not particularly interested in creating a perfect parallel between the personified form of the goddess and other facets of *śrīvidyā.* Because he is exclusively concerned with Samayācāra, he is naturally not inclined to dwell on the personified form of the goddess and her worship. He is aware of the fact that no matter how much emphasis is placed on the symbolic meaning of the goddess, the very concept of the goddess itself carries a dualistic notion: she exists as a being in time and space; she is different from those who worship her; the ritual objects offered her are different from her; and worship itself is an action directed toward her. That is why Lakṣmīdhara clearly states: ". . . this is a ritual worship. Ritual is comprised of actions and (therefore) should not be respected."[71] Right after this statement, he begins his commentary on *SL* 42 by writing: "Thus after thoroughly explaining the doctrine of Samayācāra, [now the author of the *Saundaryalaharī*] describes samayā's [physical beauty] from crown to feet."[72] This statement implies that the content of the *Saundaryalaharī,* from verse 42 onward, is not related to Samayācāra doctrine. This is probably the reason why, with the exception of verses 92 and 99, Lakṣmīdhara simply gives a word-for-word translation of the verses from this point on.

To reiterate, Lakṣmīdhara concentrates only on those verses of *SL* that can be related to Samayācāra doctrine. The essence of Samayācāra lies in this theory of *samayā's* nondual existence and her transcendence over *sadāśiva (śiva)* and *śuddhavidyā (śakti)* and all other *tattvas.* Because *samayā* alone exists, even in the practical realm, the *cakras* in the body, *śrīcakra,* the *śrīvidyā* mantra, the *mātṛkās,* the *kalās,* individual beings, and the entire universe are identical to *samayā.* As far as the soteriological goal is concerned, it can be attained only by awakening *kuṇḍalinī* and leading her from the *mūlādhāra* to the *sahasrāra,* where she unites herself with *śiva.* According to Lakṣmīdhara, all these philosophical and spiritual elements are exclusive characteristics of Samayācāra.

Discussion and Analysis

As stated earlier, Lakṣmīdhara apparently created this model while using the blueprint which already existed both in Śaiva and Śākta Tāntrism. However, we do not know exactly where the different pieces of this blueprint were originally developed, nor the process through which these pieces coalesced and attained the form in which we encounter them in Lakṣmīdhara's writings. One method of analyzing the sources from which this particular concept of Samayācāra and *śakti* may have been derived is to divide the literature into four distinct groups: the texts that Lakṣmīdhara acknowledges in his commentary; the Śaiva and Śākta texts he must have read, but does not explicitly acknowledge; the texts of Pāñcarātra Āgama that contain related concepts; and the texts of Vedic literature.

To begin with the texts he acknowledges, we find his premise that *piṇḍāṇḍa,* the individual body, and *brahmāṇḍa,* the universe, are identical in a fairly developed form in *NS*, *YH*, and *YKU*.[73] Similarly, the elaborate treatment of *cakra* theory that appears in *LD* 9-11 and 14, is reminiscent of passages in *SU*, *YH*, and *YKU*,[74] which thoroughly expound the concept of *kuṇḍalinī*, *cakras*, and the system of *nāḍīs*. These sources also contain passing references to the correlation between the esoteric planes of existence and the *cakras*. These same texts also make frequent mention of the oneness of the *cakras* with the human body, *śrīcakra*, the *śrīvidyā* mantra, *devatā*, *guru*, and one's own *ātman*.[75] The concept of *kāla*, which is only implied in *SL* but has become a significant component of *cakra* theory in *LD*, can also be traced to these sources.[76]

Turning our attention to the Śaiva and Śākta texts Lakṣmīdhara must have been familiar with but does not acknowledge, we encounter in *SVT* the concept of the oneness of *bindu*, *kalā*, *nāda*, mantra, *jīva*, *śiva*, and *kāla*.[77] Just as Lakṣmīdhara[78] considers *śiva (sadāśiva)* to be identical with *nāda*, subsuming it in *śakti*, *SVT*[79] also considers *nāda* and *sadāśiva* to be synonymous and places *nāda* in the center of *śakti*. A parallel to Lakṣmīdhara's concept of *sadāśiva* residing in *brahmanāḍī* and *sādākhyā's* transcendence is found in *SVT*.[80] According to *SVT*, *sadāśiva* is situated in the *brahmanāḍī* and *paramaśiva* transcends the *brahmanāḍī*. Lakṣmīdhara's method of raising *kuṇḍalinī* and piercing the *cakras* and his concept of *nāḍīs;* the movement of *prāṇa;* the human body being comprised of *soma*, *sūrya*, and *agni* and their oneness with *kāla*; and the whole universe being pervaded or created by *kāla* echoes *SVT*.[81] Similarly, in *NT* one finds a detailed description of *nāḍīs*, *kuṇḍalinī*, *nāda*, *bindu*, *kāla*, and *cakrabhedana*, and piercing the *cakras*—all characteristics of Samayācāra.[82]

As discussed previously, Abhinavagupta's treatment of

these subjects is amazingly close to Lakṣmīdhara's . For example, he uses the terms *sādākhyā, ṣoḍaśī,* and even *śrīvidyā.* While discussing the nature of *kuṇḍalinī śakti,* the method of awakening her, and her union with *śiva* in *sahasrāra,* he calls *kuṇḍalinī śakti* "*viśvādhāra,*" the ground of the universe.[83] Like Lakṣmīdhara, Abhinavagupta states that an aspirant leaves the path of *iḍā* and *piṅgalā,* enters *suṣumnā,* pierces all the lower *cakras,* and enters *brahmabila,* i.e., *brahmanāḍī.*[84] Eventually, he rises above *sadāśiva* and the other four *brahmans* who reside in *brahmanāḍī* and goes to the Highest, which he terms *sādākhyāṃ bhuvanam.*[85] *Parā devī brahmāṇī,* who resides in *brahmanāḍī,* obstructs the path. A *yogin* penetrates that obstruction in order to go above.[86] Lakṣmīdhara's description of *kuṇḍalinī, sadāśiva,* and the other *tattvas* as part of the *devī's* couch, *śakti* as the source of *kāla,* the concept of *mātṛikā,* the oneness between the human body and the body of *saṃvit* are similar to those found in *TĀ,* especially chapters 15 and 29.[87]

Next, we come to the texts of Pāñcarātra Āgama, which are replete with the information that Lakṣmīdhara discusses in *LD,* although he never mentions them. Because there are more than a dozen Pāñcarātra texts, some of which are voluminous, it is not possible to discuss all of them, nor is such a discussion relevant. Therefore, we have selected the *Lakṣmī-Tantra,*[88] hereafter cited as *LT,* as representative.

LT not only gives the essence but also elaborates on the contents of three major texts: *Sāttvata Saṃhitā, Jayākhya Saṃhitā,* and *Ahirbudhnya Saṃhitā. LT* combines the philosophical concepts of *Sāttvata Saṃhitā* and the ritualistic aspects of *Jayākhya Saṃhitā.* It is also one of the most important Pāñcarātra texts, as it gives a clear and systematic treatment of Pāñcarātra theories. In regard to the *śakti* principle, it shows a striking similarity to Śāktism, yet remains

Vaiṣṇavite in tone, synthesizing various concepts current in Pāñcarātra and other Tāntric traditions. Just as Lakṣmīdhara's doctrine was to do later, this text attempts to blend Sāṅkhya ideology with monistic Vedānta.

LT stands out among the vast body of Pāñcarātra texts because of its exclusive treatment of *śakti* in the form of the goddess Lakṣmī. This is one of the few Pāñcarātra texts that is cited by prominent Śākta commentators such as Bhāskararāya in his commentary on *Lalitā-Sahasranāma*, Nāgeśa Bhāṭṭa on *DS*, and Appaya Dīkṣita on *Candrakalāstutī*.

According to *LT*, Lakṣmī, who is the supreme goddess, is identical to *icchā, jñāna,* and *kriyā.* She is *pañcakṛtyakarī,* the force responsible for the fivefold functions, i.e., creation, maintenance, destruction, concealment, and grace.[89] She is *mahārājñī,* the great queen.[90] She is *hṛllekhā* (probably the three *hrīṃs* of the *śrīvidyā* mantra), *paramātmastha* (dwelling in *paramātman,* the highest self), and *cit śakti,* the power of consciousness.[91] She is *sarvaśaktimayī,* consisting of all *śaktis.* She is the leader of *śakti cakra.* She resides in the interior of *agni* and *soma,* and she is *madhyamārgānuvartinī,* traveling through the central path that is *suṣumnā.*[92] Similarly, *LT* describes the concepts of *brahma pañcakam* (five *brahmans*); the rays of *agni, sūrya,* and *soma*; and the concept of *bindu, saṃvit, mātṛkā,* and *brahmarandhra* or *brahmagranthi.*[93] Like *LD, LT* also mentions the oneness of *mātṛkās* and *agni, sūrya,* and *soma.*[94]

According to *LT*, Lakṣmī is called *mahāyoni,* the great *yoni,* the source of evolution, and Trilokajananī, the mother of the three universes, yet she is *parā,* the transcendent.[95] However, as Sanjukta Gupta writes in the introduction to her translation of *Lakṣmī Tantra, LT* establishes "the supremacy of *lakṣmī* as a philosophical principle, ranking, if not higher than Viṣnu, then at least as equal to Him. This is achieved by emphasizing the mystic tenet of unity in duality, the two-in-one accepted by the Śākta sects."[96] Describing the nature of *śakti* in *LT*, he writes, "Śakti is inherent in God just as light is inherent in the moon. She is inseparable from God yet not absolutely identical with God. . . ."[97] In *LD*, the analogies of the moon and moonlight, and fire and the heat of the fire are given to explain the inseparability and oneness of *śakti* and *śiva*, whereas in *LT*, they are used to demonstrate only inseparability. The next statement, "She is also the selfhood of the supreme Self *(paramātmam)*, i.e., of God. In other words, Lakṣmī, God's Śakti, is his essential nature. She is the divine presence. She forms the so-called body of Nārāyaṇa, consisting of six divine or ideal qualities (guṇas)."[98] Similarly, Lakṣmī is *śakti* and God is the possessor of the divine power *(śaktimat)*—a concept similar to Pūrva Kaula doctrine, as mentioned by Lakṣmīdhara.

Finally, we come to Vedic literature. Passing references to Śrīvidyā-related concepts such as *soma, kāla,* and *ṣoḍaśī* are found in the Saṃhitā portion of the Vedas. *ṚV* clearly states that there is a distinction between the *soma* obtained from herbs and the *soma* known only to the knowers of *brahman.* The latter resides in heaven *(divi)* and it is through that *soma* that the children of Aditī *(ādityāḥ)* and the earth and moon are sustained.[99] Praying to *soma,* the seer of the mantra says, "O deva, shining being [i.e., soma], they drink you, and immediately you grow again. Air is the protector of soma, [and you, soma, are] the creator of the years and months."[100] One might link this simple statement to the *candrakalā* of *LD*, which is also the creator of years and months *(saṃvatsara).* The *Yajurveda* uses the term *ṣoḍaśī* in conjunction with a statement about *trīṇi jyotīśiṃ* (three rays) penetrating the whole universe. This may be a reference to the rays of the sun, moon, and fire.[101] *The Atharvaveda*, contains references to the concept of *kāla* as *īśvara* and *prajāpatī,* and even the creator of *prajāpatī.*[102]

These passing references and the mere mention of these terms do not constitute evidence that the roots of the Samayācāra doctrine lie in the Vedas, although commentators, including Lakṣmīdhara, make this claim. They do this by extracting words, phrases, and entire passages from these ancient sources and interpreting them in a manner that supports the point they are trying to make. It is a common practice for the commentators on Indian philosophical texts to stretch the content and add materials to such a degree that the commentary becomes an independent treatise in itself. In writing such treatises, the commentators impose their ideas on the main text and validate them by quoting older texts, whose credibility has already been established. Śaṅkarācārya's *BS-B*, Abhinavagupta's *PTV* and *MVV*, and Kṣemarāja's *Vimarśinī* on the *Śiva Sūtras* and his *Uddyota* commentaries on *SVT* and *NT* are typical examples. Lakṣmīdhara's *LD* is no exception. For example, to demonstrate that the theories of *cakras, śrīcakra,* and *śrīvidyā* mantra have their roots in the Vedas, Lakṣmīdhara offers references from the *Taittirīya Saṃhitā,*[103] *Taittirīya Brāhmaṇa,*[104] and *Taittirīya Upaniṣad.*[105] However, the only direct connection between those passages and Śrīvidyā doctrine is Lakṣmīdhara's own interpretation.

If such interpretations are accepted as a valid means of locating Śrīvidyā elements in Vedic literature, we can find hundreds of such references. For example, all of the mantras from the *ṚV* that constitute the *Sarasvatī Rahasya Upaniṣad,*[106] *Vāk Sūkta,*[107] and *Śrī Sūkta*[108] can be used as a source of Śrīvidyā, or at least Śākta, ideas. Even though contemporary *śrīvidyā* adherents, especially those who are formally associated with the Śaṅkarācārya order, claim a Vedic origin for Śrīvidyā in the same fashion that Lakṣmīdhara does, this claim has by no means been substantiated. The historical connection and interaction between the Vedas and *ṣaḍ-darśana* (Nyāya Vaiśeṣika, Sāṅkhya, Yoga, Mīmāṃsā, and Vedānta), as well as between the Vedas and both Jainism and Buddhism, is well known. The nature of the relationship and the process of interaction between Tantra and Veda (Āgama and Nigama) has so far not been fully understood. It still remains a mystery how two streams of literature—Vedic and Tāntric—which were parallel in most cases and which developed in the same socio-political, cultural, economic, and geographical setting, remained so aloof from each other. Even when we come across shared ideas, we have no way of knowing how a Tāntric adherent could have adopted them, especially when these ideas did not continue to develop in the traditions that are definitely based on the Vedas. For example, the concept of *soma*, which according to the *ṚV*,[109] is consumed by the gods, appears in *Sāmbapañcāśikā* in *TS-1*[110] in almost the same language, although it does not appear elsewhere in Vedic-oriented literature.

Despite the fact that philosophers remained adamant about the ideas they advocated, vigorously refuted other ideas, and thus helped maintain distinct philosophical doctrines, the process of interaction and exchange of ideas naturally continued among the masses and the mystics. Laymen—Buddhist, Jaina, and Hindu alike—assimilated a variety of ideas such as multiple forms of the goddesses and gods, rituals, *siddhis*, *nirvāṇa*, *śūnya*, *mokṣa*, *samādhi*, and *brahman*. Spiritual seekers, especially those who placed no particular importance on religious or sectarian affiliation, served as vehicles for blending the prevalent ideas of their day. Most such spiritual seekers or mystics had little interest in propagating what they knew and did not commit their thoughts and experiences to writing. However, a few of them wrote books, and in some cases fragments of their teachings were preserved by their devotees, either in oral or written form. The literature related to such figures, including Gorakhnatha and other saints of the *natha* tradition, Kabira, Tulasīdāsa, Nānaka, Nāmadeva, and Jñāneśvara—all of whom shared the yogic ideas mentioned in *LD* and other Śaiva/Śākta texts—is representative of the ideas prevalent in the mainstream of Indian spirituality.

Today this literature is usually classified as *santa sāhitya* and is found in all the older forms of Indian vernacular. In addition to *bhakti sādhanā,* one of the major characteristics of this literature is yoga and mysticism. Every single component of yoga *sādhanā* and experience is ultimately connected to *nāda, bindu,* or *kalā* and these, in turn, are connected to *śakti.* Although philosophy was not their main concern, these saints and mystics expressed their opinions regarding ultimate truth. It is in that context that they mention the metaphysical position of *nāda, bindu,* or *kalā,* human life, the world, and the highest truth. Just as one can discern slightly different roles of *śakti* within the general ideology of Śaivism and Śāktism, these variations are also apparent in this literature. In spite of Lakṣmīdhara's lack of acknowledgment of these sources, he clearly was familiar with them and endeavored to formulate a coherent philosophy that accommodated all these yogic principles. He denounced Vāmācāra and other forms of Tantra, which were associated with *digambaras, kṣapaṇakas,* and *kāpālikas,* and claimed that Samayācāra is purely Vedic. Thus he established it as distinct, although it already existed as a prominent aspect of the general body of Śakta Tāntrism. In Samayācāra doctrine, he includes the concepts of *nāda, bindu, kalā,* the oneness among mantra, yantra, *cakras,* the deity, and the human being, and other mystical components of Yoga and Tantra.

Lakṣmīdhara is the first to meticulously unite all these concepts and give a systematic account of Samayācāra doctrine and practice. He uses *SL* as a tool and acknowledges *Subhagodaya* and *Vāmakeśvara Tantra* as a source of inspiration, but extracts "Samayācāra" concepts from Śaiva and Śākta texts, and possibly from Pāñcarātra Āgama and Santa Sāhitya.

Unlike other Śākta texts, *LD* provides a rationale for considering all these different components to be identical. Philosophically, he expounds the theory of nondualism, according to which there is only one reality, which he terms *samayā, sādākhyā, candrakalā, ṣoḍaśī,* and *śrīvidyā.* These terms explicitly transcend the level of reality usually indicated throughout Śaiva and Śākta texts by the terms *śiva* and *śakti.* In a strict sense, therefore, Lakṣmīdhara proposes Samayā Advaitavāda or Sādākhyā Advaitavāda, according to which *śakti,* known by the term *sādākhyā,* alone exists. Lakṣmīdhara's concept of *śakti* is distinguished by three major characteristics: he uses definite terms—*samayā, sādākhyā,* or *candrakalā*—to indicate the transcendental form of *śakti.* His occasional use of the term *śakti* is always in a specific context which is self-explanatory. He clearly defines the metaphysical position of *samayā/śakti*: it is a unitary state of *śuddhavidyā* and *sadāśiva,* which is purely transcendental. This unitary state does not contain the slightest trace of its two components. It is completely different from, transcendent to, and the source of *śuddhavidyā, sadāśiva,* and the rest of the empirical world. Even in the realm of *sādhanā, samayā* alone exists. The different components of *sādhanā,* such as yantra, mantra, the *cakras,* and the deity, are identical to her.

Thus, Lakṣmīdhara is the first Śrīvidyā adherent to make an attempt to give a philosophical interpretation of the elements pertaining to *sādhanā.* His clear description of the *śakti* concept, which he terms *samayā,* and its metaphysical status in relation to *śiva*, can be used as a model to delineate the philosophy of *śakti* in other schools or subschools of Śākta Tāntrism. Other Tāntric schools have made fragmentary attempts to provide a philosophical interpretation of components of their *sādhanā,* but, due to the lack of a comprehensible philosophical structure, such interpretations remain incomplete. It is not necessarily the philosophy, but rather the methodology he uses, nor is it necessarily what he expounds, but his method of expounding it that can be used to study the specific characteristics of a particular subschool of Śākta Tāntrism, as well as the distinctive notions of *śakti* therein.

CHAPTER 5

Conclusion: The Significance of Lakṣmīdhara's Concept of *Śakti*

LAKṢMĪDHARA'S WRITINGS on *śakti* cannot be properly appreciated in isolation from the traditions which he drew upon and later influenced. Śrīvidyā is historically and philosophically the most important branch of Śākta Tāntrism on the basis of its well-defined philosophical position, its high literary standards, and its coherent explanations for the practices outlined in this system. In philosophies other than Śāktism and Śaivism, the concept of *śakti* has played a role subordinate to the system's prevailing supreme principle (e.g., *apūrva*, *adṛṣṭa*, *brahman*, or *śabdabrahman*). *Śakti*, in these systems, grew out of the effort to logically explain causality. In most Śaiva and Śākta texts, however, the function assigned to *śakti* is far more central. Asserting the supremacy of either *śiva* (consciousness) or *śakti* (the creative force behind the appearance of the universe), or of their union, these texts concern themselves with such fundamental questions as whether or not *śakti* and *śiva* are inseparable, whether or not they refer to two aspects of the same absolute truth and whether they play equal roles in the manifestation of the universe.

So significant is the philosophical and metaphysical category represented by *śakti* that this concept has been employed by some scholars as a means of designating a denomination as Tāntric or non-Tāntric. As a result, Tāntrism and Śāktism are sometimes considered to be identical, though it would be more correct to describe them as intersecting, rather than coinciding, traditions. Tāntric branches such as Vaiṣṇavism, Śaivism, and Buddhism have indeed incorporated the concept of *śakti*, but she occupies a subservient position compared to her male partner, even though all Tāntric sects postulate that he is incapable of initiating any action or movement.

The Śrīvidyā school of Śākta developed on the ground of Śaiva philosophy and metaphysics, and incorporated elements from Vedic, Upaniṣadic, and Paurāṇic sources. As such, its system represents an important coalescence and clarification of some of the most prominent ideas in Indian philosophy.

Built around Tripurasundarī, one of the ten *mahāvidyās* (great goddesses), the school of Śrīvidyā holds a more prominent position than those built around the more famous goddesses, Kālī and Tārā, in part because of Śrīvidyā's inclusion or assimilation of other major goddesses within its fold. Because this is the only school in Tāntrism with explicit ties to the Vedas, and because of its interaction with two significant traditions, Śaivism and Advaita Vedānta, Śrīvidyā gained the social acceptance that has eluded the other branches of Śāktism. The adherents of Śrīvidyā were and still are Hindus well versed both in the Sanskrit language and in a wide range of philosophical literature—factors which helped Śrīvidyā to develop a sophisticated philosophy and metaphysics, and which continue to this day to lend considerable prestige and respectability to the sect.

Śrīvidyā texts, not surprisingly, explored the concept of *śakti* in some detail, providing a foundation for the philosophy that Lakṣmīdhara would later systematize. *Śakti* was variously known as *tripurā*, *tripurasundarī*, *mahātripurasundarī*, *saṃvit*, *citi*, and *parāciti*, these terms being used interchangeably to indicate the highest reality. The *tripurasundarī* simultaneously exists at three levels, the gross, the subtle, and the transcendent, which correspond, respectively, to the anthropomorphic form of the goddess, the mantric form, and the *suṣumnā nāḍī*, or the *kuṇḍalinī śakti* traveling through it. A threefold spiritual discipline *(upāsti)* corresponds to these three levels of existence—*kāyikī*, *vācikī*, and *mānasī*, i.e., physical, verbal, and mental.

Two doctrines—Ābhāsavāda and Pariṇāmavāda—developed to explain the relationship between *saṃvit* or *tripurā* and the world. The former, which is found in most of the Śrīvidyā texts, posits that *saṃvit* is like a mirror and the universe is like a reflection appearing in it. This mirror contains the whole universe inside herself, and through her *svātantryaśakti* (intrinsic autonomous power) makes them appear as though they are outside her. The latter doctrine maintains that the universe is a transformation or manifestation of *tripurā*. Indeed, *tripurā* (the cause) and the phenomenal world (the effect) are two different states of the same truth. Both of these doctrines assert that there is only one reality, *śakti*, and the world does not exist apart from her. It is either an appearance without a substance of its own (Ābhāsavāda) or a manifest state of unmanifest *śakti* (Pariṇāmavāda).

These concepts demonstrably influenced subsequent writers of the Śākta tradition; however, as did previous works, the texts use the term *śakti* loosely and do not fully define it. Thus the notion of *śakti* remained fundamentally ambiguous in Śākta doctrine until the appearance of the *LD*, and with it, a new branch of Śrīvidyā. Both the name and the main tenet of this branch, Samayācāra, derive directly from the *LD*, which expounds the premise that *samayā* (the transcendental union of *śiva* and *śakti*) is the ultimate reality.

Lakṣmīdhara wishes to posit Samayācāra as a totally independent branch of Śrīvidyā by drawing a sharp division between this and the older, Śaiva-based school known as Kaula. The conflict arose primarily from an opposition between two *ācāras* (systems of conduct and cultural values): Samaya is puritan and vegetarian; Kaula is liberal and nonvegetarian, and includes the most frequently disputed ritual elements *(pañcamakāra)*. The dispute, however, is related in a mostly one-sided manner by Samayācārins, including Lakṣmīdhara, who do not take into account what Kaulācārins themselves have to say.

This partisanship on the side of Lakṣmīdhara does not, however, take away from his enormous accomplishment of systematizing the philosophy of Śrīvidyā and of providing a coherent foundation for the practices he advocates. The lasting signficance of his work may be inferred from the fact that although the *SL* itself hardly qualifies as a Tāntric text, Lakṣmīdhara's commentary so convincingly explicates it in light of Tāntric ideas that the *SL* has come to be seen as a central document of Tāntrism.

Among the many virtues of his commentary is its exact

and highly discriminating use of terminology. Unlike other Tāntric writers, he insists on using *śakti* and the related terms *samayā*, *sādākhyā*, and *candrakalā* with precisely defined meanings. Another notable strength is the comprehensiveness of his system—a system that attempts to correlate all categories of existence and action, and to place them in relation to their ultimate cause. His objective is to demonstrate the main premise that *samayā*, or *sādākhyā*, alone is the ultimate reality. But because Śrīvidyā adherents meditate on the *cakras*, do *japa* of the *śrīvidyā* mantra, and/or worship *śrīcakra* and the personified form of *Tripurā*, Lakṣmīdhara undertakes to explain how all these components fit into the concept of nondual, transcendent Samayā. As a first step, he asserts the firmly established Tāntric belief that mantra, *cakra*, *guru*, deity, and one's own self are essentially one. He goes on to describe in detail how these elements correspond to *samayā*'s manifest and unmanifest forms.

In building his argument, Lakṣmīdhara (1) expounds the relationship between *samayā* and *kālaśakti*, i.e., the 360 rays that create the universe; (2) systematically equates *śrīcakra* with the *cakras* in the human body, thereby relating the deities residing in the various circuits of *śrīcakra* to different aspects of the human being; (3) explains how the *śrīvidyā* mantra encapsulates the entire Sanskrit alphabet, and equates the mantra with *śrīcakra*; and (4) justifies how the personified form of the goddess Tripurasundarī corresponds to the *cakras* in the human body and the *cakras* of *śrīcakra*, and explains how these are identical to each other.

The *LD* is as subtle in its arguments as it is comprehensive in its subject matter. Literature up to this time attempted with varying degrees of success to explain how *śiva* and *śakti* could be, in essence, one, even as one power or the other was held to be the ultimate truth. The *SL* itself accords primary status to *śakti*—asserting that "If *śiva* is united with *śakti*, He is able to exert his powers as Lord; if not, the God is not able to stir"—but in some verses it assigns them equal status. It is these thorny contradictions—if *śakti* is superior to *śiva*, or vice versa, then how can they hold equal status? if they are identical, why use two different terms?—that Lakṣmīdhara addresses, and he resolves them in a more coherent, philosophically sound manner than can be found elsewhere in the literature.

In constructing the Samayācāra doctrine, Lakṣmīdhara affirms the inseparability of *sadāśiva* and *śuddhavidyā*—neither can exist without the other—while proposing an entirely different category of reality, i.e., *samayā* or *sādākhyākalā*, which arises from a combination of *sadāśiva* and *śuddhavidyā*. It is from this combination or union that the processes of creation, maintenance, and dissolution originate, never from *sadāśiva* or *śuddhavidyā* alone. The transcendent *sādākhyā* alone is the nondual reality; all other *tattvas*, including *sadāśiva* and *śuddhavidyā*, evolve from this.

Many concepts expounded by Lakṣmīdhara are echoed in *TA* by Abhinavagupta, even though the latter identifies himself with the Śaiva-based Kaula tradition. Abhinavagupta's main concern is not to discuss *śakti* alone but rather to expound Trika, the triad of *śiva, śakti*, and their union. This union—beyond which there is nothing—he calls *anuttara*, which is analogous but not exactly equivalent to *samayā*.

The philosophies of these two writers are compatible in the way in which they explain the transcendence of *samayā* or *anuttara*. Yet no matter how emphatically Lakṣmīdhara and Abhinavagupta proclaim the oneness of *śakti* and *śiva*, a difference in the nature and status of *śakti* is still apparent. Lakṣmīdhara considers *samayā* or *sādākhyā* to be absolutely transcendent, with no trace of *sadāśiva* or *śuddhavidyā*, whereas Abhinavagupta views the masculine aspect as ultimately supreme. We cannot find in *TA* a clear and consistent answer to the questions of whether *śiva* predominates over *śakti* in the *anuttara* state, whether they are equal in their subordinance to *anuttara*, or whether they both completely lose their distinct identities in *anuttara*.

The *LD*, however, is consistent on this point. It is also comprehensive because it takes into consideration, and analyzes, all of the theories of *śakti* at the time. His nondualistic theory is buttressed by clear descriptions of the metaphysical relationships among *śiva, śakti,* and the transcendent form of *samayā.* His methodology includes careful philological analysis of terminology that had previously been ambiguous. And he synthesizes various philosophical writings, including Vedic, Upaniṣadic, and Paurāṇic sources, in constructing his own doctrine. For all of these reasons, the methodology developed by Lakṣmīdhara can serve as a useful model for studying the specific characteristics of the various subschools of Śākta Tāntrism, particularly the distinctive notions of *śakti* therein. Although the historical origins of Lakṣmīdhara's primary text, *SL*, may be ambiguous, his influence on the Śrīvidyā tradition, especially the Samayācāra branch of it, is indisputable.

Abbreviations of Texts

BP-L	Brahmāṇḍa Purāṇa
BS-S	Brahmasūtra Śāṅkarabhāsyam
DS	Durga Saptaśatī
GT	Gandharva Tantra
HT	Hindu Tāntrism
HTS	Hindu Tāntric and Śākta Literature
KKV	Kāmakalāvilāsa
LD	Lakṣmīdharā
LT	Lakṣmī Tantra
MMR	Mantra Aur Mātṛkāon kā Rahasya
MVV	Malinīvijaya Vārtika
NS	Nityāṣodaśikārṇava
NT	Netra Tantra
PTV	Parātriṃśikāvivaraṇa
ṚV	Ṛgveda
SL	Saundaryalaharī
ST	Śāradātilaka
SU	Subhagodaya
SVT	Svacchanda Tantra
TA	Tantrāloka
TR-J	Tripura Rahasya (Jñānakhaṇḍa)
TR-M	Tripura Rahasya (Māhātmyakhaṇḍa)
TS-1	Tantrasaṅgraha, Part I
TS-2	Tantrasaṅgraha, Part II
TS-3	Tantrasaṅgraha, Part III
VR	Varivasyārahasya
YH	Yoginī Hṛdaya
YKU	Yogakuṇḍalī Upaniṣad

Texts Quoted by Lakṣmīdhara

Amarakośa (LD 71, 74)
Maṅkhaka Sūtra (LD 3)
Aruṇopaniṣad (LD 10, 32, 40)
Aṣṭādhyāyī (by Paṇini) (LD 57, 59, 60, 67, 82)
Bhairavayāmala (LD 8, 9, 14)
Bharatamata (Bharata-nā ya-śāstra) (LD 51, 69)
Bhāgavatamatarahasya (LD 9)
Bṛhadāraṇyakopaniṣad (LD 11)
Caraṇāgama (LD 99)
Carcāstotra (by Kālidāsa) (LD 41, 82)
Dohalakautuka (LD 85)
Īśopaniṣad (LD 11)
Kamikā (Kāmikāgama) (LD 11)
Karṇāvataṃsastuti (by Lakṣmīdhara) (LD 41)
Kaṭhopaniṣad (LD 14)
Kāmakalāvidyā (Kāmakalāvilāsa) (LD 34)
Mālatīmādhava (LD 6)
Naiṣadha (Mahākāvya) (LD 47)
Nītivākyāmṛta (LD 95)
Puruṣasūkta (LD 97)
Pūrṇodaya (LD 32)
Ṛgveda (LD 5)
Raghuvaṃśa (LD 6)
Rudrarahasya (LD 9)
Rudrayāmala (LD 11)

Śrīsūkta (LD 11, 17)
Śukasaṃhitā (LD 41)
Sakalajananīstotra (LD 99)
Sanandanasaṃhitā (LD 31)
Sanatkumārasaṃhitā (LD 11, 19, 32)
Sarvajñasomeśvara (LD 67, 74)
Saṣṭhi Tantra (LD 99)
Sāmudrika (Śāstra) (LD 69)
Siddhighu ikā (LD 40)
Subhagodaya (LD 11, 17, 32, 41, 99)
Taittirīyabrāhmaṇa (LD 5, 9, 10, 11, 14, 32)
Taittirīyasaṃhitā (LD 11, 40, 99)
Taittirīyāraṇya (LD 11, 14, 32, 40, 41, 97)
Taittirīyopaniṣad (LD 11, 37, 41)
Vaśiṣṭha Saṃhitā (LD 31, 84)
Vāgbhaṭṭa (LD 53)
Vāmakeśvara Tantra (Catuḥśatī) (LD 1, 2, 5, 8, 10, 16, 19, 20, 27, 31, 35, 41)
Vāyavīyasaṃhitā (LD 11)
Yogadīpikā (LD 9)
Yogakuṇḍalī Upaniṣad (LD 10)

Transliteration Errors

Proper transliteration used in this text	*Spelling used in the notes and bibliography*
Ānandalaharī Ṭīkā	Ānandalaharī Tīkā
Bhaṭṭojidīkṣita	Bhaṭṭojidīkshita
Brahmasūtraśāṅkarabhāṣya	Brahmasūtra-Śānkarabhāṣya
Devībhāgavata	Śrīmaddevībhāgavata
Devī Pañcastavī	Devī Pañcastavi
Dīpikā	Dipikā
Gautamīya Tantra	Gautamiyatantra
Kāmadhenu Tantra	Kamadhenu Tantra
Kṣemarāja	Kṣemarāja
Mālinīvijaya	Mālinivijaya
Nirvāṇa Tantra	Nirvana Tantra
Nityāṣoḍaśikārṇava	Nityāṣodaśikārṇava
Parātriṃśikā	Parā-Trimshikā
Prapañcasārasaṅgraha	Prapañcha Sārasāra Saṅgraḥa
Ṛgveda Saṃhitā	Rig-Veda-Samhitā
Sāmbapañcāśikā	Sambapāñcāśikā
Sāyaṇācārya	Sāyaṇchārya
Svacchanda Tantra	Swacchanda Tantra
Śāradātilaka	Śardātilaka
Subhagodaya	Śrīsubhagodayastuti
Toḍala Tantra	Todalatantra
Tripurā Rahasya (Jñāna Khaṇḍa)	Tṛpurā Rahasya (Jñāna Khaṅda)
Tripurā Rahasya (Māhātmyakhaṇḍa)	Tripura Rahasya (Mahatmya Khanda)
Tripuropaniṣad	Tripurāmahopaniṣad
Yajurveda	Mūla-Yajurveda-Saṃhitā

Proper name	*Variations in published texts*
Abhinavagupta	Abhinava Gupta
Bhāskararāya	Bhāskara Ṛāya Bhāskararāya Makhin
Gopinath Kaviraj	Gopinath Kaviraja Gopinatha Kaviraja Gopīnātha Kavirāja
Kāmeśvarasūri	Kāmeśvara Sūri Kāmeśvarasūrin

Notes

CHAPTER 1

1. ". . . the worship of Tripurasundarī, the most important Tantric form of Śrī/Lakṣmī, naturally occupies a well-defined position and comes in early. This is not due to its being chronologically [sic] the first . . . but because the system is conspicuous by the literary standard of at least part of its texts, and by the mere coherence and elaboration of its doctrine. Tripurasundarī is the foremost benign, beautiful and youthful, yet motherly manifestation of the Supreme Śākti. Her *saṃpradāya* (sometimes called *saubhāgyasampradāya*, 'tradition of sweet happiness'), although presumably not the oldest, seems to have been systematized at a relatively early date. Its formulations are characterized by a high degree of technicality cultivated in order to serve an intellectualistic desire for subtle symbolism." Teun Goudriaan and Sanjukta Gupta, *Hindu Tantric and Śākta Literature* (hereafter cited as *HTS*), in *A History of Indian Literature, vol. 2: Epics and Sanskrit Religious Literature*, ed. Jan Gonda (Wiesbaden: Otto Harrassowitz, 1981), p. 58.
2. *Netra Tantram with Commentary by Kshemarāja* (hereafter cited as *NT*), ed. Madhusudan Kaul Shāstrī. Kashmir Series of Texts and Studies, no. 46 (Bombay: Tatva Vivechaka Press, 1926); *Swacchanda-Tantra* (hereafter cited as *SVT*), ed. with notes by Madhusudan Kaul Shāstrī, Kashmir Series of Texts and Studies, no. 31 (Bombay: Nirnaya-Sagar Press, 1921); *Sri Mālinivijaya Vārttikam of Abhinava Gupta* (hereafter cited as *MVV*), ed. with notes by Madhusudan Kaul Shastri, Kashmir Series of Texts and Studies, no. 32 (Srinagar: Kasmir Pratap Steam Press, 1921); Lakśmaṇadeśikendra, *The Sārdātilaka by Lakśmaṇadeśikendra with the Padārthādarśa Commentary by Raghavabhatta* (hereafter

cited as *ST*), ed. with introduction by Mukunda Jha Bakshi, Kashi Sanskrit Granthamala, 107, Tantra Śāstra Section, no. 1 (Varanasi: Chowkhamba Sanskrit Series Office, 1963); *Nityāṣoḍaśikarṇava with Two Commentaries: Rjuvimarśinī by Śīvānanda & Artharatnāvalī by Vidyānanda* (hereafter cited as *NS*), ed. Vrajavallabha Dviveda, Yoga-Tantra-Granthamālā, vol. 1, ed. Baladeva Upādhyāya (Varanasi: Varanaseya Sanskrit Vishvavidyalaya, 1968); and *Yoginī Hṛdaya with Commentaries: Dipikā of Amṛtānanda and Setubandha of Bhāskara Rāya* (hereafter cited as *YH*), 2d ed., Sarasvatī Bhavana Granthamālā, vol. 7, ed. Kshetresachandra Chattopadhyaya (Varanasi: Varanaseya Sanskrit Vishvavidyalaya, 1963).

3. What Śāktism is and whether it stands as an independent system of the philosophy of religion has not been established definitively. For example, Pushpendra Kumar offers a general definition, "Śāktism is the worship of śakti or the female principle," in *Śakti Cult in Ancient India: With Special Reference to the Purāṇic Literature* (Varanasi: Bhartiya Publishing House, 1974), p. 1. Goudriaan offers a contradictory view of Śāktism: "Sometimes it is incorrectly identified with 'the cult of female deities in general.' . . . To this should be added that inseparably connected to her is an inactive male partner as whose power of action and movement the Śakti functions . . . It is, therefore, not enough to say that Śāktas worship the female as the ultimate principle." *HT*, p. 7.

The problem is further complicated by the difficulty in determining whether literature in which the concept of *śakti* appears belongs to Śāktism or not. For example, although *śakti* as both a simple term and a comprehensive philosophical category appears in the Upaniṣads and Purāṇas, they cannot be regarded as Śākta texts. Although there is an independent body of literature (Śākta Tantras) wherein *śakti* philosophy and *sādhanā* are exclusively advocated, significant discussions on *śakti* can also be found in Śaivite and Vaiṣṇaivite Āgamas and Purāṇas. This makes it difficult to draw a definite boundary around Śāktism from the perspective of either history or literature.

Gopinath Kaviraj clearly acknowledged this difficulty: "The

Śākta literature is extensive, though most of it is of mixed character. Śiva and Śakti being intimately related, Śaiva and Śākta Tantras have generally a common cultural background, not only in practices but in philosophical conceptions as well." Gopinath Kaviraj, *Aspects of Indian Thought* (Burdwan: The University of Burdwan, 1966), p. 177.

4. Discussing this issue in great detail, Goudriaan points out: "The historical position of the term Tantra in the Tāntric tradition is therefore not entirely clear and we may assume that it only gradually came to be closely affiliated with Śākta and Śākti-oriented Śaiva literature." *HTS*, p. 7.

   In the same chapter, he also points out how difficult it is to draw a demarcation line between different traditions of Tāntrism or even to find a chronology of original Tantras and secondary Tantras; for details, see *HTS*, pp. 1-10.

   According to Brooks' observation, the kind of attention Tāntric Śāktism has received from scholars is insufficient and disproportionate; for details see, Douglas Renfrew Brooks, *The Secret of the Three Cities: An Introduction to Hindu Śākta Tantrism* (hereafter cited as Brooks, *Three Cities),* (Chicago: The University of Chicago Press, 1990), Preface ix and nn. 2 and 3 on pp. 209-210.

5. ". . . it should be kept in mind that the distinction of Śaiva/ Sākta cannot always be clearly drawn. Śāktism, the belief in and worship of the Supreme Principle as a female force or Śakti . . . as it were, grew into maturity under the cover of Śaivism where Śiva holds a similar position. This holds good at least as far as the literary development of Śākta ideology is concerned . . . it is unavoidable that some attention is also paid to tantrically oriented works which focus on the worship of Śiva or other male gods. There is no clear line of demarcation; both denominations can be distinguished but not separated." Goudriaan in *HTS*, p. 2.

   See also Goudriaan in *HT*, p. 11, and Kaviraj, *Aspects of Indian Thought*, p. 177.

6. Goudriaan in *HTS*, pp. 2-4.

7. While working with the Śrividyā school of Śākta Tāntrism in South India, Brooks shares his experience: "It is only in the living and oral tradition and through critical historical study

that a more complete picture of practice and interpretation emerges." Douglas Renfrew Brooks, "The Śrīvidya School of Śākta Tantrism: A Study of the Texts and Contexts of the Living Traditions in South India" (hereafter cited as "Śrīvidyā School") (Ph.D. dissertation, Harvard University, 1987), p. 8. For details, see pp. 6-8.

Brooks also cautions:

> What Tantric texts *say, what Tantrics say they do,* and what they *actually do* are not necessarily the same. We must not only learn to read Tantric texts and gain the confidence of Tantrics who will discuss their traditions, we must be able to criticize their interpretation and observe their practices for ourselves. . . . To go beyond a literary and speculative understanding of Tantrism and to probe a text's meanings, one must gain broad access to the secret and initiated lines of oral interpretation of which a given text is a part. . . . How insightful and accurate can a study be if the picture drawn of the whole tradition is necessarily limited by the scholar's view of an oral tradition known only partially? At best, each study is limited by the scholar's own access to living oral sources of interpretation.

Brooks, *Three Cities,* pp. 7-8.

8. Sanjukta Gupta, Dirk Jan Hoens, and Teun Goudriaan, *Hindu Tantrism* (hereafter cited as *HT*), in *Handbuch der Orientalistik,* ed. Jan Gonda (Leiden: E. J. Brill, 1979), p. 46; see also Goudriaan in *HTS*, p. 58.
9. [Śaṅkarācārya?] *The Saundaryalaharī or Flood of Beauty: Traditionally Ascribed to Śaṅkarācārya* (hereafter cited as *SL*), trans., ed., and presented in photographs by W. Norman Brown (Cambridge: Harvard University Press, 1958).
10. Lakṣmīdhara, *Lakṣmīdharā: The Commentary on the Saundaryalaharī* (hereafter cited as *LD*), in *Saundaryalaharī of Śrī Saṅkarācārya with the Commentary of Lakṣmīdhara,* 4th rev. ed., critically edited by N. S. Venkatanathacharya, Oriental Research Institute Series, 114 (Mysore: Oriental Research Institute, 1969).
11. Gerald James Larson, "The Sources for *Śakti* in Abhinavagupta's Kashmir Śaivism: A Linguistic and Aesthetic Category," *Philosophy East/West* 24 (January 1974): 41-55.

12. "*Etenāgne brahmaṇā vāvṛdhasva śaktī vā yatte cakṛmā vidā vā . . .*" *Ṛgveda* I.31.18 (hereafter cited as *ṚV*). Commenting on this mantra, Sāyaṇācārya writes, "*Śaktī vā vidā āsmadīya śāktyā,*" thus interpreting *śakti* as "capacity." *Rig-Veda-Samhitā: The Sacred Hymns of the Brāhmans, with the Commentary of Sāyaṇāchārya*, 4 vols., ed. F. Max Muller (Varanasi: Chowkhamba Sanskrit Series Office, 1966), 1:31:18. [Note: All references to the *Ṛgveda* are given by *maṇḍala: sūkta:* mantra.]
13. "*Pra te pūrvāṇi karaṇāni vocaṃ pra nūtanā maghavan yā cakartha. Śaktīvo yadvibharā rodasī ubhe jayannapo manave dānu citrāḥ.*" *ṚV* 5:31:6. According to Sāyaṇācārya, "*Śaktīvaḥ śaktiman śaktir vajraṃ karma vā*"; *śakti* means *vajra* or *karma*.
14. "*Dīrghaṃ hyaṅkuśaṃ yathā śaktiṃ vibharṣi mantumaḥ.*" *ṚV* 10:134:6.
15. "*Parāsya śaktir vividhaiva śrūyate svābhāvikī jñānabalakriyā ca.*" *Śvetāśvatara Upaniṣad*, in *Upaniṣat-Saṁgrahaḥ: Containing 188 Upaniṣads*, ed. with Sanskrit introduction by J. L. Shastri (Delhi: Motilal Banarsidass, 1970), 6:8.
16. Mark S. G. Dyczkowski, *The Canon of the Śaivagāmà and the Kubjikā Tantras of the Western Kaula Tradition* (hereafter cited as *The Canon of the Śaivagāma*) (Albany: State University of New York Press, 1988), p. 8.
17. "*Tato' tikopapūrṇasya cakriṇo vadanāttataḥ. Niścakrāma mahattejo brahmaṇaḥ śaṅkarasya ca . . . nāgahāram dadau tasyai dhatte yaḥ pṛthīvīmimām. Anyairapi surair devī bhūṣaṇairāyudhaistathā.*" *Durgāsaptaśatī with Seven Sanskrit Commentaries: Durgāpradīpa, Guptavatī, Caturdharī, Śāntanavī, Nāgojībhaṭṭī, Jagaccandracandrikā, Daṃśoddhāra* (hereafter cited as *DS*) (Delhi: Butala & Co., 1984), 2:9-30.
18. When Śakti appears with a particular god, she assumes the same name and form as that god. For instance:

    Brahmeśaguhaviṣṇūnāṃ tathendrasya ca śaktayaḥ.
    Śarīrebhyo viniṣkramya tadrūpaiścaṇḍikaṃ yayuḥ.
    Yasya devasya yadrūpaṃ yathā bhūṣaṇavāhanam.
    Tadvadeva hi tacchaktir asurān yoddhum āyayau.
    DS 8:12-13.

In some instances, Śakti creates her male partner from her own body and his physical appearance and weapon, etc., resemble that of Śakti's. For example, see "Lalitopākhyāna" of *Brahmāṇḍa Purāṇa* in *Brahmāṇḍa Purāṇa of Sage Kṛṣṇa Dvaipāyana Vyāsa* (hereafter cited as *BP-L*), ed. J. L. Shastri (Delhi: Motilal Banarsidass, 1973), and "Prādhānika Rahasya" in *Durgā Saptaśatī* (Gorakh Pur: Gita Press, n.d.), pp. 195-197.

19. "*Aiśvarya vacanaḥ śaśca ktiḥ parākrama eva ca. Tatsvarūpā tayor dātrī sā śaktiḥ parikīrtitā.*" *Śrīmaddevībhāgavatam Mahāpurāṇa*, ed. Rāmatej Pāṇḍeya (Kashi: Paṇḍit-Pustakālaya, n.d.), 9:2.10.
20. "*Sā devī paramā śaktiḥ parabrahmasvarūpiṇī . . .*" *BP-L* 10:90; "*Jaya brahmamaye devi brahmātmakarasātmake . . .*" *BP-L* 13:3; furthermore: "*Yadadvaitaṃ paraṃ brahma sadasadbhāvavarjitam . . . tvāmeva hi praśaṃsanti pañca brahmasvarūpiṇīm.*" *BP-L* 15:6-9.
21. "*Hetuḥ samastajagatāṃ triguṇāpi doṣair na jñāyase hariharādibhirpyapārā. Sarvāśrayākhilam idaṃ jagadaṃśabhūtam avyākṛtā hi paramā prakṛtistvamādyā.*" *DS* 4:6. Also see *BP-L* 13:5-28 and *Śrīmaddevībhāgavatam Mahāpurāna*, 9:1.5-8.
22. "*Ekaivāhaṃ jagatyatra dvitīyā kā mamāparā. Paśyaitā duṣṭa mayyeva viśantyo mad vibhūtayaḥ. Tataḥ samastāstā devyo brahmāṇīpramukhā layam. Tasyā devyāstanau jagmurekaivāsīt tadāmbikā.*" *DS* 10:3-4.
23. "*Nityaiva sā jaganmūrtistayā sarvamidam tatam. Tathāpi tatsamutpattir bahudhā śrūyatām mama . . . utpanneti tadā loke sā nityāpyabhidhīyate.*" *DS* 1:47-48; also see *DS* 1:54-69; 2:9-12; 4:1-26; 5:38-43; 11:1-34.
24. "*Jayadevi jaganmātarjaya devi parātpare. Jaya kalyāṇanilaye jaya kāmakalātmike. . . . Prasīda viśveśvari viśvavandite prasīda vidyeśvari vedarūpiṇi. Prasīda māyāmayi mantravigrahe prasīda sarveśvari sarvarūpiṇi.*" *BP-L* 13:1-28.
25. Gaṅgānātha Jhā, *The Prābhākara School of Pūrva Mīmāmsā* (Allahabad: n.p., 1911; reprinted, Delhi: Motilal Banarsidass, 1978), p. 91.
26. Ibid., p. 166.

27. Jayanta Bhaṭṭa, *Nyāya-Mañjarī: The Compendium of Indian Speculative Logic*, vol. 1, trans. Janaki Vallabha Bhattacharyya (Delhi: Motilal Banarsidass, 1978), pp. 81-85.
28. *Encyclopedia of Indian Philosophies: Indian Metaphysics and Epistemology: The Tradition of Nyāya-Vaiśeṣika Up to Gaṅgeśa*, ed. Karl H. Potter (Princeton: Princeton University Press, 1977), p. 340.
29. Ibid., p. 65.
30. George Chemparathy, *An Indian Rational Theology: Introduction to Udayana's Nyāyakusumāñjali* (Vienna: Gerold & Co., 1972), p. 49.
31. Gopikamohan Bhattacharyya, *Studies in Nyāya-Vaiśeṣika Theism* (Calcutta: Sanskrit College, 1961), pp. 18-28.
32. H. Ui, *Vaiśeṣika Philosophy According to the Daśapadārtha-Śāstra: Chinese Text with Introduction, Translation and Notes*, 2d ed., edited by F. W. Thomas, Chowkhamba Sanskrit Series, vol. 22 (Varanasi: Chowkhamba Sanskrit Series Office, 1962), pp.10, 123-126.
33. "*Nahi tayā vinā paremeśvarasya sraṣṭṛtvaṃ siddhyati. Śaktirahitasya tasya pravṛtyanupapatteḥ.*" *Brahmasūtra-Śānkarabhāsyam with the Commentaries: Bhāṣyaratnaprabhā of Govindānanda, Bhāmatī of Vācaspatimiśra, Nyāya-Nirṇaya of Ānandagiri* (hereafter cited as *BS-B*), ed. J. L. Shastri (Delhi: Motilal Banarsidass, 1980), 1:4.3.
34. "*Paripūrṇaśaktikaṃ tu brahma . . . tasmād ekasyāpi brahmaṇo vicitraśaktiyogāt kṣīrādivat vicitrapariṇāma utpadyate.*" *BS-B* 2:1.24.
35. "*Asya jagato nāmarūpābhyām . . . janmasthitibhaṅgaṃ yataḥ sarvajñāt sarvaśakteḥ kāraṇād bhavati.*" *BS-B* 1:1.2.

    "*Ekasyāpi brahmaṇo vicitraśuktiyogāt utpadyate vicitro vikāraprapañcam ityukam. Tatpunaḥ katham avagamyate vicitraśaktiyuktaṃ paraṃ brahmeti. Taducyate. Sarvopetā ca taddarśanāt. Sarvaśaktiyuktā ca parā devatetyabhyupagantavyam. Kutaḥ. Taddarśanāt. Tathā hi darśayati śrutiḥ sarvaśakti yogaṃ parasyāḥ devatāyāḥ.*" *BS-B* 2:1.30.
36. Although Śaṅkarācārya proposes the theory of Vivartavāda, occasionally he uses the term *parināma*, such as "*pariṇāma-prakriyāyām,*" *BS-B* 2:1.14; and "*vicitrapariṇāma utpadyate,*" *BS-B* 2:1.24.

37. "... *Nahi tayā vinā ... avidyātmikā hi bījaśaktir avyaktaśabda nirdeśyā parameśvarāśrayā māyāmayī mahāsuṣuptiḥ ...*" *BS-B* 1:4.3.
38. Gaurinath Sastri, *The Philosophy of Word and Meaning: Some Indian Approaches with Special Reference to the Philosophy of Bhartṛhari* (Calcutta: Sanskrit College, 1959), p. 13.
39. Ibid., pp. 12-16, 28-44.
40. "*Śaktirnipuṇatā lokaśāstrakāvyādyavekṣaṇāt. Kāvyajña-śikṣayābhyāsa iti hetustadudbhave.*" (*Kāvyaprakāśa* 1:3). "*Śaktiḥ kavitvabījarupaḥ saṃskāraviśeṣah. Yāṃ vinā kāvyaṃ na prasaret, prasṛtaṃ vopahasanīyaṃ syāt.*" (*Sampradāya Prakāśinī* of Śrīvidyācakravartin). Mammaṭa, *The Poetic Light: Kāvyaprakāśa of Mammaṭa: Text with Translation and Sampradāyaprakāśinī of Śrīvidyācakravartin*, vol. 1, 2d rev. ed., trans. R. C. Dwivedi (Delhi: Motilal Banarsidass, 1977).
41. Ānandavardhana, *Dhvanyāloka of Ānandavardhana*, with a foreword by K. R. Srinivasa Iyengar, trans. and ed. K. Krishnamoorthy (Dharwar: Karnatak University, 1974), 1:1 and 6 and 2:20-23.
42. Kanti Chandra Pandey, *Abhinavagupta: An Historical and Philosophical Study*, 2d ed., rev. & enl., Chowkhamba Sanskrit Studies, vol. 1 (Varanasi: Chowkhamba Sanskrit Series Office, 1963) pp. 692-732; also see Gopinath Kaviraj, *Aspects of Indian Thought*, pp. 1-44, and Jagadish Chandra, *Dhvāniprasthāna meṃ Ācārya Mammaṭa kā Avadāna* in Banaras Hindu University Sanskrit Series, vol. XI, ed. Biswanath Bhattacharya (Varanasi: Banaras Hindu University, 1977), pp. 41-44.
43. For instance, in *DS* 1:78-87, 2:4-8, 5:7-82, and 13:12, and *BP-L* 12:61-68, *śakti* is evoked. Then in *DS* 1:89-91, 2:10-13, 5:84-87, and 13:13-15 and *BP-L* 12:69-75, she materializes in response. On other occasions (i.e., in *DS* 8:12-23), she appears instantly in order to destroy demonic forces.
44. For examples of *śakti's* intermingled characteristics as a goddess and a philosophical category, see the following sources: *DS*, 4:2-27, 5: 9-82, 11:3-35; *BP-L* 13:1-28, 30:11-42; *Tripura Rahasya: Mahatmya Khandam, with Hindi Translation* (hereafter cited as *TR-M*), Gurumandal Series, no. 28 (Calcutta:

Gurumandal Granthamala, 1970), 8:2-30, 30:17-28, 40:11-21.

45. Sudhendu Kumar Das, *Śakti or Divine Power: A Historical Study Based on Original Sanskrit Texts* (Calcutta: University of Calcutta, 1934).
46. Jadunath Sinha, *Shakta Monism* (Calcutta: Sinha Publishing House, 1966).
47. *Encyclopedia of Religion*, ed. Mircea Eliade (New York: Macmillan Publishing Co., 1987), s.v. "The Hindu Goddess," by David Kinsley, pp. 53-54.
48. Gopinath Kaviraj, *Bhāratīya Saṃskṛti Aura Sādhanā*, vol. 1, vol. 2, 2d ed. (Patna: Bihāra-Rāṣṭrabhāṣā-Pariṣad, 1964); *Tāntrika Vāṅmaya Meṃ Śāktadṛṣṭi*, 2d ed. (Patna: Bihāra-Rāṣṭrabhāṣā-Pariṣad, 1963); and *Aspects of Indian Thought*, pp. 175-215 and 216-228.
49. Kailāśa Pati Miśra, *Kāśmīra Śaiva Darśana: Mūla Siddhānta* (Varanasi: Arddhanārīśvara Prakāśana, 1982); Baladeva Upādhyāya, *Bhāratīya Darśana: An Authentic and Comprehensive Exposition of the Doctrines of the Different Schools of the Indian Philosophy-Vedic and Tāntric*, 2d ed., foreword by Gopīnātha Kavirāja (Varanasi: Chaukhambha Orientalia, 1979), pp. 431-527; Kamalakar Mishra, *Significance of the Tantric Tradition* (Varanasi: Arddhanārīśvara Publications, 1981); and Sangam Lal Pandey, *Bhāratīya Darśana kā Sarvekṣaṇa* (Allahabad: Central Book Depot, 1981).

   Kaviraj's voice can be heard even in the writings of notable modern scholars in the field, such as Teun Goudriaan. As Brooks remarks:

   > It is evident, for example, that Goudriaan's contribution in *HTSL* depends to a large extent on Dwiveda and Kaviraj and that his remarks on the authorship and content of texts are frequently based on manuscript catalogues and bibliographical sources such as Kaviraj's *Tāntrika Sāhitya*. This is not to suggest that all of his study is based on these compilations (he, in fact, does not discuss how he proceeded with his work) but it is certain that certain errors are merely repetitions of other's work he deems reliable.

50. Wendell Charles Beane, *Myth, Cult and Symbols in Śākta Hinduism: A Study of the Indian Mother Goddess* (Leiden: E. J. Brill, 1977); Ernest A. Payne, *The Śāktas: An Introductory*

and *Comparative Study* (New York: Garland Publishing, 1979).

51. Narendra Nath Bhattacharyya, *History of the Śākta Religion* (New Delhi: Munshiram Manoharlal Publishers Pvt. Ltd., 1974); *The Indian Mother Goddess*, 2d ed., rev. & enl. (New Delhi: Manohar Book Service, 1977).
52. D. C. Sircar, *The Śākta Pīṭhas*, 2d rev. ed. (Delhi: Motilal Banarsidass, 1973).
53. Goudriaan in *HT*, p. 5.
54. Douglas Renfrew Brooks, *Auspicious Wisdom: The Texts and Traditions of Śrīvidyā Śākta Tantrism in South India* (Albany: State University of New York Press, 1992); *The Secret of the Three Cities;* and "Srividya School"; Mark S. G. Dyczkowski, *The Canon of the Śaivāgama* (Albany: State University of New York Press, 1988); *The Doctrine of Vibration* (Albany: State University of New York Press, 1987); and *The Stanzas on Vibration* (Albany: State University of New York Press, 1992); Paul Eduardo Muller-Ortega, *The Triadic Heart of Śiva: Kaula Tantricism of Abhinavagupta in the Non-Dual Shaivism of Kashmir* (Albany: State University of New York, 1989); André Padoux, *Vāc: The Concept of the Word in Selected Hindu Tantras* (Albany: State University of New York, 1990); and Jaideva Singh, *Abhinavagupta: A Trident of Wisdom* (Albany: State University of New York Press, 1989); *Spanda Kārikās* (Delhi: Motilal Banarsidass, 1980); *Pratyabhijnāhṛdayam* (Delhi: Motilal Banarsidass, 1963); and *Śiva Sūtras* (Delhi: Motilal Banarsidass, 1963).
55. Abhinavagupta, *The Tantrāloka of Abhinavagupta with the Commentary of Jayaratha* (hereafter cited as *TĀ*), 8 vols., enl. ed., edited by R. C. Dwivedi and Navjivan Rastogi (Delhi: Motilal Banarsidass, 1987).
56. K.C. Pandey, *Abhinavagupta*; V. Raghavan, *Abhinavagupta and His Works* (Varanasi: n.p., 1980); B[alajin] N[ath] Pandit, *Śrī Kāśmīra Śaiva Darśana* (Jammu: Shri Ranbir Kendriya Sanskrit Vidyapitha, 1973); Miśra, *Kāśmīra Śaiva Darśana*; Harvey Paul Alper, "Abhinavagupta's Concept of Cognitive Power: A Translation of the Jñānaśaktyāhnika of the Īśvarapratyabhijñāvimarśinī with Commentary and Introduction" (Ph.D. dissertation, University of Pennsylvania, 1976).

CHAPTER 2

1. Tripurā, or Tripurasundarī, is one of the ten *māhavidyās* in Śākta Tāntrism, although the term *śrīvidyā* is currently more popular. The term *śrīvidyā* might have become widely used as a consequence of the text, *Śrīvidyā Ratna Sūtrāni* by Gauḍapāda, (if this text is really by Gauḍapāda, the teacher of Ādi Śaṅkara). But oddly enough, Śaṅkara does not use this term even once in *SL*. According to Lakṣmīdhara, the term *śrī* is connected with the *bījākṣara śrīṃ* found in the most sacred mantra of Tripurasundarī: ". . . *śrībījātmikā vidyā śrīvidyeti rahasyaṃ* . . ." (*LD* 32). This mantra has sixteen syllables, the sixteenth, *śrīṃ*, being the most secret. Because the mantra has sixteen letters, another term for this *mahāvidyā* is Ṣoḍaśī, the *vidyā* consisting of sixteen letters. For the mythological origin of this term, see *LD* 32; also see *TR-M* 53:42-47.
2. Andre Padoux, *Vāc: The Concept of the Word in Selected Hindu Tantras*, trans. by Jacques Gontier (Albany: State University of New York Press, 1990), pp. 31-32.
3. Ibid., p. 31.
4. Goudriaan in *HT*, p. 6.
5. John Woodroffe, *Principles of Tantra: The Tantra-Tattva of Śrīyukta Śiva Candra Vidyārṇava Bhattacārya Mahodaya*, part 1, 5th ed. (Madras: Ganesh & Co., 1978), 71; also see Goudriaan in *HT*, pp. 7-9; and Brooks, *Three Cities*, pp. 3-5.
6. Brooks, *Three Cities*, p. 5.
7. Omar V. Garrison, *Tantra: The Yoga of Sex* (New York: Causeway Books, 1964); Robert K. Moffet, *Tantric Sex* (New York: Berkeley Publishing Corp., 1974); and Marcus Allen, *Tantra for the West*, (Mill Valley, CA: Whatever Publications, 1981).
8. "Standard Tāntric *sādhanā*" here means the practices that are described in acclaimed Tāntric texts (such as the *Śāradātilaka*, *Kulārṇava Tantra*, *NS*, *YH*, *TĀ*, or *Tantrarāja Tantra*), upheld by a recognized tradition, and accompanied by a sound philosophy.
9. Gupta in *HT*, p. 121.
10. The Āryasamāja alone seems to be free from Tāntric influence. Although Sikhism did not originally believe in idol wor-

ship, temple construction, or pilgrimages to holy shrines, it has replaced these Hindu Tāntric elements with the worship of the *Grantha Sāhib* (their holy scripture), *gurudvāras*, and pilgrimages to their own holy places, such as Harmandir Sahib, (Golden Temple) in Amritsar and Hemkunt Sahib in the Garhwal Himalayas. Moreover, recitation of *Grantha Sāhib*, *Japjī*, and *Sukhamanī*; *japa* or *simaran* of *nāma*, the holy name or a mantra; and practice of *nāda* yoga can be considered to be Tāntric elements.

11. Agehananda Bharati, *The Tantric Tradition* (New York: Samuel Weiser Inc., 1970), pp. 16-17.
12. Goudriaan in *HT*, p. 9.
13. Bhattacharyya, *History of the Śākta Religion*, p. 6.
14. B. Bhattacharya, *Śaivism and the Phallic World*, 2 vols. (New Delhi: Oxford & IBH Publishing Co., 1975), pp. 709-711.
15. Bhattacharyya, *History of the Śākta Religion*, p. 6.
16. In Goudriaan's words, "But while dealing with such hypothetical matters, it is very easy to overshoot the mark by undue generalization." *HT*, p. 17.
17. Ibid., p. 20.
18. "Returning to the question of the antiquity of Tantric literature, we have to admit that the answer still quite escapes us. Assumptions made up till now were based upon hypothetical reasoning, outright guesswork, or faulty datings of manuscripts, but we can as yet hardly produce something better. Farquhar held that Śākta ritual and theology were already developed in about 600 A.D., but he based himself mainly on a faulty dating of a manuscript of the *Kubjikāmatatantra*. Eliade says that Tantrism is present everywhere in India from the sixth century onwards; this is presumably based on unproven early dates for the Pāñcarātra text *Jayākhyasaṃhitā* and the Buddhist *Guhyasamājatantra*." *HTS*, p. 20.
19. Padoux, *Vāc*, p. 31.
20. *The Atharvaveda*, introduction by M. C. Joshi, trans. Devi Chand (Delhi: Munshiram Manoharlal Publishers Pvt. Ltd., 1982).
21. "There is a possibility that Hindu Tantric literature existed already in the fifth cent. A.D. or even earlier. . . . Of the early Buddhist Tantras, the Guhyasamāja has been dated—on

scanty evidence—as early as the third cent. A.D. (B. Bhattacharya). Tantric elements like Dhāranis (spells in a certain kind of structured prose) were included in Buddhist texts which have been translated into Chinese in the fifth century." Goudriaan in *HT*, p. 20.

22. "Without doubt both Hindu and Buddhist Tantrism were based upon older traditions handed down and developed by people who perhaps in some cases did not care much about their denominational position. Moreover, it seems certain that the Buddhist doctrinal tradition can never have developed an offshoot so completely foreign to itself like Tantrism on its own accord. The Tantric deities and practices in Buddhism must have been derived from other sources, viz. Brahmanic ritual and doctrinal speculation, yoga culture of the siddhas, or popular beliefs often introduced in Hinduism and Buddhism alike." Ibid., p. 21.
23. Brooks, *Three Cities*, pp. 4-5.
24. Demonstrating the popularity of the goddess worship, Bhattacharyya writes: "It was so deep-rooted in the Indian mind that even in sectarian religions such as Vaiṣṇavism and Saivism, etc., the female principle had to be given a prominent position. Even the basically atheistic systems like Buddhism and Jainism could not avoid this popular influence. Later Buddhism is, in fact, nothing but a disguised Tantric cult of the female principle." Bhattacharyya, *The Indian Mother Goddess*, pp. 222-223.
25. Goudriaan in *HT*, p. 6.
26. Bhattacharyya, *History of the Śākta Religion*, p. 73; also see idem, *The Indian Mother Goddess*, p. 223.
27. Goudriaan in *HT*, p. 7.
28. J. Desmond Clark, Johnathan Mark Kenoyer, J. N. Pal, and G. R. Sharma, "Baghor I: A Possible Upper Paleolithic Shrine in Central India," *Anthro Quest* 24 (Winter, 1982): 13.
29. Bhattacharyya, *The Indian Mother Goddess*, pp.1-9, 35-76.
30. *Aditirdyauraditirantarikṣamaditirmātā sa pitā sa putraḥ. Viśve devā aditiḥ pañcajanā aditirjātamaditirjanitvam. ṚV* 1.89.10.
31. Das, *Śakti or Divine Power*, pp. 7-58.
32. *Kena Upaniṣad*, in *Upaniṣat-Saṁgrahaḥ*, chaps. 3 and 4.
33. *Śvetāśvatara Upaniṣad*, in *Upaniṣat-Saṁgrahaḥ*, 6:8.

34. Kaviraj, *Aspects of Indian Thought*, p. 177.
35. Goudriaan in *HT*, p. 18.
36. Bhattacharyya, *History of the Śākta Religion*, p. 77.
37. Kaviraj, *Aspects of Indian Thought*, p. 177.
38. Ibid.
39. Sircar, *The Śākta Pīṭhas*, pp. 17-42.
40. Ibid.
41. Goudriaan in *HT*, pp. 36-38.
42. "*Kālī tārā mahāvidyā ṣoḍaśī bhuvaneśvarī. Bhairavī chinnamastā ca vidyā dhūmāvatī tathā. Bagalāmukhī siddhavidyā mātaṅgī kamalātmikā. Etā daśa mahāvidyāḥ siddhavidyāḥ prakīrtitāḥ.*" *Muṇḍamālā Tantra*, in *Tantrasaṅgraha Part III*, (hereafter cited as *TS-III*), ed. by Dr. Rāmaprasāda Tripāthī in *Yogatantra-Granthamala*, vol. 6 (Varanasi: Sampurnanand Sanskrit Vishvavidyalaya, 1979), 1:7-8.

    [Note: In *TS-III*, there are two versions of *Muṇḍamālā Tantra* entitled *Prathamuṇḍamālā Tantra* and *Dvitīyamuṇḍamālā Tantra*. This reference is from *Dvitīyamuṇḍamạlā Tantra*); also see Goudriaan in *HT*, p. 65.]
43. S. Shankaranarayan, *The Ten Great Cosmic Powers: Daśa Mahāvidyās*, 2d ed. (Pondicherry: Dipti Publications, 1975), pp. 6-7.
44. "*Śṛnu cārvaṅgi subhage kālikāyāśca bhairavam. . . . kamalāyāḥ dakṣiṇāṃśe viṣṇurūpam sadāśivam. Pūjayet parameśāni sa siddho nātra saṃśayaḥ.*" *Toḍalatantra*, in *Tantrasaṅgraha, Part II* (hereafter cited as *TS-II*), ed. by Gopinaha Kaviraja in *Yogatantra-Granthamala*, vol. IV, (Varanasi: Varanaseya Sanskrit Vishvavidyalaya, 1970), 1:1-16.
45. "*Kālī tārā chinnamastā sundarī bagalāmukhī. Mātaṅgī bhuvanā lakṣmī dhūmrā tripurabhairavī. Etā eva mahāvidyā siddhavidyā yugāntarāt . . .*" *Śaktisaṅgama Tantra*, ed. by Rama Datta Shukla (Prayag: Kalyan Mandir Press, n.d.), 1:101-102.
46. Rājdeva Nandana Siṃha, *Śākta Pramoda* (Bombay: Khemarāja Śrīkṛṣṇadāsa, Śrī Veṅkaṭeśvara Steam Press, 1973); see also Goudriaan in *HTS*, pp. 70, 81, 97, and 145, and in *HT*, p. 65.
47. Douglas Renfrew Brooks, *Auspicious Wisdom: The Texts and Traditions of Śrīvidyā Śākta Tantrism in South India*

(hereafter cited as *Auspicious Wisdom*), (Albany: State University of New York Press, 1992), p. xv.

48. Goudriaan in *HTS*, p. 86.
49. Ibid., p. 58.
50. In the Yajurveda, Śrí and Lakṣhmī have separate identities, though both are closely associated as consorts of Puruṣha (Nārāyaṇa), but in the Khila of *ṚV* (Śrī-sūkta) one single deity is addressed as both, the two names being used interchangeably.

    The word "Lakṣmī" occurs in *ṚV* only once (10:71.2); "Śrī" occurs 82 times. The concept of Śrī came into prominence much earlier than the concept of Lakṣhmī. Śrī in Vedic literature was more an inner quality and deeper power. Lakṣhmī was associated with physical signs *(lakṣhaṇas)* of auspicious presence, especially on the face and in speech.
51. *"Ārādhitā vatsarāṇāmarbudānyake vinśatiḥ.*
    Prasannā chandayāmāsa vareṇa tripurā parā.
    Tayā vṛtañca sāyujyam tataḥ prāha parāmbikā.
    Vatse tvayā vinā viṣṇuraprabhuḥ paripālane.
    Śrī vidyetyahamākhyātā śrīpuram me puram bhavet.
    Śrī cakram me bhaveccakram śrīkramaḥ syānmama kramaḥ.
    Śrī sūktam etad bhūyānme vidyā śrīṣoḍaśī bhavet.
    Mahālakṣmītyaham khyātā tvattādātmyena saṃsthitā."
    TR-M, 53:42-47.
52. "... *etasyaiva bījasya nāma śrīvidyeti. Śrībījātmikā vidyā śrīvidyeti rahasyam....*" *LD* 32, p. 83.
53. *"Kāmeśvarī tvam devaśca bhavet kāmeśvarastathā.*
    Rājarājātmanām nastvamīśanāccāpisāmpratam.
    Rājarājeśvarī tvam vai rājarājeśvarastvayam.
    Tvam vai tripurasundarī caiṣa tripurasundaraḥ."
    TR-M 55:74-75.
54. "... *caturājñākośabhūtām naumi śrītripurāmaham." NS* 1:12;
    "... *yābhirviracitābhistu saṃmukhām tripurā bhavet.*" *NS* 3:2;
    "... *Tripurā paramā śaktirādyā jātāditaḥ priye." NS* 4:4;
    "... *Tripurā trividhā devī brahmaviṣṇvīśa rūpiṇī." NS* 4:11;
    "*Ramate svayam avyaktā tripurā vyaktim āgatā ...*"
    NS 4:16; "... *Evam devī tryakṣarā tu mahātripurasundarī.*"
    NS 4:18.

55. "... *Trividhastripurādevyāḥ saṅketaḥ parameśvari.*" *YH* 1:6; "... *kathitastripurādevyāḥ jīvanmuktipravartakaḥ.*" *YH* 1: 86.
56. "... *cakram kāmakalārūpam prasāraparamārthataḥ.*" *YH* 1:24.
57. *"Iti kāmākalāvidyā devīcakrakramātmikā seyam. Viditā yena sa mukto bhavati mahātripurasundarīrūpaḥ."* Puṇyānandanātha, *Kāmakalā-Vilasa with Commentary of Natanānandanātha* (hereafter cited as *KKV*), ed. Sadāshiva Mishra, trans. Arthur Avalon, Tantrik Texts, vol. 10, ed. Arthur Avalon (Calcutta: Āgamānusandhāna Samiti Sanskrit Press Depository, 1922), 8; *"Vadyāpi tādṛgātmā sukṣmā sā tripurasundari devī* ..." *KKV* 19; *"Āsīnā vindumaye cakre sā tripurasundarī devī*..." *KKV* 37; also see *KKV* 25 and 54.
58. "*Vajreśvarī tṛtīyā ca turyā tripurasundarī.*" *Gandharva Tantra* (hereafter cited as *GT*), in *Tantrasaṅgraha, Part III*, (herafter cited as *TS-III*). References to Tripurā found in *GT* 2:9, also see 2:32; 7:45-68; Lalitā in *GT* 7:72. Identifying Tripurā with goddess Durgā *GT* 2:10-11 says: "*Tripureti samākhyātā* ... *durgā sā parameśvarī. Tripureti samākhyātā saundaryātiśayāt tathā.*"
59. Altering Śaṅkara's opinion about the goddess appearing at *maṇipūra* in her usual personified form (i.e., holding *dhanuṣ, bāṇa, pāśa,* and *aṅkuśa* in her four hands), Lakṣmīdhara describes her as Daśabhujā, the goddess with ten hands holding ten different weapons in *LD* 41, p. 121. This description of Daśabhujā seems to be referring to Durgā.
60. Motilal Sharma, "Daśa Mahāvidyā," in *Kalyāṇa: Śakti Aṅka* (Gorakh Pur: Gita Press, Saṃvat, 1991), p. 112.
61. Gupta in *HT*, p. 122.
62. Shankaranarayan, *The Ten Great Cosmic Powers*, p. 9.
63. Gīrvāṇendra Saraswathi, *Prapañcha Sārasāra Saṅgraḥa of Gīrvāṇendra Saraswathi*, pt. 1 (hereafter cited as *PSS*), ed. K. S. Subramania Sastry, Tanjore Sarasvati Mahal Series, no. 98 (Tanjore: Shri S. Gopalan, 1962), chaps. 8, 9, and 12.
64. Vidyāraṇya, *Śrīvidyārṇava Tantra*, ed. Bhadrashil Sharma, (Prayag: Kalyāṇa Mandir Press, 2023 Vikrama Saṃvat), chap. 7.
65. Two bījas most commonly serving as part of the *śrīvidyā* mantra, *śrī* and *hrī*, without their *bhūta-lipi* nasalizations,

occur together as early as the *Taittirīya Upaniṣad* (1:11.3) and as late as DS (1:79). *Śrī* is also contrasted with Lakśhmī in *DS* 4:5. The *Devyatharva Śīrṣa* identifies Durgā as part of Śrīvidyā.

66. Goudriaan in *HTS*, p. 58 and Gupta in *HT*, p. 122.
67. Brooks, *Auspicious Wisdom*, p. xiv.
68. For example, see Lakṣmīdhara quoting *ṚV*, *Taittirīya Samhitā*, *Taittirīya Brāhmaṇṁa*, and *Taittirīya Āraṇyaka* in *LD* 5, 18, 32, 40, and 99.
69. Brooks, "Śrīvidya School," pp. 83-181.
70. Ibid., p. 84.
71. Ibid., pp. 89-90.
72. Ibid., p. 92.
73. Ibid., pp. 93-95.
74. Ibid., pp. 96-97.
75. Ibid., p. 105.
76. Ibid., p.106. Alexis Sanderson gives a succinct history of Śaivism in Kashmir. According to him, there were two "radically opposed" schools of Śaivism during the tenth century A.D.: nondualistic Trika-Krama and dualistic Śaiva Siddhānta. The nondualistic Trika–Krama school was influenced by the "Kāpālika culture of the cremation grounds and the erotico-mystical soteriology of the Kaulas." In order to stay "pure," the Śaiva Siddhānta rejected the *ācāra* (conduct) of the Kāpālikas and Kaulas. However, between the two extremes of nondualistic Trika-Krama and dualistic Śaiva-Siddhānta, another Śaiva school existed which, according to Sanderson, was the principal one in Kashmir. It worshipped *svacchandabhairava* and his consort, *aghoreśvarī*. Subsequently, the Trika–Krama school and the cult devoted to *svacchandabhairava* consolidated, which resulted in what is now popularly known as Kashmir Śaivism. Meanwhile, as Sanderson writes:

    The new nondualism also entered the Kaula cult of the goddess Tripurasundarī, or Śrīvidyāṃ, which rose to eminence in Kashmir during the eleventh century. This Kashmirian tradition of the Śrīvidyāṃ, which, by the twelfth century, had spread to the Tamil country, came to be adopted in the Trika circles with the result that the Trika became less a system of Tāntric worship than a matrix of metaphysics and soteriological theory. (*Encyclopedia of Religion*, s.v. "Śaivism in Kashmir," by Alexis Sanderson.)

77. Brooks, *Śrīvidyā School*, p. 116.
78. Ibid., p. 131.
79. Ibid., p. 134.
80. Ibid., p. 147.
81. Brooks, *Auspicious Wisdom*, p. 73-74.
82. Brooks, *Three Cities*, p. 67
83. According to Goudriaan (*HTS* 147-148 and *HT* 26 and 44) Lakṣmīdhara is probably also the author of *Śaiva Kalpadhruma*, who, in the colophones, says he is a worshipper of *śiva* at Ekamra (Bhuvaneśvara, Orissa). In the colophones of his commentary on the *SL*, Lakṣmīdhara mentions Gajapati Vīrarudra (Pratāparudra Gajapati) of Orissa as his patron. This association would place him in the early sixteenth century A.D. The compiler of the *Bibliography of Indian Philosophies*, Karl H. Potter, mentions that an Advaita text, *Advaita Makaranda*, is also catalogued under Lakṣmīdhara but so far no one has suggested the possibility that the author of this text was also the author of *LD* .
84. "*Kulācāro nāma bāhyapūjāratiḥ.*" *LD* 8, p. 16.
85. Brooks, *Three Cities*, p. 28.
86. Gupta translates the word *prāṇapratiṣṭhā* as "meditating on the replacement of the worshipper's mundane self by his divine self." Gupta in *HT*, p. 140.
87. Ibid., pp. 143-144.
88. Ibid., pp. 145-146.
89. *Vaidikī sandhyā; śiva pūjā*, the worship of *śiva;* the ritual worship of *śrīcakra* preceded by *antarmātṛkānyāsa*, *bahirmātṛkānyāsa*, *vaśinyādīnyāsa*, *pīthanyāsa*, *Ṛṣyādīnyāsa*, and the worship of each *cakra* of *śrīcakra* while offering water, sandalwood paste, flowers, incense, candles, fruits, sweets, betel leaf, etc., are common in *śrīcakra* worship whether the practitioner belongs to the left or right hand Kaula group. This part of *śrīcakra* worship is common even among so-called *samayācārins* today. The main difference between these two groups is that the *vāmācārins* worship

śrīcakra from left to right (i.e., clockwise) whereas the *dakṣiṇacārins* do the opposite. Further differences are based on the specific line of gurus *(paramparā).* What really distinguished *vāmācārins* from *dakṣiṇacārins* and *samayins* is the *cakra pūjā*, which is usually performed at night under the direct supervision of the teacher. This *cakra pūjā* involves purification of *bindu,* the ritual wine (often done by *cakreśvara*, the Tāntric master); an invocation of, and offering to, *ānandabhairava* and *ānandabhairavī*; *mārjana*, cleansing the body, subtle elements, senses, and mind with purified wine; and *bindu-svīkāra*, accepting the *bindu* (offering the wine to the soul, which is identical to *brahman*). Then the actual worship with the *pañcamakāras* begins. New initiates are allowed to worship *śakti* only up to the fifth chalice. A master, who is *pūrṇābhiṣkta,* can go to the seventh chalice. Only the adept of the highest calibre *(sāmrājyābhiṣkta)* can go all the way to the eleventh, and final, chalice if he wishes.
[Note: I gathered this information from a Tāntric adept, Pramathānanda Natha (known locally as Dolai Baba), and his students at Kamakhya, Assam.]

90. While sitting in a meditative pose, the aspirant balances the chalice on *trikhaṇḍā mudrā*, which is formed by extending the thumb, index finger and little finger, and folding the remaining two fingers against the palm. He recites the following prayer before offering the wine to the fire of *kuṇḍalinī*: *Ahantā pātra bharitam idantā para-māmṛtam. Parāhantāmaye vahnau juhomi śiva rūpadhṛk. . . . Śrīkuṇḍalīrūpacidagnikuṇḍe vācam sudhāñcaiva samarpayāmi.*
91. "*Samayācāro nāma āntarapūjāratiḥ . . . sā kuṇḍalinī punaḥ svasthānam etya svādhisthānam prāpya svapitīti tatparyam.*" *LD* 8, pp. 16-17; and "*Atra samayimatam nirūpyate . . . ata eva samayimate bāhyārādhanam dūrata eva nirastam . . .*" *LD* 41, pp. 117-119.
92. "*Tantrāṣṭake traivarṇikānām sūdrādīnāñca adhikārosti . . . tatpratipādakam tantram kaulamārgaḥ . . .*" Ibid. 31, pp. 78-79; and "*. . . tattu avaidikamārgatvāt smarṇārham api na bhavati . . .*" Ibid. 41, p. 117.
93. "*Bāhyapūjāyām eva ṛṣichandaḥprabhṛtijñānapurvakatvam . . . kartavyam iti niyamyate . . .*" Ibid. 32, pp. 96-97.

94. "*Kaulāḥ ādhāracakrapūjāratāḥ* . . ." *Ibid. 32, p. 97; and "Ataḥ teṣām ādhāracakram eva pūjyam. Tatra sthitā kuṇḍalinī śaktiḥ kaulinī ityucyate . . . samayinām sahasrakamale samayāyāḥ samayasya ca śambhoḥ pūjā."* Ibid. 41, pp. 116-117.
95. "*Teṣām ṣaṭcakrapūjā na niyatā apitu sahasrakamala eva pūjā . . . samayinām caturvidhaikyānusandhānam eva bhagavatyāḥ samārādhanam* . . ." Ibid. 41, p. 119.
96. "*Samhārakrameṇa lekhanam kaulamarga eva . . . sṛṣṭikramastu samayamārgaḥ* . . ." Ibid. 11, pp. 32-33.
97. "*Catuṣṣaṣṭhyā catuṣaṣṭhi saṅkhyākayaiḥ mahāmāyāśambarādibhiḥ . . . iti pancasaṃhitāḥ śubhāgamapañcakam* . . ." Ibid. 31, p. 73.
98. "*Tatra śubhāgamapañcake ṣoḍaśanityā nām pratipādanam mūlavidyānām antarbhāvam aṅgīkṛtya aṅgatayā. . . . candrajñānavidyāyām ṣoḍaśanityāḥ pradhānatvena pratipādita iti* . . ." Ibid. 31, pp. 78-79.
99. "*Ato navavidhaikyam bhairavībhairavayoḥ jñātavyam iti kaula mata rahasyam* . . ." Ibid. 34, pp. 100-105; and "*Samayānāma śambhunā sāmyam pañcavidham yātīti samayā . . . pañcavidham sāyam* . . ." Ibid. 41, pp. 117-119.
100. "It is hardly surprising that the *samayin* Lakṣmīdhara does not mention the Kaula-oriented *Tripurā Upaniṣad* in his work. As a result, we have no way of assessing his opinion on the use of the term 'Upaniṣad' for Kaula-oriented texts. This too is hardly surprising since he mentions Kaula sources only in general terms so that he can distance the Samaya school from their teachings and assert the supremacy of Samaya ideology and disciplines." Brooks, *Three Cities*, p. 28.
101. "*Eṣām vai bhūtānām pṛthivī rasaḥ . . . tasmast striyam adha upāsīta . . . tasya vedirupastho lomāni barhiścarmādhiṣavaṇe samiddho madhyataḥ . . . māṃsaudanam pācayitvā sarpiṣmantam aśnīyātām īśvarau janyitavai aukṣeṇa vārṣabheṇa vā." Bṛhadāraṇyaka Upaniṣad*, in *Upaniṣat-Saṁgrahaḥ* 6:4:1-18.
102. For example, *vāmācārins* recite the following Vedic *mantras* at various stages of *cakra pūjā*: "*Om ārdraṁ jvalati jyotir ahamasmi jyotir jvalati* . . ." *Mahānārāyaṇṁa Upaniṣad* in *Upaniṣat-Saṁgrahaḥ* 5:10; "*Om yaśchandasām ṛṣabho*

viśvarupa . . ." Ibid. 7:5; also see *Taittirīya Upaniṣad*, in *Upaniṣat-Saṁgrahaḥ*, 1:4.1.

103. Brooks, *Three Cities*, p. 29.
104. "Kaulas who favor external forms of ritual and sanction the use of the convention-defying behaviors also accept the superiority of ritual internalization *(antaryāga)*. Bhasṃkararāya, for example, in his Upaniṣad commentaries discusses at length the transformative qualities of external worship and the necessity of gradual internalization. Contemporary practitioners explain this position by saying that external rites should continue in order to maintain discipline and as an example for those who may never reach the higher state of internalization." Brooks, *Auspicious Wisdom*, p. 24.
105. Brooks, *Three Cities*, p. 29.
106. Śaiva texts, such as *SVT* 4:360-402 with Kṣemarāja's *Uddyota* commentary, and *NT* chaps. 7 and 8 with Kshemarāja's *Uddyota* commentary, as well as the writings of Abhinavagupta, which are major sources of Kaula *sādhanā*, give a thorough treatment of *kuṇḍalinī śakti* and the *cakras* and describe the methods of awakening *kuṇḍalinī* and leading her to the highest *cakra* while piercing the six lower *cakras*. Furthermore, the followers of Kaula *sādhanā* seem to have a great respect for Vedic exhortations as evinced in the *cakra pūjā*, during which Vedic mantras are recited during the offering of wine, meat, fish, and roasted grains.
107. Brooks, *Auspicious Wisdom*, p. 23.
108. The idea of a Śrīvidyā practitioner aspiring to achive a state of oneness is clearly found in Śrīvidyā texts that are not necessarily Samayācāra oriented. Referring to Amṛtananda's *Yoginīhṛdayadīpikā*, Brooks writes, "Kaulas are those who identify five elements in their spiritual lives, the so-called *śrīpañackam* frequently referred to by contemporary practitioners: (1) the Self *(ātman)* identified with the universal Brahman; (2) the guru; (3) the *śrīvidyā*, that is, the fifteen-or sixteen-syllable mantra; (4) Śrīmātā or the Auspicious Mother, that is, Devī in her beneficent aspects; and (5) the *śrīcakra*. . . . In the Setubandha Bhāskararāya continues this line of thought when he says that a Kaula is one who has made the identification of knower, knowing, and the object

of knowledge with the conscious self, the same definition he gives for a Śrīvidyā adept." Ibid., p. 22.

109. Mark S. G. Dyczkowski, *The Doctrine of Vibration: An Analysis of the Doctrines and Practices of Kashmir Shaivism* (Albany: SUNY Press, 1987), pp. 9-14.
110. "The Samaya-Kaula opposition is, however, primarily one of Ācāra 'systems of conduct,' not of the literary tradition." *HTS*, p. 18; for further details see also pp. 49-52 and Goudriaan in *HT*, pp. 45-46.
111. Gopinath Kaviraj, *Tāntrika Sāhitya: Vivaraṇātmaka Granthasūcī*, Hindi Samiti Granthamālā, 200 (Lucknow: Rājarṣi Puruṣottama Dāsa Ṭaṇḍana Hindī Bahavana, 1972), p. 49.
112. Goudriaan in *HT*, p. 45.
113. "We are left either to conclude that Lakṣmīdhara and his Samayācāra did not survive, that it was absolutely secretive, or that it produced only a theoretical interpretation of key Śrīvidyāṃ elements with no corresponding practical formulations. In fact, contemporary Samayins—who are our only clue to the historical practice—do not follow Lakṣmīdhara's interpretation to the letter and do not create ritual handbooks to meet the rather special situation arising with the *śricakra's* repositioning." Brooks, *Three Cities*, p. 220.
114. "*Mahāvedhaḥ śaivaḥ sādākhyāyāḥ prakāśa rūpo . . .*" *LD* 41, p. 120.
115. "*Gato'yam śaṅkarācāryo vīramāheśvaro gatah. Ṣaṭ cakrabhedane ko vā jānīte mat pariśramam.*" *LD* 100, p. 204.
116. At some point in the history of interaction between Śrividyā and Śaivism, these two systems came so close to each other that many of the Śrīvidyāṃ texts look like Śaivite texts, and vice versa. For example, Śrīvidyāṃ texts, such as commentaries on *YH* and *NS* by Śaiva adepts, *KKV* and Cidvallī, and *TR* (Jñānṉakhanda) are heavily Śaivite in tone. On the other hand, Śaivite texts such as *Parātriṃśikā* and *Malinīvijaya Vārttika*, are heavily Śākta in tone. Consequently, the commentators from both groups use these texts as their common source.
117. *SL*, p. v.
118. Ibid., p. vi.

119. [Śaṅkarācārya?] *Saundarya-Laharī of Śrī Śaṃkarācārya with Commentaries: Saubhāgyavardhanī of Kaivalyāśrama, Lakṣmīdharā of Lakṣmīdharācārya, Aruṇāmodinī of Kamesvarasūrin*, foreword by G. P. Ramaswami Aiyar, trans. and notes by R. Anantakṛṣṇa Śāstri and Karrā Rāmamūrthy Gāru (Madras: Ganesh & Co., 1957), p. 11.

120. [Śaṅkarācārya?] *Saundarya-Laharī (The Ocean of Beauty) of Śrī Śaṃkara-Bhagavatpāda.* 3rd. ed., trans., and commentary by S. Subrahmanya Sastri and T. R. Srinivasa Ayyangar (Adyar: Theosophical Publishing House, 1965), pp. 9-13; [Śaṅkarācārya?] *Saundarya-Laharī kā Hindī Anuvāda*, 3rd. ed., trans., and commentary by Viṣṇutīrtha (Rishikesh: Yogaśrī Pīṭha, 1970), p. 18.

Commentators such as Lakṣmīdhara, Kaivalyāśrama, Kāmeśavasūri, Acyutānanda, and modern Indian adherents such as S. Subrahmanya Sastri, T. R. Srinivasa Ayyangar, and Swami Viṣṇutīrtha, consider Ādi Śaṅkara to be the author of *SL*. Brown mentions another view: "The dissident human ascription is found in the commentary called Sudhāvidyotinī, whose author's name is variously given as Arijit or Aricchit. He says that the *Saundaryalaharī* was composed by his father Pravara or Pravarsena, a king in the Dramiḍa country, son of a king named Dramiḍa by his learned (vedavatī) wife; this king had a minister named Śuka. Even this tradition has its miraculous elements. King Pravara is otherwise unknown to me and Arijit's claim cannot be strengthened by supplementary evidence." *SL*, p. 25.

121. *SL*, p. 30.

122. "These disputes have never reached a satisfactory historical conclusion. From at least the fifteenth century, Śaṅkara is clearly identified with Śrīvidyāṃ tradition and the contemporary Śaṅkara *maṭhas* in both North and South India support the belief that he was a Śrīvidyāṃ adept (but not solely a Śrīvidyāṃ worshipper). Bhāskararāya and other Śrīvidyā adepts do not distinguish Śaṅkara who authored the *Brahmasūtrabhāsya* and other strictly *advaitic* works, from the Śākta-oriented Śaṅkara who penned *Saundaryalaharī,* though they are also not particularly interested in the former." Brooks, *Three Cities*, p. 273.

123. *SL*, p. 30.
124. Lakṣmīdhara's *Lakṣmīdharā*, Kaivalyaśrama's *Saubhāgyavardhinī*, Kāmeśvarasūri's *Aruṇāmodinī*, Ānandagiri's *Ānandagirīyā*, Mādhava Vaidya's *Tātparyadīpinī*, *Padārthacandrikā* (author unknown), Rāmakavi's *ḍiṇḍima Bhāsya*, Narasiṃhasvāmin's *Gopālasundarī*, and Gaurīkānta's *Ānandalaharī Tīkā* are published in *Saundaryalaharī of Śrī Śaṅkara Bhagavatpādācārya with Commentaries (in Sanskrit): Lakṣmīdharā, Saubhāgyavardhanī, Aruṇāmodinī, Ānandagirīyā, Tātparyadīpinī, Padārthacandrikā, ḍiṇḍima Bhāṣya, Gopālasundarī and Ānandalaharī Tīkā.* ed. A. Kuppuswami (hereafter cited as *Saundaryalaharī*, ed. A. Kuppuswami), (Tiruchirapalli: The Ministry of Education and Social Welfare, Government of India, 1976).

The following three commentaries were obtained from the India Office Library, London: Acyutānanda Śarman, *Ānandalaharī Tīkā (Vyākhyā)*, (Calcutta, 1885) Microfilm, VT 396(c); Mahādeva Vidyāvāgīśa Bhaṭṭacārya *(Ānandalaharī) Tattvabodhinī* (Sanskrit MS 2624, ff.61, Eggling 2524: I.O. 2196, n.d.). Jagadīśa Tarkālaṅkāra, *Ānandalaharīvyākhyā* (Sanskrit MS 2623 ff.58, Eggling 2623: I.O. 659, n.d.).
125. Gauḍapāda, *Śrī Subhagodayastuti*, in app. I of Shastri, Shiva Shankara Awasthi, *Mantra Aur Mātṛkāon kā Rahasya: Significance of Mantras and Mātṛkās According to Tāntrism* (hereafter cited as *MMR*), Vidyabhawan Rastrabhasha Granthamala, 95 (Varanasi: Chowkhamba Vidyabhawan, 1966), 241-249.
126. *"Paropi śaktirahitaḥ śaktaḥ kartum na kiñcana . . . śaktaḥ syāt parameśāni śaktyā yukto bhavedyadi."* *LD* 11, p. 29. (Note: With a slightly different rendering, the same verse is found in *NS* 4:6. For complete citation see Note 26 of Chapter 3.)
127. For a complete list of the texts quoted by Lakṣmīdhara, see pages 150-51.
128. It is to be noted, however, that the traditional adherents of Śrīvidyā, especially those who are initiates in the order of Śaṅkarācārya, claim that *SL* is one of the most profound Tāntric texts and contains all important tenets of Samayācāra. The text of an interview with Swami Veda

Bharati, an acclaimed Śrīvidyā practitioner, demonstrates this traditional view:

On the basis of internal evidence in *SL*, it would be inaccurate to say that *SL* is not a Tantra text proper. Although it is a very short text, the Ānanda-Laharī (AL) portion alone effectively states in summary form all the central tenets of Samayācāra. One might go so far as to say that larger texts of Samaya as well as the oral tradition elaborate on what has already been stated in *SL*. One may safely assume then, that *SL* is a full statement of Samayācāra in a versified "*sūtra*" form, which the other texts as well as the commentators like Lakṣmīdhara only expand and expound in further detail.

To cite some examples:

1. Where the theory of the philosophy of *śrīcakra* is given in verse 8, the description fits not the *mūlādhāra* but the *sahasrāra*. Even though verse 9 starts with the *mūlādhāra*, its goal is to conquer, subdue, and subordinate *(jitavā)* the Kula path and to dwell in the *sahasrāra*. It could be interpreted, by *dhvani* theory, to suggest that followers of Samaya should defeat the adherents of Kaula. Given the dialectic tradition of the philosophers of India, such an interpretation is on a firm historical basis.
2. In verse 10, what grace is sprinkled on the lower *cakras* comes from her feet at the highest pedestal. Verse 11 provides the biggest proof where *śrīcakra* is drawn according to the Samaya tradition with five *śakti* triangles and four *śiva* triangles.
3. In verse 14, the location of the *devi's* feet is again at the highest pedestal.
4. In verse 21, even though the force in the *agni, sūrya,* and *candra maṇḍalas* are her form, she herself dwells beyond these. And in verse 25, all the deities stand honoring her there.
5. Verse 26 conforms to the *yoga sūtra* tradition of *samādhi.* As all the deities and elements are dissolved in the process of *prati-sarga*, the supreme force dwells in fullest joy. Here, by *dhvani,* the author again challenges the adherents of the Kaula system as following temporary forces.

6. Verse 27 is of course the fullest possible definition of *antaryāga*, and the total refutation of external ritual.
7. In verse 31, any power that comes to the *kula* seat in the *mūlādhāra (kṣiti-tala)* is by the grace of her who is far above the dependencies *(para-tantra)* that are produced by practices on the *kaula* path.
8. In verse 33, again, the *yāga* is in *śivāgni*, in *sahasrāra*.
9. It is significant that even though a number of descriptions of the *kuṇḍalinī* path begin with the *mūlādhāra* in *AL* (e.g., verse 9), where actual meditation process is taught in verses 35-41, the description begins at the sixth *cakra*, completely opposite to the Kaula system of meditation.
10. It is clearly reiterated in verse 36, as was said in verse 21, that the *devī* is beyond the three sections into which the *cakras* are divided: the *agnimaṇḍala*, the *sūrya maṇḍala*, and the *candra maṇḍala (raviśaśiśucīnām aviṣaye)*.
11. While describing the techniques for meditating on the *cakras*, *SL* mentions the word "samayā" twice and this term is used in the cases of the two *cakras*—the *mūlādhāra* and the *svādhiṣṭhāna*—which the kaulas consider their domain.

My remarks, which are certainly not exhaustive, clearly demonstrate that *SL* is a Tāntric text and offers a complete knowledge of theory as well as practice, which a practitioner of Samayācāra requires.

CHAPTER 3

1. Here we have selected the version of the *Subhagodaya* (hereafter cited as *SU)* found in the app. of Awasthi, *MMR*.
2. Durvāsas, *Tripurasundarīmahimnastotra*, found in app. 1 of Awasthi, *MMR*, pp. 211-219.
3. Kālidāsa, *Pañcastavī* (the group of five *stotras* entitled "Laghustuti," "Ghaṭastava," "Carcāstuti," "Ambāstuti," and "Sakalajananīstava") found in app. 1 of Awasthi, *MMR*, pp. 250-268.
4. Śīvānanda, *Ṛjuvimarśinī*, commentary on *NS*.

5. Amṛtānanda, *Dipikā*, commentary on *YH*.
6. Vidyānanda, *Artharatnāvalī*, commentary on *NS*.
7. Puṇyānanda, *KKV*, along with Naṭanānanda's *Cidvallī*, the commentary on *KKV*.
8. Bhāskararāya, *Setubandha*, commentary on *YH*, and Bhāskararāya, *Varivasyā-Rahasya and its Commentary Prakāśa*, 4th ed., edited by Pandit S. Subrahmanya Sastri (Madras: The Adyar Library and Research Centre, 1976).
9. *TR-M* 30:17-21; *Tripurā Rahasya (Jñāna-khaṇḍṁa* (hereafter cited as *TR-J*) Swāmī Śrī Sanātanadevaji Mahārāja (Varanasi: Chowkhamba Sanskrit Series Office, 1967). 4:94, 99-100; 15:90-91; 18:29-45, 59, 64-65, 77-86; 22:67-69, 79-81, 112.
10. In his introduction to *NS*, pp. 84-86, Vrajavallabha Dviveda gives seventeen different meanings of the term "*tripurā*" compiled from: *Ns;* Vidyānanda's *Artharatnāvalī*; Bhāskararāya's *Setubandha*; Naṭanānanda's *Cidvallī*; *Tripurāraṇava*; *Kālikā Purāṇa* and Bhāskararāya's *Saubhāgyabhāskara*, a commentary on *Lalitā-Sahasranāman*. These sources derive the meaning of "*tripurā*" not through the etymology *(vyutpatti)* of the word, but through pseudo-etymology *(nirukti)*. The purpose of such pseudo-etymological interpretation is simply to indicate that *tripurā* pervades and transcends the threefold world.
11. "*Iha khalu śrītripurasundaryāḥ sthūlasūkṣmapararūpabhedena trividhāyaḥ upāstirupāḥ kriyā api trividhā kāyikī vācikī mānasī ceti.*" Bhāskararāya, *Bhāvanopaniṣat*, in *LD*, app. 2, p. 269.
12. Brooks, *Śrīvidyā School*, p. 183.
13. "*Deśakālākāraiḥ aniyantritasvabhāvatvāt . . . saṃvideva mahātripurasundarīpadābhilapyā. Saṃvideva bhagavatī svāntaḥ sthitaṃ jagad bahiḥ prakāśayati. . . .*" Vrajavallabha Dviveda in the introduction to *NS*, pp. 84-85.
14. "*Sṛṣṭau vā pralaye vāpi nirvikalpaiva sā citiḥ.*
Pratibimbasya bhāve vāpyabhāve veva darpaṇaḥ.
Evaṃvidhaikarūpāpi citiḥ svātantryahetutaḥ.
Svāntarvibhāsayed bāhyam ādarśe gaganaṃ yathā."
TR-J 14:57-58.
15. "*Nityasambandhaḥ samavāyaḥ. Ayutasiddhavṛttiḥ. Yayor dravyayor madhye ekam avinaśyadavastham aparāśritam*

evātiṣṭhate tāvayutasiddhau. Yathā avayavāvayavinau guṇaguṇinau kriyākriyāvantau jātivyaktī viśeṣanityadravye ceti." Annambhaṭṭa, *Tarkasaṅgraha* (Varanasi: Harikṛṣṇanibandhabhawanam, 1969), p. 107.

16. *"Tathā citir jagatsattā tataḥ sarvaṃ citirbhavet. Adhikaṃ bhāsate yattu tannairmalyamahatvataḥ."* *TR-J* 11:54; *"Darpaṇapratibimbānāṃ cidātmānanyatā yathā. Cidātmapratibimbānāṃ cidātmānanyatā tathā."* *TR-J* 11:63; *"Yadastīti bhāti tattu citireva maheśvarī. Evaṃ jagaccidātmarūpaṃ te samyagīritam."* *TR-J* 11:85.
17. Śri Bhāskararāya Makhin, *Varivasyā-Rahasya* (hereafter cited as *VR*), ed. with English translation by Pandit S. Subrahmanya Sastri (Adyar: The Adyar Library and Research Centre, 1976).
18. *". . . tena cāreṇa santuṣṭā punarekākinī satī. Ramate svayamavyaktā tripurā vyaktimāgatā . . ."* *NS* 4:15-16.
19. *"Bījāvasthāyām aṅkurakāṇḍapatra puṣpaphalādivāt śaktyavasthāyām antaḥ sadātmanā vartate kāryarūpaḥ prapañca iti."* *Ṛjuvimarśinī* on *NS* 4:5.
20. *"Prakṛtipariṇāmavāde guṇānām sāmyaṃ vaiṣamyam upaiti, atra tu svatantrā citiḥ svasvātantryeṇa avikṛtā satī tattadrūpeṇa svātmānaṃ prakāśayatīti na vaiṣamyāvakāśaḥ."* Vrajavallabha Dviveda in the introduction to *NS*, p. 90.
21. Ibid.
22. *"Tripurā paramā saktirādyā jātāditaḥ priye. Sthūlasūkṣmavibhedena trailokyotpattimāṛkā."* *NS* 4:4.
23. *"Kavalīkṛtaniśśeṣatattvagrāmasvarūpiṇī . . ."* *NS* 4:5.
24. *"Bijāvasthāyām aṅkurakāṇḍapatrapuṣpaphalādivat śaktyavasthāyām antaḥ sadātmanā vartate kāryarūpaḥ prapañcaḥ . . ."* *Ṛjuvimarśinī* on *NS* 4:5.
25. Ibid.
26. *"Paro hi śaktirahitaḥ śaktaḥ kartum na kiñcana. Śaktastu parameśāni śaktyā yukto yadā bhavet. Śaktyā vinā śive sūkṣme nāma dhāma na vidyate . . ."* *NS* 4:6-7.
27. *Ṛjuvimarśinī* and *Artharatnāvalī* on *NS* 4:5-7.
28. See Chapter 2, pp. 44-45 of this manuscript.
29. *"Eṣā sā paramā sāktirekaiva parameśvarī. Tripurā trividhā devī brahmaviṣṇvīśarūpiṇī.*

Jñānaśaktiḥ kriyāśaktiricchāśaktyātmikā priye.
Trailokyaṃ saṃsṛjatyeṣā tripurā parikīrtyate."
NS 4:10-12.

30. "*Tathāpi naitena sa śaktipāramyavādīti bhramaitavyam . . . śivapāramyapakṣapāti tvam ātmano vyanakti* . . ." Vrajavallabha Dviveda in the introduction to *NS*, p. 90.
31. "*Sā jayati śaktirādyā nijasukhamayanityanirupamākārā. Bhāvicarācaravījam śivarūpavimarśanirmalādarśaḥ.*" *KKV* 2, see also *VR* 2:67-68, as well as the *Prakāśa* commentary; *SL* 34, 35, and 41; and *SU* 44.
32. *Śiva Sūtras: The Yoga of Supreme Identity: Text of the Sūtras and the Commentary Vimarśinī by Kṣemarāja*, trans. with introduction and notes by Jaideva Singh (Delhi: Motilal Banarsidass, 1979), 1:1; Kṣemarāja, *Pratyabhijñāhṛdaya*, 2d ed., trans., notes, and introduction by Jaideva Singh (Delhi: Motilal Banarsidass, 1979) sutra 1; and also see *YH* 1:9-11, *KKV* 1-3, and *VR* 1:4.
33. ". . . *bahuśaktitvamapyasya tacchaktyaivāviyuktā. . . . tenādvayaḥ sa evāpi śaktimatparikalpane. . . . ko bhedo vastuto vahanerdagdhṛpaktṛtvayoriva. Na cāsau paramārthena na kiñcidbhāsnādṛte. Nahyasti kiñcittacchiktitadvabhadepi vāstavaḥ.*" *TĀ* 1:68-71; see also *TĀ* 3:106-10; and Abhinavagupta, *MVV*, ed. with notes by Madhusudan Kaul Shastri, Kashmir Series of Texts and Studies, no. 32 (Srinagar: Kasmir Pratap Steam Press, 1921), 1:17.
34. ". . . *evam śaktimacchabdavyavahāropi nāyam, sopi hi param śaktilakṣhaṇamarthamurarīkṛtyaiva vartate* . . ." *Viveka* commentary on *TĀ* 2:24-26.
35. "*Śivaḥ śaktyā yukto yadi bhavati śaktaḥ prabhavitum na cedevam devo na khalu kuśalaḥ spanditum api* . . ." *SL* 1.
36. Bhaṭṭojidīkshita, *Vaiyākaraṇa Siddhāntakaumudī of Bhaṭṭojidīkshita*, 5th ed., edited by Gopāla Shastrī Nene, Haridas Sanskrit Series, 11 (Varanasi: Chaukhamba Sanskrit Series Office, 1977), see "Avyayaprakaraṇa" under sūtra "Svarādinipātmavyayam."

It is to be noted, however, that *SL* 39 and 41 use the accusative *(samayām)* and instrumental *(samayayā)* forms of *samayā*, respectively. It is agreed that *samayā*, also as a feminine gender noun, has not been included in lexicons. All this proves is that the lexicons have failed to notice the particular philosophical usage of the term.

37. Monier Monier-Williams, *Sanskṛit-English Dictionary: Etymologically and Philologically Arranged with Special Reference to Cognate Indo-European Languages*, new enl. ed. (Oxford: Clarendon Press, 1899; reprint ed., Delhi: Munshiram Manoharlal Publishers, 1981), s.v. "samayā" and "samaya."
38. Goudriaan, *HT*, p. 45; also see *TĀ* 4:64, 15:459, 19:31, 35, 48, 55, and 29:197 and 199.
39. The term *samayin* occurs in *SU* 3, 7, 12, 13, 15, 22, 28-32, 35, 38, 40-42, 45, and 51; the term *samaya* in *SU* 7; and the term *samayamārga* in *SU* 49.
40. The term *subhagā* occurs in *SU* 52; *sādākhyā* in *SU* 24, 35, and 36; and *candrakalā* or *aindavakalā* in *SU* 1, 5, 20, 23, 26, and 49.
41. ". . . *mahākālātītām kalitasaraṇīkalpitatanum* . . ." *SU* 1; ". . . *kulam tyaktvā rauti sphuṭati ca mahākālabhujagī* . . ." *SU* 6; ". . . *sūryaśaśinor agamye raśmīnām samayasahite tvam viharase.*" *SU* 7, and "*Mahākaulestasmānna hi tava śive kālakalanā.*" *SU* 9.
42. "*. . . samayasahite tvaṃ viharase.*" *SU* 7.
43. "*Kālo aśvo vahati saptaraśmiḥ sahasrākṣo ajaro bhūmiretāh.*
Tamārohanti kavayo vipaścitas tasya cakrā bhuvanāni viśvā.
Sapta cakrān vahati kāla eṣa saptāsya nābhīramṛtaṃ nvakṣaḥ.
Sa imā viśvā bhuvanānyañjayat kālaḥ sa īyate prathamo nu devaḥ." *The Atharvaveda* 19:53.1-2.
"*Kāle tapaḥ kāle jyeṣtham kāle brahma samāhitam.*
Kālo hi sarvasyeśvaro yaḥ pitāsītprajāpateḥ."
The Atharvaveda 19:53.8.
For details, see *The Atharvaveda* 19:53.1-8 and 19:54.1-5.
44. Beane, *Myth, Cult and Symbols*, pp. 150-168; and Motilal Sharma, "Daśa Mahāvidyā," in *Kalyāṇa: Śakti Anka*, pp. 98-105.
45. John Woodroffe, *Tantrarāja Tantra: A Short Analysis*, 3rd. ed. (Madras: Ganesh & Co., 1971), pp. 118-121.
46. "*Kalāmuhūrtakāṣṭhāharmāsartuśaradātmane . . .*" *BP-L* 13:6.
47. "*. . . caturvidhā śabdamayī parāśaktirvijṛmbhate.*" *TR-M* 58:9; "*Śabdaḥ kālamayaḥ sarvo . . .*" *TR-M* 58:25.
48. "*Kecittu ekapañcāśata tattvānyāhuḥ . . . guṇāḥ sattvarajas-*

tamāṃsi . . ." *LD* 11, pp. 28-29.

49. "*Eteṣu sarveṣu tattveṣu katicana tattvāni kutracid antarbhavanti . . . etāni pañcaviṃśati tattvāni sarvasammatāni.*" Ibid., p. 29.
50. "*Śuddhavidyā tu sadāśivena yuktā satī sādākhyākaleti vyavahṛyate. Ato bhagavatī caturviṃśati tattvānyatikrāntā sadāśivena pañcaviṃśena sārdhaṃ viharamāṇā ṣaḍviṃśatattvātmatām āpannā paramātmeti gīyat . . .*" *LD* 9, p. 20.
[Note: Although Lakṣmīdhara does not cite the source of his commentary on *SL* 9 and 11, he is clearly echoing *SU* 2-5.]
51. See footnote 49 of Chapter 3.
52. Ibid., p. 29.
53. Ibid.
54. *SL* 34.
55. "*Yadā sṛṣṭisthitilayeṣu ānandabhairavasya parānandasañjñikasya paracitsvarūpāyāśca mahābhairavyāḥ prayatnaḥ utpadyate, tadā bhairavīprādhānyāt pradhānaṃ prakṛtiśabdavācyā mahābhairavīti, tasyāḥ pradhānatvaṃ śeṣitvaṃ; ānandabhairavasya apradhānatvaṃ guṇabhāvaḥ śeṣatvaṃ. Yadā sarvopasaṃhāre prakṛteḥ tanmātrāvasthitau bhairavyāḥ svātmani antarbhāvāt bhairavasya śeṣitvaṃ tadā bhairavyāḥ śeṣatvaṃ iti.*" *LD* 34, p. 105.
56. "*Ānandabhairavamahābhairavyoḥ tādātmye siddhe navātmatā dvayoḥ samānā.*" Ibid.
57. "*Ataḥ śeṣaśibhāvaḥ āpekṣikaḥ.*" Ibid.
58. "*. . . Uttara kaulamate pradhānameva jagatkartṛ. Pradhānatvādeva śeṣabhāvo nāsti śivasyābhāvāt . . .*" *LD* 35.
59. "*. . . Evaṃ prapañcaṃ kāryarūpaṃ svasyām āropya kāraṇarūpeṇa avasthitā . . .*" Ibid.
60. "*. . . bhāvena icchayā bibhṛṣe icchayaiva sisṛkṣādikāyāṃ śaktiḥ śiva iti rūpadvayam aṅgīkṛtaṃ.*" *Aruṇāmodinī* on *SL* 35, published in *Saundaryalaharī*, ed. A. Kuppuswami, p. 317.
61. "*Anyathā tvam evaiketyabhiprāyaḥ.*" Ibid.
62. "*Ataḥ manaḥ prabhṛtīnāṃ śaktipariṇāmaḥ, tattvānāṃ svarūpapariṇāmaḥ. Evaṃ prapañcaṃ kāryarūpaṃ svasyāṃ āropya kāraṇarūpeṇa avasthitā. Sā ca ādhārakuṇḍalinī ityabhidhīyate.*" *LD* 35.
63. "*Iha khalu śaṅkarabhagavatpūjyapādāḥ samayatattvavedinaḥ*

samayākhyāṃ candrakalāṃ ślokaśatena prastuvanti." *LD* 1, p. 2.

64. "*Śivaśaktyormelanaṃ ṣaḍviṃśaṃ sarvatattvātītaṃ tattvāntaram iti purastānnivedayiṣyate. Tasmānmelanādeva jagadutpattisthitilayāḥ, na kevalādeveti . . .*" Ibid., p. 3.
65. "*Śuddhavidyā tu sadāśivana yuktā satī sādākhyākaleti vyavahriyate. Ato bhagavatī caturviṃśati-tattvavānyatikrāntā sadāśivena pañcaviṃśena viharamāṇā ṣaḍviṃśatattvātmatāṃ āpannā paramātmeti gīyate. Etad uktaṃ bhavatisādākhyākalā pañcaviṃśena sadāśivena militā ṣaḍviṃśā bhavati, melanasya tattvāntaratvāt. Na cobhayormelanaṃ ubhayātmakaṃ.*" *LD* 9, p. 20.
66. "*Avinābhāvasambhandhaṃ yo jānāti sa cakravit . . . avinābhāvasambandhaḥ tasmādbindu-trikoṇayoḥ.*" Ibid., p. 22.
67. "*. . . sarvatattvātītaṃ tattvāntaraṃ . . .*" *LD* 1, p. 3; "*Tasya tādātmyarūpatvāt tattvāntaram eveti rahasyam.*" *LD* 9, p. 20; "*Ataśca sarvatattvātītam śivaśaktisampuṭam. Tasmādeva jagadutpattiḥ.*" *LD* 11, p. 29.
68. "*Samayānāma śambhunā sāmyaṃ pañcavidhaṃ yātīti samayā. Samayatvaṃ śambhorapi-pañcavidhṃ sāmyaṃ devyā saha yātīti. Ataḥ ubhayoḥ samaprādhānyenaiva sāmyaṃ vijñeyam.*" *LD* 41, p. 117.
69. In *LD* 41, Lakṣmīdhara continues explaining how and in which particular verses of *SL* these fivefold "equivalencies or samenesses," *sāmya*, have been described: *Adhiṣṭhāna-samayā* means "equivalency or sameness in foundation," i.e., the *cakras* where *śakti* and *śiva* equally reside. *Śakti* and *śiva* are eternally united in the *sahasrāra* as well as in all six other *cakras*, as mentioned in verses 9, 36-41.

    Anuṣṭhāna-samayā means equivalency in function or activity. In the process of manifestation, *śakti* and *śiva* participate together and play equal roles. In verse 41, the world consists of both father and mother, *śiva* and *śakti.*

    Avasthāna-samayā means taking their places equally in every aspect of the universe. During the cosmic dance *(mahātāṇḍava)*, which is followed by the withdrawal or destruction of the world, *śakti* and *śiva* play equal roles. As they participate in the dance, *śakti* performs in the delicate, *lāsya* style and *śiva* in the vigorous *mahātāṇḍava* style in verse 41. Dancing side by side, *śiva*, as the eternal consuming fire *(saṁvarta agni)*, angrily burns up the world with his fierce gaze, while *śakti* through her glance, moist with compassion, provides the cooling antidote in verse 39.

Avasthāna-samayā has also been described by the phrase *yamārādhyan bhaktyā* in verse 36, the phrase *śaśikiraṇa-sārūpya saraṇīṃ* in verse 37, and the phrase *sphurannānā-ratnābharaṇa pariṇaddhendra dhanuṣaṃ* in verse 40.

Rūpa-sāmya and *nāma-sāmya* mean equivalency in form and name. Equivalency in form is demonstrated by the fact that in their personified forms as *kāmeśvara* and *kāmeśvarī*, or as *ānandabhairava* and *ānandabhairavī*, they resemble each other. Their color, complexions, facial expressions, physical gestures, weapons, etc., are alike. Similarly, their names *kāmeśvara-kāmeśvarī, ānandabhairava-ānandabhairavī*, and *samaya-samayā*, etc., match.

In commenting on verse 41, Lakṣmīdhara quotes specific words from various verses of *SL* which, according to him, describe the oneness in name and form of *śakti* and *śiva*. For instance, the words *taḍitvantaṃ* in *SL* in verse 40 refer to both *taḍitvān*, masculine-gender *śiva* and *taḍitvatī*, a feminine gender *śakti*. Similarly, *hutabhukkaṇika* in verse 78, *śuddhasphaṭ ikaviśadaṃ* in verse 37, and *tapanaśaśiko ṭidyutidharaṃ* and *paraṃ śambhū* in verse 36 describe their oneness in name.

70. *"Ānandabhairavamahābhairavyoḥ parānandaparāsañjñayoḥ tādātmye siddhe navātmatā dvayoḥ samānā. Ataḥ śeṣaśeṣibhāvaḥ āpekṣikaḥ . . ." LD* 34.
71. *". . . tadubhayayāmalasphuritabhāvavisargamayam hṛdaya-munutarāmṛtakulam mama saṃsphuratāt." TĀ 1:1; "Tay-oryadyāmalam rūpam sa saṅghaṭṭa iti smṛtaḥ. Ānandaśaktiḥ saivoktā yato viśvam vijṛmbhate." TĀ* 3:68; also see 3:143, 201-208, 234.
72. *"Śaktimānañjyate yasmānna śaktirjātu kencit.*
Icchā jñanam kriyā ceti yatpṛthakpṛthagañjyate.
Tadeva śaktimatsvaiḥ svairiṣyamāṇādikaiḥ sphuṭam . . ."
Ibid., 3:106-107.
73. *". . . Rūpam bhāti param prakāśanividam devaḥ sa ekaḥ*

śivaḥ. Tatsvātantryarasātpunaḥ śivapadādbhede vibhāte param yadrūpam bahudhānugāni tadidam tattavam vibhoḥ śasane." TĀ 9:1-2; *"Vastutaḥ sarvabhāvāna karteśānaḥ paraḥ śivaḥ . . ." TĀ* 9:8; *". . . ekaikatrāpi tattvesmin sarvaśaktisunirbhare. Tattatprādhānyayogena sa sa bhedo nirūpyate. Tadhāhi svasvatantratvaparipūrṇatayā vibhuḥ." TĀ* 9: 51-52

74. Larson, "The Sources for Śakti," pp. 51-52.
75. Ibid., p. 44.
76. Ibid., p. 49.
77. *"Naiṣā śaktirmahādevī na paratrāśrito yataḥ. Na caiṣa śaktimāndevo na kasyāpyāśrayo yataḥ." TĀ* 2:24; Also Notes 33 and 72 of this chapter.
78. *"Vimalakalāśrayābhinavasṛṣtimahājananī bharitatanuśca pañcamukhaguptarucirjanakaḥ. Tadubhayāmalasphuritabhāvavisargamayam hṛdayamnuttarāmṛtakulam mama saṃsphurāt." TĀ* 1:1, also see 3:66-103, and 3:136-234.
79. K. C. Pandey, *Abhinavagupta*, p. 590.
80. Ibid., pp. 636-637.
81. Ibid., p. 643.
82. In describing the nature of *anuttara* and its intrinsic components, Padoux writes:

    We have not been able to find a satisfactory translation of *anuttara*. One could say unexcelled or unsurpassed. R. Gnoli translates it by 'Senza Superiore.' Abhinavagupta, at the beginning of the PTV (pp. 19-32), gives sixteen different interpretations or sixteen possible ways of apprehending the senses and meanings of *anuttara*. . . . One could also be tempted to render *anuttara* as 'transcendent,' except that there is no such thing really as transcendence in nondualistic Śaivism. As we shall see later on, there is, for Abhinavagupta or Jayaratha, a particular interplay between transcendence and immanence. The primary principle, the *anuttara,* is both *viśvottīrṇa,* beyond manifestation, unimpeded pure consciousness, and *viśvamaya* or *viśvarūpa,* assuming the form of the universe, that is, pervading it, being its essence or substratum. It can be envisaged as either or both of them.

    Such a conception of the primary principle of the universe is not, of course, peculiar to Abhinavagupta and is much earlier than he. Padoux, *Vāc*, p. 235.

83. "*. . . devaḥ sa ekaḥ śivaḥ.*" *TĀ* 9:1.
"*. . . karteśānaḥ paraḥ śivaḥ.*" *TĀ* 9:8.

84. "*. . . kāryakāraṇabhāvo yaḥ śivecchāparikalpaitaḥ.*" *TĀ* 9:7.

85. Some of the specific verses that indicate the supremacy of śiva are *TĀ* 9:1, 7, 8, 21, 35, and 38.

86. Padoux, *Vāc* p. 244.

87. Ibid., p. 240.

88. "*Akulasyāsya devasya kulaprathanaśālinī.*
Kaulīnī sā parā śaktiraviyukto yayā prabhuḥ." *TĀ* 3:67.

89. "*Śaktayo jagat kṛtsnam śaktimāṃstu maheśvaraḥ . . .*" *TĀ* 5:40.

90. Jayaratha, *Viveka* on *TĀ* 3:67, pp. 76-78.

91. "*No śāntam nāpyuditam sāntoditasūtikāraṇam paraṃ kaulam . . .*" *TĀ* 29:117.
"*. . . śāntoditātmakam dyāmatha yugapadudeti śaktiśaktimatoḥ.*" *TĀ* 29:19.
"*. . . ubhayamapi vastutaḥ kila yāmalamiti tathoditam śāntam.*" *TĀ* 29:120.

92. "*. . . sukumārahṛdayānām āgāmikānaṃ sammoho mā bhūditi. . . . vastutastu sthitameva sarvatattvānām abhidhānam.*" *Viveka* on *TĀ* 11:28.

93. "*. . . yattu sarvāvibhāgātma svatantraṃ bodhasundaram.*
sapta triṃśam tu tatprāhustattvam paraśivābhidham . . ." *TĀ* 11:21-22.

94. "*Kramatāratamyayogāt saiva hi saṃvidvisargasaṃghaṭṭaḥ.*
Taddhruvadhāmānuttaramubhayātmakajagadudārasānandam.
No śāntam nāpyuditam śāntoditsūtikāraṇam param kaulam . . .
śantoditātmakam dvayamatha yugapadudeti śaktimatoḥ." *TĀ* 29:116-119.

95. "*. . . tasyāpyuktanayād vedyabhāve'tra partikalpite.*
Yadāste hyanavacchinnam tadaṣṭātriṃśam ucyate." *TĀ* 11:22-23.

96. "*. . . tām parāṃ pratibhāṃ devīm saṅgirante hyanuttarām.*" *TĀ* 3:66.

97. "*. . . niratiśayasvātantryaiśvaryacamatkāramayī.*" *Viveka* on *TĀ* 3:66.

98. See Note 88 of Chapter 3.

99. "*Tayoryad yāmalaṃ rūpaṃ sa saṅghaṭṭa iti smṛtaḥ.*

Ānandaśaktiḥ saivoktā yato viśvaṃ visṛjyate." *TĀ* 3:68.

100. *"Parāparātparam tattvam saiṣā devī nigadyate. Tatsāraṃ tacca hṛdayaṃ sa visargaḥ paraḥ prabhuḥ. Devīyāmalaśāstre sā kathitā kālakarṣiṇī. Mahāḍāmarake yāge śrīparā mastake tathā."* *TĀ* 3:69-70.

101. K. C. Pandey, *Abhinavagupta*, pp. 682-686.

CHAPTER 4

1. "*. . . śivaśaktayor melanam ṣaḍviṃśam sarvatattvātītam tattvāntaram iti . . . tasmanmelanad eva jagadutpattisthiti layāḥ . . .*" *LD* 1, p. 3; "*. . . anekakoṭi brahmāṇḍapiṇḍaṇḍāvacchinnamayūkhānām uparyeva vartamānatvāt . . .*" *LD* 14, p. 49; and "*. . . sarvabhūtātmakam sarvamantrātmakam sarvatattvātmakam sarvāvasthātmakam sarvadevātmakam sarvavedārthātmakam sarvaśabdātmakam sarvaśaktyātmakam triguṇātmakam trikhaṇḍam triguṇātītam sādākhyāparaparyāyam . . .*" *LD* 32, p. 96.
2. *Yogakuṇḍalī Upaniṣad* (hereafter cited as *YKU*) in *Upaniṣat-Saṁgrahaḥ.*
3. "*. . . Tacca piṇḍāṇḍabrahmāṇḍayoḥ aikyānusandhānamahimnā . . . ayamarthaḥ–piṇḍāṇḍabrahmāṇḍayoraikyaṃ jñātavyam. . . .*" *LD* 99, pp. 200-201; "*. . . Te ca marīcayaḥ asmin brahmāṇḍe piṇḍāṇḍe ca ṣaṣṭyuttaraśatasaṅkhyātāḥ evam anantako ṭipiṇḍāṇḍabrahmāṇḍeṣu . . .*" *LD* 14, p. 49; and "*Brahmāṇḍasthita-piṇḍāṇḍasthita-candra sūryayoḥ aikyāt . . .*" *LD* 41, p. 122.
4. "*. . . Mūlādhāra-svādhiṣṭhāna-maṇipūrānāhata-viśuddhyājñātmakāni ṣaṭcakrāṇi . . .*" *LD* 9, p. 19.
5. "*Etāni pṛthvyagnijalapavanākāśamanastattvātmakāni. Tāni tattvāni teṣu cakreṣu tanmātratayāvasthitāni. Tanmātrāstu gandharūparasasparśaśabdātmakāḥ. Ājñācakrasthitena manastattvena ekādaśendriyagaṇaḥ saṅgṛhītaḥ.*" *LD* 9, pp. 19-20.
6. "*Piṇḍāṇḍamatītya vartate sahasrārakamalam . . .*" *LD* 14, p. 48.
7. "*. . . Ādhārasvādhiṣṭhānamaṇipūrānāhataviśuddhyājñācakrātmakaṃ śrīcakraṃ trikhaṇḍaṃ somasūryānalātmakam. Mūlādhārasvādhiṣṭhānacakradvayam ekaṃ khaṇḍam.*

Maṇipūrānāhatacakradvayam ekaṃ khaṇḍham. Viśuddhyājñācakradvayam ekaṃ khaṇḍam. Atra prathama-khaṇḍopari agnisthānam. Tadeva rudragranthirityucyate. Dvitīyakhaṇdopari sūryasthānam. Tadevaviṣṇugranthi-rityucyate. Tṛtīyakhaṇḍopari candrasthānam. Tadeva brahmagranthirityucyate." *LD* 14, p. 47.

8. *"Āgnīṣomātmakaṃ cakram agnīṣomamayaṃ jagat. Agnāvantarbabhau bhānuḥ agnīṣomamayaṃ smṛtam. Trikhaṇḍaṃ mātṛkācakraṃ somasūryānalātmakam . . ."* *LD* 11, p 34.
9. *"Evam somasūryānalāḥ piṇḍāṇḍabrahmāṇḍe āvṛtya vartante."* *LD* 14, p. 48.
10. *"Piṇḍāṇḍabrahmāṇḍayoraikyāt piṇḍāṇḍavṛtireva brahmāṇḍāvṛtiriti rahasyam. Evaṃ piṇḍāṇḍamatītya vartate sahasārakamalam. Tacca jyotsnāmayo lokaḥ. Tatratyaścan-dramā nityakalaḥ."* Ibid.
11. *"Tava upari māyāśuddhavidyāmaheśvarasadāśivātmaka-tattva-catusṭayaṃ brahmagranthyantarabhāvi . . ."* *LD* 92, p. 186.
12. There are two reasons to believe that the *brahmagranthi* is situated above the *ājñā cakra* and below the *sahasrāra*:

    1. Lakṣmīdhara clearly states: *"Tṛtiyakhaṇḍopari can-drasthānaṃ tadeva brahmagranthi,"* "at the top of the third division is the place of the moon and that is the *brahmagranthi*." *LD* 14. He uses a similar passage in *LD* 99: *"Ājñā cakrānte ekaṃ brahmagranthyātmakam."* "At the end of the *ājñā cakra* is the *brahmagranthi.*"

    2. By stating "*Manastattvātmake ājñācakre catuṣṣaṣṭiḥ*" (*LD* 14), he completes the enumeration of 360 *kalās*, which in different proportions belong to the six *cakras* of the fiery, solar, and lunar divisions. These 360 *kalās* constitute the world. By mentioning that their place is at the top of *ājñā cakra* and by considering them to be the components of the goddess' couch, (*LD* 8 and 92), Lakṣmīdhara must mean that they are between the *ājñā* and *sahasrāra cakras* and that is where the *brahmagranthi* could be located.
13. "*Tānyeva mañcasya catuṣpadāni. Śuddhavidyāyāḥ sadāśivatattvābhiniveśāt tacchāyāpattyā sahasrakamalāntar-gataḥ śivaḥ sadāśivātmā anurāgavaśāt śuddhavidyāyāḥ*

saṃvalanāt tādātmyaṃ pratīyate." *LD* 92, p. 186; "*Śivādīnāṃ mañcopadhānatvapatadgrahāvasthāpannatvaṃ kāmarūpatvāddevānam atyantāsannasevārthaṃ* . . ." *LD* 8, p. 17.

14. Padoux, *Vāc*, pp. 309-312.
15. ". . . *Ādhāram andhatāmiśram. Svādhiṣṭhānam tu sūryakiraṇa samparkāt miśralokaḥ. Maṇipūrastu agnisthānatve'pi tatra sthite jale sūryakiraṇapratibimbāt miśraka eva lokaḥ. Anāhataṃ jyotirlokaḥ. Evam anāhatacakra paryantaṃ jyotistamomiśrako lokaḥ. Viśuddhicakraṃ cāndro lokaḥ. Ājñācakraṃ tu candrasthānatvāt sudhālokaḥ, anayorlokayoḥ sūryakiraṇasamparkat jyotsnā nāsti. Sahasrakamalaṃ tu jyotsnāmaya eva lokaḥ. Tatra sthitaścandro nityakalā yuktah . . . kalā sādākhyā.*" *LD* 32, pp. 85-86; and "*Tacca jyotsnāmayo lokaḥ. Tatratyaścandrama nityakalaḥ.*" *LD* 14, p. 48.
16. ". . . *Baindavasthānaṃ sudhāsindhuḥ saraghā iti bahudhā prapañcitaṃ pūrvameva.*" *LD* 41, p. 117; "*Sahasrakamalaṃ bindvatītaṃ baindavasthānātmakaṃ sudhāsindhvaparaparyāyaṃ sarghāśabdavācyam.*" *LD* 41, p. 120 ; ". . . *śirassthitaṃ candramaṇḍalaṃ sarvayogaśāstraprasiddham. Tattu samayināṃ mate śrīcakrameva.*" *LD* 10, pp. 23-24; and ". . . *Baindavāparaparyāya-saraghāśabdavācya-sudhāsindhau śivaśaktyor melanam iti.*" *LD* 92, p. 186.
17. "*Idam atrānusandheyaṃ–śrīvidyāyāḥ candrakalāvidyāparanāmadheyāyāḥ pañcadaśatithirūpatvāt ṣaṣṭyuttaratriśataṃ mayūkhāḥ divasātmakāḥ, tena samvatsaro lakṣyate. Tasya kālaśaktyātmakasya saṃvatsarasya prajāpatirūpatvāt, prajāpateḥ jagatkartṛtvāt, marīcīnāṃ jagadutpattilayakaratvam.*" *LD* 14, p. 49.
18. ". . . *Sūryacandrāgnayaḥ bhagavatīpādārabindodbhūtānanta koṭikiraṇamadhye katipayān kiraṇānāhṛtya bhagavatīprasādasamāsādita jagatprakāśanasāmarthyāt jaganti prakāśayanti. Ataśca sarvalokātikrāntaṃ candrakalācakraṃ baindavasthānam iti.*" Ibid.
19. "*Atredam anusandheyam ādharasvādhiṣṭhānamaṇipurānāhataviśuddhyājñā-cakrātmakam śrīcakram trikhaṇḍam somasūryānalātamakam. Maṇipūra svādhiṣṭhānacakradvayam ekaṃ khaṇḍam. Maṇipūrānāhatacakradvayam ekaṃ*

khaṇḍam. Viśudhyājñācakradvyam ekaṃ khaṇḍam . . . ādharackare mahītattvātmake vahneḥ ṣaṭpañāśajjvālāḥ . . ." *LD* 14, pp. 47-48.

20. *"Parā trikoṇātmikā paśyantī aṣṭakoṇarūpini . . . kalāh pañcāśat, ṣaṣṭyuttaratriśatasaṅkhyakā vā."* *LD* 41, pp. 119-120.
21. *". . . pañcāśadvarṇātmaka-ṣaṣṭyuttara triśatasaṅkhyāparigaṇitamahākālātmaka-pañcadaśakalātītā sādākhyā śrīvidyāparaparyāyā citkalāśabdavācyā brahmavidyāparaparyāyā bhagavatī nādabindukalātītaṃ bhāgavataṃ tattvam iti tattvavidrahasyam."* Ibid., p. 120.
22. In Tāntric literature the terms *nāda, bindu,* and *kalā* are used in a variety of ways. *Nāda* usually refers to unarticulated primordial sound, which manifests in three stages, *paśyantī, madhyamā,* and *vaikharī.* It is also the potentiality of *śabdabrahman. Bindu* means "drop." It refers to the concentrated or condensed state of energy, the foundational energy from which the empirical world emerges. *Bindu* is the central point in *śrīcakra.* In the Gorakṣanātha school, it also means "mercury, sexual energy, and a mystical state of meditation which a *yogi* penetrates before reaching the *sahasrāra. Kalā* refers to the power of particularization, delimitation, or the capacity of the nondual *śakti* to assume many forms. For details, see Padoux, *Vāc,* pp. 89-124 and Brooks, *Three Cities,* pp. 248-249.
23. *". . . bhidyamānāt parād bindoravyaktātmā ravo' bhavat." ST,* 1:11; *"Śabdabrahmeti taṃ prāhuḥ sarvāgamaviśāradāḥ . . ." ST,* 1:12; *". . . caitanyaṃ sarvabhūtānām śabdabrahmeti me matiḥ." ST,* 1:13; *"Sarvadevamayī devī sarvamantramayī śivā. Sarvatattvamayī sākṣāt sūkṣmātsūkṣmatarā bibhuḥ." ST,* 1:55; *"Tridhāmajananī devī śabdabrahmasvarūpiṇī. Dvicatvāriṃśad varṇātma pañcāśadvarṇarūpiṇī." ST* 1:56; *"Guṇitā sarvagātreṣu kuṇḍalī paradevatā. Viśvātamnā prabhuddhā sā sūte mantramayam jagat." ST,* 1:57; *"Sā prasūte kuṇḍalinī śabdabrahmamayī vibhuḥ." ST,* 1:111); and *". . . krameṇānena sṛjati kuṇḍalinī varṇamālikām." ST,* 1:113.
24. "*Śabdabrahma param brahma śabdāstiṣṭhanti tatra vai...śaktiḥ sarveṣu deveṣu devīṣu ca śucismite.*" *Bhūtaśuddhi Tantra,* in *TS-III,* ed. Rāmaprasāda Tripāṭhī. Yogatantra-Granthamālā,

vol. 6. (Varanasi: Sampurnananda Sanskrit Vishvavidyalaya, 1979), 3:46-48.

25. "... *mahākālī paramātma caṇakāra rūpataḥ ... hartapādādi rahita candrasūryāgnirūpiṇī.*" *Nirvana Tantra* in *TS-II*, 10:26-53.

26. *Toḍalatantra* in *TS-II*, 2:2-14, 8:11-22; *Kāmadhenu Tantra* in *TS-II*, 1:7-10, 8:6-23, and 10:25, 27, 30; *Vātulaśuddhākhya Tantra* in *Tantrasaṅgraha, Part 1* (hereafter cited as *TS-I*), ed. Gopinatha Kavirāja, Yogatantra-Granthamālā, vol. 3 (Varanasi: Varanaseya Sanskrit Vishvavidyalaya, 1970), 3:1-3 and 5:2, *Anubhavasūtra* in *TS-I*, 6:44-56; *Virūpākṣapañcāśikā* in *TS-I*, 21; Durvāsas, *Tripurasundarīmahimnastotra*, found in app. 1 of Awasthi, *MMR*, 6, 27-28; Kālidāsa, *Laghustuti* in Ibid., 1-2, 15-16; Kālidāsa, *Carcāstuti* in Ibid., 16-17; Kālidāsa, *Ambāstuti* in Ibid., 3, 6, 18-20, and 25-27; Kālidāsa, *Sakalajananīstava* in Ibid., 7-19, 26-28, and 34-35; Dīpakanātha, *Tripurasundarīdaṇḍaka* in the app. of *NS*, 1 and 26; Sīvānanda, *Saubhāgyahṛdayastotra* in Ibid., 3-5; *Saubhāgyasudhodaya* in Ibid.; *NS* 1:1-13; *YH* 1:13; *KKV* 8-25; and *VR* 1:5, 32-36, 2:83-109.

27. Sastri, *Philosophy of Word and Meaning*, pp. 29-37 and 62-65.

28. "*Nādaḥ parāpaśyantīmadhyamāvaikharīrūpeṇa caturvidhaḥ iti prāgevoktam.*" *LD* 41, p. 119.

29. "*Nādātītatattvaṃ tu tripurasundaryādiśabdābhidheyam ...*" Ibid.

30. "*Asyārthaḥ ye mayūkhāḥ ṣaṣṭhyuttaratriśatasaṅkhyākaḥ śarīrāṇi kālātmakāni ṣaṣṭyuttaratriśatasaṅkhyākāni dināni, tānyeva saṃvatsaraḥ, saṃvatsaro vai prajāpatiḥ iti śruteḥ.*" *LD* 11, p 37; "*Tasya kālaśaktyātmakasya saṃvatsarasya prajāpatirūpatvāt, prajāpateḥ jagatkartṛtvāt, marīcīnām jagadutpatti-stiti layakaratvam. Te ca marīcayaḥ asmin brahmāṇḍe piṇḍāṇḍe ca ṣaṣṭhyuttara saṅkhyākāḥ ... ataśca sarvalokātikrāntaṃ candrakalācakraṃ baindvasthānam iti.*" *LD* 14, p. 49; and "... *Ṣaṭṣyuttara-triśatasaṅkhyā-parigaṇita-mahākālātmaka-pañcadaśakalāt ītā sādākhyā śrīvidyā ...*" *LD* 41, p. 120.

31. "... *śivaśabdena navayonicakramadhye caturyonyātmakam ardhacakram ucyate. Śaktiśabdena avaśiṣṭaṃ pañcayonyātmakam ardhacakram ucyate.*" *LD* 1, p. 3.

32. "... *etasmāccakrādeva jagadutpatti-sthiti layā bhavanti*..." Ibid.
33. "... *iti siddhānuvādaḥ na tvāropastutiḥ*..." *LD* 14, p. 49.
34. In commenting on *SL* 11, Lakṣmīdhara gives various methods of drawing *śrīcakra*. The first one is called *saṃhārakrama*, "the order of dissolution or withdrawal." According to this order, the *śrīcakra* is drawn from the outer to the inner, i.e., first one draws the outer circle and then the other progressively more internal *cakras*. Another method is called *sṛṣṭikrama*, "the order of creation." According to this method, *śrīcakra* is drawn from the inner to the outer, from the subtle to the gross. According to Lakṣmīdhara, Samayins worship the *śrīcakra* of *sṛṣṭikrama*.
35. *SL* 11 and *LD* 11.
36. "... *Trikoṇāṣṭakoṇadaśakoṇayugala-caturdaśakoṇātmakāni śakticakrāṇi. Aṣṭadalaṣoḍaśadala-mekhalātrayabhūpura-trayātmakāni catvāri śivacakrāṇi.*" *LD* 11, p. 31.
37. "*Ityādau śakticakrāṇi trikoṇāṣṭakoṇa-daśāradvitaya-caturdaśakoṇātmakāni pañcacakrāṇi. Śivacakrāṇi tu aṣṭadalaṣoḍaśadalamekhalātritaya-bhūpura-trayāmkāni. Ataḥ śakticakrāṇām bāhyataḥ śivacakrāṇi. Śivasya bāhyatvāyogāt tāni śivacakrāṇi bindurūpeṇākṛṣya śakticakrāntare sthāpitāni. Ata eva binduḥ śivacakracatuṣṭayātmakaḥ śakticakreṣu pañcasu vyaśnuvānaḥ samāpataḥ iti śivaṣaktyoraikam iti kecit.*" *LD* 9, p. 21.
38. "*Anye tu bindutrikoṇayoraikaṃ, aṣṭakoṇāṣṭadalāmbujayoḥ, daśārayugmaṣoḍaśadalāmbujayoḥ, caturdaśārabhūpurayoraikaṃ, anena prakāreṇa śivaśaktyoraikamāhuḥ.*" Ibid.
39. "*Ataśca trikoṇam ādhāraḥ, aṣṭakoṇaṃ svādhiṣṭhānaṃ, daśāraṃ maṇipūram, dvitīyadaśāram anāhataṃ, caturdaśāraṃ viśuddhicakraṃ, śivacakracatuṣṭayam ājñācakraṃ, bindusthānaṃ caturasraṃ sahasrakamalaṃ iti siddham.*" *LD* 32, p. 86.
40. "*Akule viṣusajñe ca śākte vahnau tathā punaḥ. Nābhāvanāhate śuddhe lambikāgre bhruvo'ntare.*" *YH* 1:25; and "... *Akulādiṣu purvoktasthāneṣu paricintayet. Cakreśvarīsamāyuktaṃ navacakraṃ puroditam*..." *YH* 2:8. Also see Amṛtānanda's *Dipikā* and Bhāskararāya's *Setubandha* on these verses of *YH*.

According to *Gautamīya Tantra,* these additional *cakras* are known as *kailāsa* and *rodhinī* and are located above the *ājñā cakra*: "*Dvidalaṃ hasadvyakṣarasaṃ-yuktaṃ paṅkajaṃ sumanoharam. Kailāsākhyaṃ tadūrddhe tu rodhinī tu tadūrddhataḥ.*" Maharshi Gautama, *Gautamiyatantram,* ed. Bhagiratha Jha, Krishnadas Prachyavidya Granthamala, 5 (Varanasi: Chowkhamba Sanskrit Series Office, 1977), 32:56.

41. *"Nava yonayo navadhātvātmakāḥ. Tathā coktaṃ kāmikāyam–tvagasṛṅmāṃsa-medosthidhātavaḥ śaktimūlakāḥ.*
Majjāśuklaprāṇajīvadhātavaḥ śivamūlakāḥ.
Navadhāturayaṃ deho navayonisamudbhavaḥ.
Daśamī yonirekaiva parā śaktistadīśvarī. Iti
Daśamo yoniḥ baindavasthānam, tadīśvarī tasya dehasyetyarthaḥ." LD 11, p. 27.
42. The description of the deities in various *cakras* given in the present work is based on *LD* 11, 17, 31, and 32, and *Bhāvanopaniṣat* with Bhāskararāya's commentary.
43. The particular formation of *śrīcakra* in which the *bindu* is surrounded by a square instead of being surrounded by the central triangle belongs to the variation of *sṛṣṭikrama* of *śrīcakra* accepted by the *samayācārins,* as Lakṣmīdhara claims. According to the most popular variations of *śrīcakra*, the *bindu* is located inside the central triangle. In accepting this particular variation, Lakṣmīdhara is clearly establishing the supremacy of *śakti* by stating that "all *śiva cakras* are extracted and placed in the *bindu.*" See *LD* 9, p. 21 and *LD* 32, p. 86.

   See also Brooks, *Three Cities,* "Appendix: The Cakras of the Body and the Śrīcakra."
44. The three most famous variations of the *śrīvidyā* mantra—*known as kādividyā, hādividyā,* and *sādividyā*—all consist of fifteen letters. They begin with the letters *ka, ha,* and *sa,* from which they derive their names. In addition, there are variations of the *śrīvidyā* mantra named after the person first practicing them: Munūpāsitā, Candropāsitā, Kubreropāsitā, Lopāmudropāsitā, Manmathopāsitā, Agstyopāsitā, Nandikeśopāsitā, Śūryopāsitā, Viṣṇūpāsitā, Ṣaṇmukopāsitā, Śivopāsitā, and Durvāsasopāsitā. Some of these mantras con-

sist of fifteen, seventeen, eighteen, twenty-two, twenty-eight, and thirty-two letters and are also named accordingly—*pañcadaśākṣarī, saptadaśākṣarī*, and *aṣṭādaśakṣarī*, etc. *PSS*, pp. 222-229.

45. See chap. 2, n. 1.
46. *"Pūrṇodayamatānusāreṇa tu–somasūryānalātmakatayā cakrasya trikhaṇḍatvaṃ evaṃ mantrasyāpi trikhaṇḍatvaṃ suprasiddham. Candrasya kalāḥ ṣoḍaśa indukhaṇḍe antarbhūtah." LD* 32, pp. 87-88.

    "Atredam anusandheyam–śivaḥ śaktiḥ kāmaḥ kṣitiriti varṇacatuṣṭayam āgneyaṃ khaṇḍam. Raviḥ śītakiranaḥ smaraḥ haṃsaḥ śakra iti varṇapañcakaṃ sauraṃ khaṇḍam. Ubhayoḥ kaṇḍayoḥ madhye rudrasthānīyaṃ hṛllekhābījam. Parāmāraharaya iti varṇatrayeṇa saumyaṃ khaṇḍaṃ nirupitam. Saumyasaurakhaṇḍayor madhye viṣṇugranthistnānīyaṃ bhuvaneśvarībījam." LD 32, pp. 81-82.
47. *"Turīyam ekākṣaraṃ candrakalākhaṇḍam. Saumyacanrakalākaṇḍayor madhye brahmasthānīyaṃ hṛllekhābījam." LD* 32, p. 82. *". . . eko varṇaḥ ṣoḍaśakalātmakaḥ pradhānabhūta iti . . ."* Ibid.
48. *". . . evam mantreṇa sarvā mātṛkāh ṁsaṅgṛhitā iti." LD* 32, p. 87.
49. *"Etāḥ pañcāśatakalāḥ pañcāśadvarṇātmakāḥ pañcadaśākṣarīmantre antarbhūtāh." LD* 32, p. 86.
50. *"Tathā hi–ṣoḍaśasvarāḥ kādayaḥ tāntāḥ ṣoḍaśa, thādayaḥ sāntāśca ṣoḍaśa. ṣoḍaśatrikaṃ ṣoḍaśanityāsu antarbhūtam. Hakāraḥ ākāśabījaṃ baindavasthāne nilīnam. Lakāraḥ antasthāsvantarbhūto'pi kakāreṇa pratyāhārārthaṃ punargṛhītaḥ. Kṣakārastu kakārasakārasamudāyarūpatvāt. Kakārādayaḥ sāntāḥ ṣoḍaśanityāsu antarbhūtāḥ svarasahitāḥ." LD* 32, p. 87.
51. *"Akāreṇa pratyāhṛtaḥ kṣakāraḥ akṣamāleti gīyate. Ataḥ kṣakāreṇa sarvā mātṛkāḥ saṅgṛhītāḥ bhavanti."* Ibid.
52. *"Ata eva antimakhaṇḍe sakalahrīm iti kakāralakārayoryoge kalāśabdaniṣpattiḥ, kaṣayoryoge kṣakāraniṣpattiriti, evaṃ mantreṇa sarvā mātṛkāḥ saṅgṛhītā iti tātparyam."* Ibid.
53. *"Ataśca ṣoḍaśanityānām mantragata-ṣoḍaśavarnātmakatvaṃ, ṣoḍaśavarṇānāṃ pañcāśadvarṇātmakatvaṃ, pañcāśadvarṇānāṃ sūryacandrāgnikalātmakatvaṃ sūryacandrāgnirūpeṇa trikhaṇḍm iti aikyacatuṣṭayam anusand-*

heyam." Ibid.

54. "*Evaṃ cakramantrayorapi. Yathā hrīṅkāratryaṃ śrībījaṃ ca śivacakracatuṣṭayātmakatrikoṇe bindurūpeṇa antarbhūtam. Sakaleti varṇatrayeṇa saṅgṛhītamātṛkā, akṣamālātmikā, mātṛkā ubhayamapi yathāyogaṃ cakre antarbhūtam. Tathāhi–antasthāścatvāraḥ, ūṣmāṇaścatvāraḥ–evamaṣṭau varṇāḥ vargapañcamān vihāya daśārayugme antarbhūtāḥ. Vargapañcamāstu anusvārarūpeṇa bindāvantarbhūtāḥ. Caturdaśāre caturdaśasvarā antarbhūtāḥ. Anusvāravisargayoḥ bindāvanrbhāvaḥ.*" Ibid.
55. "*Tāstu viśuddhicakre ṣoḍaśāre prāgādikrameṇa ṣoḍaśadikṣu paribhramanti.*" *LD* 32, p. 89.
56. This particular description is based on *LD* 32, pp. 87-89, and represents the view of Samayācārins who draw and worship *śrīcakra* in *sṛṣṭikrama*. In *LD* 31, however, Lakṣmīdhara explains the specific ways of demonstrating the oneness of *nityākalās*, the *tithis* of the fortnights, with *śrīcakra* and the *śrīvidyā* mantra when *śrīcakra* is drawn and worshipped in three other ways: *meruprastāra*, *kailāsaprastāra*, and *bhūprastāra*.

    For details, see: "*Idānīṃ ṣoḍaśanityānām śrīcakre aṅgatayā antarbhāvo nirūpyate . . . ityādiśloka-vyākhyānāvasare kathitāni.*" *LD* 31, pp. 79-80.
57. "*Ata eva darśādikalānāṃ trikhaṇḍatvaṃ spaṣṭam. Darśā dṛṣṭā darśatā viśvarūpā sudarśanā–eṣa āgneyaḥ khaṇḍaḥ. Āpyāyamānā āpyāyamānā āpyāyā sūnṛtā irā–eṣa sauraḥ khaṇḍaḥ. Āpūryamāṇā āpūryamāṇā pūrayantī pūrṇā paurṇamāsīti–eṣa cāndraḥ khaṇḍaḥ tṛtīyo nirūpitaḥ.*" *LD* 32, pp. 88-89.
58. "*Darśā kalā śivatattvātmikā. Dṛṣṭā kalā śaktitattvātmikā. Darśatā kalā māyātattvātmikā. Viśvarūpā kalā śuddhavidyātattvātmikā. Sudarśanā kalā jalatattvāmikā. . . . nityākalā sādākhyātattvātmikā.*" *LD* 32, p. 89. While describing the nature of *ṣoḍaśī*, the sixteenth *kalā*, in the beginning of the paragraph, Lakṣmīdhara states: "*ṣoḍaśyāḥ cidrūpātmikāyāḥ kalāyāḥ sādākhya-tattvarūpatvāt adhidevatāntaraṃ nāsti.*" *LD* 32, p. 88.
59. "*Āpūryamāṇāyāḥ kalāyāḥ candrakhaṇḍāntssthitāyā api saurakhaṇḍe antarbhāvaḥ. Irākalāprabhedatvāt*

irāpūryamāṇyoḥ aikyam iti anusandheyam." Ibid., p. 89.

60. *"Stāstu viśuddhicakre ṣoḍaśāre prāgādikrameṇa ṣoḍaśadikṣu paribhramanti." LD* 32, p. 89.

61. *"Pūrṇodayamatānusāreṇa tu–somasūryānalātmakatayā cakrasya trikhaṇḍatvaṃ evaṃ mantrasyāpi trikhaṇḍatvaṃ suprasiddham. Candrasya kalāḥ ṣoḍaśa indukhaṇḍe antarbhūtah." LD* 32, pp. 87-88.

"Atredam anusandheyam–śivaḥ śaktiḥ kāmaḥ kṣitiriti varṇacatuṣṭayam āgneyaṃ khaṇḍam. Raviḥ śītakiranaḥ smaraḥ haṃsaḥ śakra iti varṇapañcakaṃ sauraṃ khaṇḍam. Ubhayoḥ kaṇḍayoḥ madhye rudrasthānīyaṃ hṛllekhābījam. Parāmāraharaya iti varṇatrayeṇa saumyaṃ khaṇḍaṃ nirupitam. Saumyasaurakhaṇḍayor madhye viṣṇugranthistnānīyaṃ bhuvaneśvarībījam." LD 32, pp. 81-82.

62. *"Ājñācakragatacandre pañcadaśakalāḥ pratiphalanañca."* Ibid., p. 86.

63. *"Śrīcakrarūpacandrabimbe ekaiva kalā sā paramākalā . . . sādākhyākalā śrīvidyāparaparyāya nāda bindukalātī tā."* Ibid.

64. *"Bindusthānaṃ sudhāsindhuḥ pañcayonyaḥ suradrumāḥ.*
Tatraiva nīpaśreṇī ca tanmadhye maṇimaṇḍapam.
Tatra cintāmaṇikṛtaṃ devyā mandiram uttamam.
Śivātmake mahāmañce maheśanopabarhaṇe.
Atiramyatare tatra kaśipuśca sadāśivaḥ.
Bhṛtakāśca catuṣpādā mahendraśca patadgrahaḥ."
LD 8, p. 16.

65. *"Pāśāṅkuśau tadīyau tu rāgdveṣātmakau smṛtau.*
Śabdaśparśādayo bānāḥ manastasyābhavaddhanuḥ.
Karaṇendriyacakrasthām devīṃ saṃvit svarūpiṇim . . ."
LD 41, p. 124.

66. *". . . śivārkamaṇḍalaṃ bhittvā drāvyantīndumaṇḍalam.*
Tadudbhūtāmṛta-syandi-paramānandananditā.
Kulayoṣit kulaṃ tyaktvā paraṃ varṣaṇam etya sā.
Iti bhairavayāmale vāmakeśvaramahātantre."
LD 8, p. 16.

67. Brown, *SL* 10.

68. *"Atha ca suṣṭhu rājate prakāśata iti suro jīvaḥ; sa eva viṭapī, āpādamastakaṃ vistīrya vartamānatvāt tasya vāṭyā veṣṭanena parito vṛte dhṛte; tadabhāve dehasthityabhāvāt. Kiñca maṇimayā maṇivatprakāśamānāḥ dvīpāḥ devatānivāsa-*

sthānatvād dvīpatulyā mūlādhārādisthānaviśeṣāḥ . . . Nayanti śarIīaṃ gamanāgama-navyāpārairiti nīpaḥ prānāpānavyānodānasamānākhyā mukhyaprānāḥ, nāgakūrmakṛkaradevadattadhanañjayopaprāṇāśca; nitarām pāti śarīram iti vā nīpaḥ purvoktā indriyādhiṣṭhānadevatāśca . . ." *Aruṇāmodinī* on *SL* 8 in *Saundaryalaharī*, ed. A. Kuppuswami.

69. *"Śṛṣṭicakraṃ sudhāsindhuḥ saubhāgyaṃ suravāṭikā. Daśārayugalaṃ ratnadvīpaṃ nīpavanaṃ tathā. Cintāmaṇigṛhaṃ ramyam aṣṭāram parameśvari. Trikoṇaṃ mañcarūpaṃ tu bindukaṃ tu sadāśivaḥ."* Narasiṃhasvāmin, *Gopālasundarī*, on *SL* 8, in *Saundaryalaharī*, ed. A. Kuppuswami.
70. *". . . pretāḥ prakarṣeṇa itāḥ devīśarīra-saṃsargātiśayaṃ prāptāḥ."* *Ānandalaharī Tīkā* on *SL* 8 in *Saundaryalaharī*, ed. A. Kuppuswami.
71. *"Iyam upāsanā. Vidhiḥ kriyātmako nādaraṇīyaḥ."* *LD* 41, p. 124.
72. *"Evaṃ samayamataṃ samyak prapañcya samayāyāḥ bhagavatyāḥ kirīṭaprabhṛti pādāntaṃ varṇayati . . ."* Ibid..
73. "*Gaṇeśagrahanakṣatrayoginīrāśirūpiṇīm. Devīm mantramayīm naumi mātṛkām pītharūpiṇim.*" *NS* 1:1; also see *YH* 2:57-68; and *YKU* 1:81, 2:49, 3:13, and 3:22.
74. "*Yadā candrārkau nijasadanasaṃrodhanavaśād aśaktau pīyūṣasravaṇa haraṇe sā ca bhujagi. Prabuddhā kṣutkruddhā daśati śaśinam baindavagatam sudhādhārāsāraiḥ snapayasi tanum baindavakale.*" *SU* 4; and "*idam kālotpattisthitilayakaram padmanikarm trikhandam śrīcakram . . . śāstramuditam,*" *SU* 50; also see *YH* 2:69-72; and *YKU* 1:67-86, 2:42-49, 3:1-35.
75. "*. . . tathā mantraḥ samastāśca vidyāyāmatrasaṃsthitaḥ . . . śivagurvātmanām aikyānusandhānāt tadātmakam . . . ittham mantrātmakam cakram devatāyāḥ param vapuḥ.*" *YH* 2:47-56; also see *KKV* 8 and 15-17; *SU* 4, 10-13, 38, and 50.
76. *"Bhavāni tvam vande bhavamahiṣi saccitvapuḥ parākārām devīm amṛtalaharīm aindavakalām . . . mahākālātītām kalitasaraṇīkalpitatanum sudhāsindhorantarvasatim aniśam vāsaramayīm."* *SU* 1; *"Kumarī yanmandram dhvanati ca tato yoṣid apara kulam tyaktvā rauti sphuṭati ca mahākālabhujagī . . ."* *SU* 6; *"Śatam cāṣṭau vahneḥ śatamapi kalāḥ*

ṣoḍaśaraveḥ . . . mahākaulestasmānna hi tava śive kālakalanā." *SU* 9; also see *KKV* 17; and *NS* 1:1.

77. "*Evam bindukalā jñeyā nādaśaktyātmikāśca yaḥ. Vyāpinyādyātmikā yāśca vyāpyavyāpakabhedataḥ . . . Tasminyuktaḥ pare tattve sārvajñyādiguṇānvitaḥ. Śiva eko bhaveddevi avibhagena sarvataḥ.*" *SVT* 4:245-402; see also 5:56-86.
78. "*Tanmadhyagataśivatattvaṃ nāda ityucyate.*" *LD* 99, p. 197.
79. "*. . . nāde vācyaḥ sadāśivaḥ . . .*" *SVT* 4:265.
80. "*...mūrdhvam devaḥ sadāśivaḥ. Tattvadvrayasamāyukto yāvadbrahambilam gatah . . . Unmanā tataḥ. Tatparam tu param tattvam pramāṇaparivarjitam.*" *SVT* 4:346-348.
81. "*Pradhānā daśa yaḥ proktā nāḍyaśca varānane. Tāsām madhye tu deveśi vāyavo ye vyavasthitaḥ . . .*" *SVT* 7:13-158.
82. *NT* chaps. 7 and 8.
83. "*. . . nirodhikāmimām bhitvā sadākhyam bhuvanam param . . .*
Nādaḥ suṣumnādhārastu bhitvā viśvamidam jagat.
Adhaḥ śaktayā vinirgacchedūrvaśaktyā ca mūrdhataḥ.
Nādyā brahmabile līnaḥ . . .
. . . tām bhitvā codharvakuṇdalī.
Śaktiḥ suptāhisadṛśī sā viśvādhāra ucyate . . .
. . . iti ṣodaśabhuvaneyam tattvayugam śāntyatītā syāt."
TĀ 8:386-427.
84. Ibid.
85. "*Nirodhikāmimām bhitvā sādākhyam bhuvanaṃ paraṃ.*" Ibid., 8:386.
86. "*Suṣumnordhve brahmabila samjñāvaraṇam tridṛk.*
Tatra brahmā sitaḥ śūlī pañcāsyaḥ śaśiśekharaḥ.
Tasyotasaṇge parā devī brahmāṇī mokṣamārgagā.
Roddhrī dātrī ca mokṣasya tām bhitvā cordhvakuṇḍalī."
TĀ 8:394-395.
87. "*. . . śabdarāśirmālinī ca śiva śaktyātmakam tvidam.*" *TĀ* 15:133; "*Māyottīrṇam hi yadrūpam brahmādīnām puroditam. Āsanam tvetadeva syānnatu māyāñjanāñjitam . . . Sadāśivam mahāpretam mūrtim sārdhrākṣarām yajet. Paratvena parāmūrdhve gandhapuṣpādibhistviti.*" *TĀ* 15:308-322; "*. . . madhyagā kila yā devī saiva sadbhāvarūpiṇī. Kālasaṇkarṣiṇī ghorā. . . . Parā tu mātṛkā devī mālinī mad-*

hyagoditā. Madhye nyasyetsūryarucim sarvākṣaramayīm-parām." *TĀ* 15:331-333; *"Kuṇḍam śaktiḥ śivo liñgam melakam paramam padam. . . . Madhyasthanālagumphitasarojayugaghaṭṭanakramādagnau. Madhyasthapūrṇa sundaraśaśadharadinakarakālaughasañghaṭṭāt."* *TĀ* 29:141-152;

"Deha eva param liṇgam sarvatattvātmakam śivam.
Devatācakrasañjuṣtam pūjādhāma taduttamam.
Tadeva maṇḍalam mukhyam tritriśūlābjacakrakham.
Tatraiva devatā cakram bahirantaḥ sadā yajet."
TĀ 29:171-172.

88. *Lakṣmī-Tantra: A Pāñcarātra Āgama* (hereafter cited as *LT*), ed. and introduction by V. Krishnamacharya (Adyar: Adyar Library and Research Centre, 1959).
89. *"Tadevam paramonmeṣarūpāham vitatodayā. Icchajñānakriyārūpā pañcakṛtyakarī vibhoḥ."* *LT* 27:14.
90. *"Mahārājñī tathaivāham anayaiva trayīparā. Ṛgyajuḥsāmasaṅghāte cintye saure ca maṇḍale."* *LT* 25:42.
91. *"Hṛllekhā paramātmasthā yā śaktirbhuvaneśvarī. Cicchaktiḥ śāntirūpā ca ghoṣaṇī ghoṣa sambhavā."* *LT* 25:46.
92. *"Mūlabhūtām parāhantām viṣṇostaddharmadharmiṇīm. Sarvaśaktimayīm tāṃ māṃ śakticakrasya nāyikām. Prakāśānandayor antaranusyūtam anusmaret. Agniṣomadvayāntaḥsthām madhyamārgānuvartinīm."* *LT* 45:99-100.
93. *"Catasro dhāraṇā jñeyāsta etāstattvakovidaiḥ. Śādikṣāntam tu vijñeyam viśuddham brahmapañcakam."* *LT* 19:16; also see 28-32; 23:45; 32:36, 44, and 60; 35:33, 45, and 70; and 40:5-6.
94. *"Śubhairvarṇamayaiḥ padmairagnīṣomamayaiḥ kṛtām. Bibhratīm vanamālāñca kaṇṭhātpādāvalambinīṃ."* *LT* 23:28.
95. *"Kuryād vikasitañcaiva mudraiṣā balaṣudana. Mahāyonyabhidhāna ca trilokajananī parā."* *LT* 45:110.
96. *Lakṣmī Tantra: A Pāñcarātra Text,* trans. and notes by Sanjukta Gupta, Orientalia Rheno-Traiectina, vol. 60, ed. J. Gonda and H. W. Obbink (Leiden: E. J. Brill, 1972), xxii.
97. Ibid., xxv.
98. Ibid.
99. "*. . . divi somo adhiśritaḥ.*
Somenādityāḥ balinaḥ somena pṛthivī mahī.
Atho nakṣatrāṇām eṣām upasthe soma āhitaḥ.

Somaṃ manyate papivān yatsampiṃṣantyoṣadhim. ṣomaṃ yaṃ brāhmaṇo vidurna tasyāśnāti kaścana." *Ṛ*V 10:85:1-3.

100. *"Yattvā deva prapibanti tata āpyāyase punaḥ. Vāyuḥ somasya rakṣitā samānāṃ māsa ākṛtiḥ."* *ṚV* 10:85:5.

101. *"Yasmānna jātaḥ paro anyo asti ya āviveśa bhuvanāni trīṇi jyotīṣiṃsacate sa ṣoḍaśī." Mūla-Yajurveda Saṃhitā*, ed. Siddheśvara Bhaṭṭācārya. Banaras Hindu University, Sanskrit Series, vol. 8 (Varanasi: Banaras Hindu University, 1973) 37:9:9.

102. *"Kālo aśvo vahati saptaraśmiḥ sahasrākṣo ajaro bhūmiretāh.*
Tamārohanti kavayo vipaścitas tasya cakrā bhuvanāni viśvā.
Sapta cakrān vahati kāla eṣa saptāsya nābhīramṛtaṃ nvakṣaḥ.
Sa imā viśvā bhuvanānyañjayat kālaḥ sa īyate prathamo nu devah." The Atharvaveda 19:53:1-2.
"Kāle tapaḥ kāle jyeṣtham kāle brahma samāhitam.
Kālo hi sarvasyeśvaro yaḥ pitāsītprajāpateḥ."
The Atharvaveda 19:53:8.
For details, see *The Atharvaveda* 19:53:1-8 and 19:54:1-5.

103. "*Tasmācchūdro yajñe anavakḷptaḥ*" quoted in *LD* 11, p. 42; *"Tadeṣābhyuktā apāṃ rasamudayaṃṁsan sūrye śukram sanābhṛtam apām rasaya yo rasaḥ. Tam vo gṛhṇāmyuttamam.*" quoted in *LD* 40, p. 114; and *"Tasmadrudraḥ paśūnām adhipatiḥ."* quoted in *LD* 99, p. 195.

104. *"Lokasya dvāram arcimatpavitram jyotiṣmadbhrājamānam mahasvat. Amṛtasya dhārā bahudhā dohamānam caraṇam no loke sudhitām dadhātu."* quoted in *LD* 10, p. 25; *"Saṃvatsaro vai prajāpatiḥ,ṁ*" quoted in *LD* 11, p.37; and *"Ayañca lokasya dvāram arcimat pavitram*" quoted in LD 14, p. 49.

105. "*Brahmā śivo me astu sadāśivom*" is quoted in *LD* 11, p. 40; "*Tasmad vā estasmādātmana ākāśasambhūtaḥ.*" quoted in *LD* 37, p. 108; and "*Ātmana ākāśaḥ sambhūtaḥ ākāśād vāyuḥ vāyoragniḥ agnerāpaḥ adbhyaḥ pṛthivī*" is quoted in *LD* 41, p. 123.

106. The ten mantras that constitute the *Sarasvatīrahasya Upaniṣad* are taken from *ṚV* 6:61:4; 5:43:11; 1:3:10-12; 1:164:45; 8:100:10-11; 10:71:4;, and 2:41:16.

107. *ṚV* 10:125:1-8.

108. *Ṛ V* Khailikāni Sūktāni 8:1-29.
109. "*Satyenottabhitā bhūmiḥ sūryeṇottabhitā dauḥ.*
Ṛtenādityāstiṣṭhanti divi somo adhi śritaḥ.
Somenādityā balinaḥ somena pṛthivī mahī.
Atho nakṣkatrāṇāmeṣām upasthe soma āhitaḥ.
Somam manyate papivān yatsampiṣamtyoṣadhim.
Somam yam brāhmaṇo vidurna tasyāśnāti kaścana.
Ācchdvidhanairgupito bārhataiḥ soma rakṣhitaḥ.
Grāvṇāmicchṛṇvantiṣṭhasina te aśnāti pārthivaḥ.
Yattvā deva prapibamti tata āpyāyase punaḥ.
Yajuḥ somasya rakṣhitā samānām māsa ākṛtiḥ."
Ṛ V 10:85:1-5.
110. "*Yasmin somaḥ surapitṛnarairanvaḥ pīyamānaḥ kṣīṇaḥ kṣīṇaḥ praviśati yato vardhate capi bhūyaḥ. Yasmin vedā madhuni saraghākāravadbhānti cāgre taccāṇḍoṃśoramitamamṛtam maṇḍalastham prapadye.*" *Sāmbapañcāśikā* in *TS-I*, 8, p. 28.

BIBLIOGRAPHY

Abhinavagupta. *Sri Mālinivijaya Vārttikam of Abhinava Gupta.* Edited with notes by Madhusudan Kaul Shastri. Kashmir Series of Texts and Studies, no. 32. Srinagar: Kasmir Pratap Steam Press, 1921.

———. *The Tantrāloka of Abhinavagupta with the Commentary of Jayaratha.* 8 vols, enl. ed. Edited by R. C. Dwivedi and Navjivan Rastogi. Delhi: Motilal Banarsidass, 1987.

———. *Viveka.* Commentary on *Para-Trimśikā.* In *Parā-Trimshikā with Commentary, the Latter by Abhinava Gupta.* Edited with notes by Mukunda Rāma Shāstrī. Kashmir Series of Texts and Studies, no. 18. Bombay: Tatva-Vivechaka Press, 1918.

Allen, Marcus. *Tantra for the West.* Mill Valley, CA: Whatever Publicatons, 1981.

Alper, Harvey Paul. "Abhinavagupta's Concept of Cognitive Power: A Translation of the Jñānaśaktyāhnika of the Īśvarapratyabhijñāvimarśinī with Commentary and Introduction," Ph.D. dissertation, University of Pennsylvania, 1976.

Amṛtānanda. *Cidvilāsāstava.* In the Appendix of *Nityāṣodaśikārṇava with Two Commentaries: Ṛjuvimarśinī by Śīvānanda & Artharatnāvalī by Vidyānanda.* Edited by Vrajavallabha Dviveda. In *Yoga-Tantra-Granthamālā*, vol. 1. Edited by Baladeva Upādhyāya. Varanasi: Varanaseya Sanskrit Vishvavidyalaya, 1968.

———. *Dīpikā.* Commentary on *Yoginī Hṛdaya.* In *Yoginī Hṛdaya with Commentaries: Dīpikā of Amṛtānanda and Setubandha of Bhāskara Rāya.* 2d ed. In *Sarasvatī Bhavana Granthamālā*, vol. 7. Edited by Kshetresachandra Chattopadhyaya. Varanasi: Varanaseya Sanskrit Vishvavidyalaya, 1963.

———. *Saubhāgyasudhodaya*. In the Appendix of *Nityāṣodaśikārṇava*.

Anandagiri. *Ānandagirīyā*. Commentary on the *Saundaryalaharī*. In *Saundaryalaharī of Śrī Śaṅkara Bhagavatpādācārya with Commentaries (in Sanskrit): Lakṣmīdharā, Saubhāgyavardhanī, Aruṇāmodinī, Ānandagirīyā, Tātparyadīpinī, Padārthacandrikā, ḍiṇḍima Bhāṣya, Gopālasundarī and Ānandalaharī Tīkā*. Edited by A. Kuppuswami. Published with the financial assistance from the Ministry of Education and Social Welfare, Government of India. Tiruchirapalli: A. Kuppuswami, 1976.

Ānandavardhana. *Dhvanyāloka of Ānandavardhana*. Foreword by K. R. Srinivasa Iyengar. Translated and edited by K. Krishnamoorthy. Dharwar: Karnatak University, 1974.

Annambhaṭṭa. *Tarkasaṅgraha*. Varanasi: Harikṛṣṇanibandhabhavanam, 1969.

Anubhavasūtra. In *Tantrasaṅgraha, Part I: Virūpāksapañcāśikā, Sambapāñcāśikā, & Tripurāmahimnastotra with Commentries, Spandapradīpikā, Anubhavasūtra & Vātulaśuddhākhyatantra*. Edited by Gopinatha Kaviraja. In *Yogatantra-Granthamālā*, vol. 3. Edited by Badarinath Shukla. Varanasi: Varanaseya Sanskrit Vishvavidyalaya, 1970.

The Atharvaveda. Introduction by M. C. Joshi. Translated by Devi Chand. New Delhi: Munshiram Manoharlal Publishers, 1982.

Awasthi, Shiva Shankara. *Mantra Aur Mātṛkāon kā Rahasya: Significance of Mantras and Mātṛkās According to Tāntrism*. Vidyabhawan Rastrabhasha Granthamala, 95. Varanasi: Chowkhamba Vidyabhawan, 1966.

Beane, Wendell Charles. *Myth, Cult and Symbols in Śākta Hinduism: A Study of the Indian Mother Goddess*. Leiden: E. J. Brill, 1977.

Bhandarkar, R. G. *Vaiṣṇavism Śaivism and Minor Religious*

Systems. Varanasi: Indological Book House, 1965.

Bharati, Agehananda. *The Tantric Tradition*. New York: Samuel Weiser Inc., 1970.

Bharati, Swami Veda. Interview with an acclaimed Śrīvidyā practitioner. Sadhana Mandir, Ram Nagar, Rishikesh, U. P. India

Bhāskararāya [Makhin]. Commentary on *Bhāvanopaniṣat*. In *Saundaryalaharī of Śrī Śaṅkarācārya with the Commentary of Lakṣmīdhara: Bhāvanopaniṣat with the Commentary of Bhāskararāya and Devī Pañcastavi*. 4th rev. ed. Critically edited by N. S. Venkatanathacharya. Oriental Research Institute Series, 114. Mysore: Oriental Research Institute, 1969.

———. Commentary on *Lalitā-Sahasranāman*. In *Lalitā-Sahasranāman with Bhāskararāya's Commentary*. Translated by R. Ananthakrishna Sastry. Adyar: Theosophical Publishing House, 1951.

———. Commentary on *Tripuropaniṣad*. In *Tripurā Mahopaniṣad*. 2d ed. Edited by Ramādatta Śukla. Prayag: Kalyāna Mandir Prakāśana, Saṃvat 2033, n.d.

———. *Setubandha*. Commentary on *Yoginī Hṛdaya*. In *Yoginī Hṛdaya*.

———. *Varivasyā-Rahasya and Its Commentary, Prakāśa*, 4th ed. Edited and translated by Pandit S. Subrahamanya Sastri. Madras: The Adyar Library and Research Centre, 1976.

Bhaṭṭa, Jayanta. *Nyāya-Mañjarī: The Compendium of Indian Speculative Logic*, vol. 1. Translated by Janaki Vallabha Bhattacharyya. Delhi: Motilal Banarsidass, 1978.

Bhaṭṭacārya, Mahādeva Vidyāvāgīśa. *(Ānandalaharī) Tattvabodhinī* (Sanskrit MS 2624, ff.61, Eggling 2524: I:O: 2196, n.d.). India Office Library, London, n.d.

Bhattacharyya, B. *Śaivism and the Phallic World*. 2 vols. New Delhi: Oxford & IBH Publishing Co., 1975.

Bhattacharyya, Gopikamohan. *Studies in Nyāya-Vaiśeṣika*

Theism. Studies, no. 5. Calcutta Sanskrit College Research Series, no. 14. Calcutta: Sanskrit College, 1961.

Bhattacharyya, Narendra Nath. *History of the Śākta Religion*. New Delhi: Munshiram Manoharlal Publishers, 1974.

———. *The Indian Mother Goddess*. 2d ed., rev. & enl. New Delhi: Manohar Book Service, 1977.

Bhaṭṭojidīkshita. *Vaiyākaraṇa Siddhāntakaumudī of Bhaṭṭojidīkshita*. 5th ed. Edited by Gopāla Shastrī Nene. Haridas Sanskrit Series, 11. Varanasi: Chowkhamba Sanskrit Series Office, 1977.

Bhūtaśuddhi Tantra. In *Tantrasaṅgraha, Part III*. Edited by Rāmaprasāda Tripāṭhī. In *Yogatantra-Granthamālā*, vol. 6. Edited by Bhāgīratha Prasāda Tripāṭhī. Varanasi: Sampurnanand Sanskrit Vishvavidyalaya, 1979.

Brahmāṇḍa Purāṇa of Sage Kṛṣṇa Dvaipāyana Vyāsa. Edited by J. L. Shastri. Delhi: Motilal Banarsidass, 1973.

Brahmasūtra-Śānkarabhāsyam with the Commentaries: Bhāṣyaratnaprabhā of Govindānanda, Bhāmatī of Vācaspatimiśra, Nyāya-Nirṇaya of Ānandagiri. Edited by J. L. Shastri. Delhi: Motilal Banarsidass, 1980.

Brooks, Douglas Renfrew. *Auspicious Wisdom: The Texts and Traditions of Śrīvidyā Śākta Tantrism in South India*. Albany: State University of New York Press, 1992.

——— *The Secret of the Three Cities: An Introduction to Hindu Śākta Tantrism*. Chicago: The University of Chicago Press, 1990.

———. "The Srividya School of Sakta Tantrism: A Study of the Texts and Contexts of the Living Traditions in South India." Ph.D. dissertation, Harvard University, 1987.

Chandra, Jagadish. *Dhvaniprasthāna meṃ Ācārya Mammaṭa kā Avadāna*. Banaras Hindu University Sanskrit Series, vol. 11. Edited by Biswanath Bhattacharya. Varanasi: Banaras Hindu University, 1977.

Chemparathy, George. *An Indian Rational Theology: Introduction to Udayana's Nyāyakusumāñjali*. Edited by

George Oberhammer. Publications of the De Nobili Research Library, vol. 1. Vienna: Gerold & Co., 1972.

Cidvilāsāstava. In the Appendix of *Nityāṣodaśikārṇava.*

Clark, J. Desmond; Kenoyer, Jonathan Mark; Pal, J. N.; and Sharma, G. R. "Baghor I: A Possible Upper Paleolithic Shrine in Central India." *Anthro Quest* 25 (Spring, 1983): 13.

Das, Sudhendu Kumar. *Śakti or Divine Power: A Historical Study Based on Original Sanskrit Texts.* Calcutta: University of Calcutta, 1934.

Devyatharva Śīrṣa. In *Durgāsaptaśatī.* Gorakh Pur Bita Press, n.d.

Dīpakanātha. *Tripurasundarīdaṇḍaka.* In the Appendix of *Nityāṣodaśikārṇava.*

Durgāsaptaśatī with Seven Sanskrit Commentaries: Durgāpradīpa, Guptavatī, Caturdharī, Śāntanavī, Nāgojībhaṭṭī, Jagaccandracandrikā, Daṃśoddhāra. Delhi: Butala & Co., 1984.

Durvāsas. *Tripurāsundarīmahimnastotra.* In *Tantrasaṅgraha, Part I.*

Dyczkowski, Mark S. G. *The Canon of the Śaivāgama and the Kubjikā Tantras of the Western Kaula Tradition.* Albany: State University of New York Press, 1988.

———. *The Doctrine of Vibration: An Analysis of the Doctrines and Practices of Kashmir Shaivism.* Albany: State University of New York Press, 1987.

———. *The Stanzas on Vibration.* Albany: State University of New York Press, 1992.

Encyclopedia of Indian Philosophies: Indian Metaphysics and Epistemology: The Tradition of Nyāya-Vaiśeṣika Up to Gaṅgeśa. Edited by Karl H. Potter. Princeton: Princeton University Press, 1977.

The Encyclopedia of Religion. Edited by Mircea Eliade. New York: Macmillan Publishing Co., 1987. S.v. "Gāṇapatyas" by Paul B. Courtright, "Hindu Goddesses" by David Kinsley, "Śaivism in Kashmir" by Alexis

Sanderson.

Gandharva Tantra. In *Tantrasaṅgraha, Part III*.

Garrison, Omar V. *Tantra: The Yoga of Sex*. Madras: Ganesh & Co., 1978.

Gauḍapāda. *Śrī Subhagodayastuti*. In Appendix I of Awasthi, Shiva Shankara. *Mantra Aur Mātṛkāon kā Rahasya: Significance of Mantras and Mātṛkās According to Tāntrism*. In *Vidyabhawan Rastrabhasha Granthamala*, 95. Varanasi: Chowkhamba Vidyabhawan, 1966.

———. *Śrīvidyā Ratna Sūtrāni*. Varanasi: Krishnananda Sagar, 1985.

Gaurīkānta. *Ānandalaharī Tikā*. In *Saundaryalaharī* (Tiruchirapalli).

Gautama. *Gautamiyatantram of Maharshi Gautama*. Edited by Bhagiratha Jha. Introduction by Shesharaja Sharma Regmi. In *Krishnadas Prachyavidya Granthamala*, 5. Varanasi: Chowkhamba Sanskrit Series Office, 1977.

Goudriaan, Teun. "Hindu Tantric Literature in Sanskrit." In Goudriaan, Teun; and Gupta, Sanjukta. *Hindu Tantric and Śākta Literature*. In *A History of Indian Literature*, vol. 2: *Epics and Sanskrit Religious Literature*, pt. 1. Edited by Jan Gonda. Wiesbaden: Otto Harrassowitz, 1981.

———. "Introduction, History and Philosophy." In Gupta, Sanjukta; Hoens, Dirk Jan; and Goudriaan, Teun. *Hindu Tantrism*. In *Handbuch der Orientalistik*. Edited by Jan Gonda. Leiden: E. J. Brill, 1979.

Gupta, Sanjukta. "Modes of Worship and Meditation." In Gupta, Sanjukta,; Hoens, Dirk Jan; and Goudriaan, Teun. *Hindu Tantrism*. In *Handbuch der Orientalistik*. Edited by Jan Gonda. Leiden: E. J. Brill, 1979.

Hariharananda. *Shrividya-Ratnakarah with Shrisaparya-Mantrabhashya-Wanchhakalpalata-Laksharchana and Allied Subjects*. Edited by Sitaram Kaviraj. Calcutta: Bhaktisudha Sahitya Parishad, 2029 Vikrama Saṃvat, n.d.

Jayaratha. *Viveka*. Commentary on *Tantrāloka*. In *The*

Tantrāloka of Abhinavagupta with the Commentary of Rājānaka Jayaratha. Allahabad: Luzon & Co., 1981.

Jhā, Gaṅgānātha. *The Prābhākara School of Pūrva Mīmāmsā.* Allahabad: n.p., 1911; reprint ed., Delhi: Motilal Banarsidass, 1978.

Kaivalyāśrama. *Saubhāgyavardhanī.* Commentary on the *Saundaryalaharī.* In *Saundaryalaharī* (Tiruchirapalli).

Kālidāsa. *Ambāstuti.* In Appendix I of Awasthi, *Mantra Aur Mātṛkāon kā Rahasya.*

———. *Carcāstuti.* In Appendix I of Awasthi, *Mantra Aur Mātṛkāon kā Rahasya.*

———. *Laghustuti.* In Appendix I of Awasthi, *Mantra Aur Mātṛkāon kā Rahasya.*

———. *Pañcastavī.* In Appendix I of Awasthi, *Mantra Aur Mātṛkāon kā Rahasya.*

———. *Sakalajananīstava.* In Appendix I of Awasthi, *Mantra Aur Mātṛkāon kā Rahasya.*

Kāmadhenu Tantra. In *Tantrasaṅgraha, Part II: Nirvāṇatantra, Todalatantra, Kāmadhenu Tantra, Phetkārinītantra, Jñānasankalinitantra & Devīkalottarāgama with Commentary of Niranjana Siddha.* Edited by Gopinatha Kaviraja. In *Yogatantra-Granthamālā*, vol 4. Edited by Badarinath Shukla. Varanasi: Varanaseya Sanskrit Vishvavidyalaya, 1970.

Kāmeśvarasūri. *Aruṇāmodinī.* In *Saundaryalaharī* (Tiruchirapalli).

Kaviraj, Gopinath. *Aspects of Indian Thought.* Burdwan: University of Burdwan, [1966].

———. *Bhāratīya Saṃskṛti Aura Sādhanā*, 2 vols. 2d ed. of vol. 1. Patna: Bihāra-Rāṣṭrabhāṣā-Pariṣad, 1964.

———. *Tāntrika Sāhitya: Vivaraṇātmaka Granthasūcī.* Hindī Samiti Granthamālā, 200. Lucknow: Rājarṣi Puruṣottama Dāsa Ṭaṇḍana Hindī Bhavana, 1972.

———. *Tāntrika Vāṅmaya Meṃ Śāktadṛṣṭi.* Patna: Bihāra-Rāṣṭrabhāṣā-Pariṣad, 1963.

Kena Upaniṣad. In *Upaniṣat-Saṁgrahaḥ.*

[Kṣemarāja]. *Pratyabhijñāhṛdaya.* 2d. rev. ed. Translation, notes and introduction by Jaideva Singh. Delhi: Motilal Banarsidass, 1977.

———. *Uddyota.* Commentary on *Netra Tantra.* In *Netra Tantram.*

———. *Uddyota.* Commentary on *Swacchanda Tantra.* In *Swacchanda-Tantra.*

Kumar, Pushpendra. *Śakti Cult in Ancient India: With Special Reference to the Purānic Literature.* Varanasi: Bhartiya Publishing House, 1974.

Lakśmaṇadeśikendra. *The Śārdātilakam by Lakśmaṇadeśikendra with the Padārthādarśa Commentary by Raghavabhaṭṭa.* Edited with introduction by Mukunda Jha Bakshi. In *Kashi Sanskrit Granthamala,* 107. Tantra Śāstra Section, no. 1. Varanasi: Chowkhamba Sanskrit Series Office, 1963.

Lakṣmīdhara. *Lakṣmīdharā: The Commentary on the Saundaryalaharī.* In *Saundaryalaharī* (Mysore).

Lakṣmī-Tantra: A Pāñcarātra Āgama. Editing and introduction by V. Krishnamacharya. Adyar: Adyar Library and Research Centre, 1959.

Lakṣmī Tantra: A Pāñcarātra Text. Translation and notes by Sanjukta Gupta. Orientalia Rheno-Traiectina, vol. 60. Edited by J. Gonda and H. W. Obbink. Leiden: E. J. Brill, 1972.

Lalitā-Sahasranāman with Bhāskararāya's Commentary. Translated by R. Ananthakrishna Sastry. Adyar: The Theosophical Publishing House, 1951.

"Lalitopākhyāna." In *Brahmāṇḍa Purāṇa of Sage Kṛṣṇa Dvaipāyana Vyāsa,* ed. J. L. Shastri. Delhi: Motilal Banarsidass, 1973.

Larson, Gerald James. "The Sources for Śakti in Abhinavagupta's Kashmir Śaivism: A Linguistic and Aesthetic Category." In *Philosophy East/West* 24 (January 1974): 41-55.

MacDonell, A. A. *Vedic Mythology.* Strassburg: n.p., 1898;

reprint ed., Delhi: Motilal Banarsidass, 1974.

Mahānārāyana Upaniṣad. In *Upaniṣat-Saṁgrahaḥ.*

Maitreyī Upaniṣad. In *Upaniṣat-Saṁgrahaḥ.*

Malinīvijaya Vārttika of Abhinava Gupta. Edited by Pandit Madhusudan Kaul Shastri. Srinagar: Luzac & Co, 1921.

Mammaṭa. *The Poetic Light: Kāvyaprakāśa of Mammaṭa: Text with Translation and Sampradāyaprakāśinī of Śrīvidyācakravartin,* vol. 1. 2d. rev. ed. Translated by R. C. Dwivedi. Delhi: Motilal Banarsidass, 1977.

Mishra, Kamalakar. *Significance of the Tantric Tradition.* Varanasi: Arddhanārīśvara Publications, 1981.

Miśra, Kailāśa Pati. *Kāśmīra Śaiva Darśana: Mūla Siddhānta.* Varanasi: Arddhanārīśvara Prakāśana, 1982.

Moffet, Robert K. *Tantric Sex.* New York: Berkeley Publishing Corp., 1974.

Monier-Williams, Monier. *Sanskṛit-English Dictionary: Etymologically and Philologically Arranged with Special Reference to Cognate Indo-European Languages.* new enl. ed. Oxford: Clarendon Press, 1899; reprint ed., Delhi: Munshiram Manoharlal Publishers, 1981. S.v. "samayā" and "samaya."

Mūla-Yajurveda Saṃhitā. Edited by Siddheśvara Bhaṭṭācārya. Banaras Hindu University Sanskrit Series, vol. 8. Varanasi: Banaras Hindu University, 1973.

Muller-Ortega, Paul Eduardo. *The Triadic Heart of Śiva: Kaula Tantricism of Abhinavagupta in the Non-Dual Shaivism of Kashmir.* Albany: State University of New York Press, 1989.

Muṇḍamālā Tantra. In *Tantrasaṅgraha, Part III.*

Narasiṃhasvāmin. *Gopālasundarī* in *Saundaryalaharī* (Tiruchirapalli).

Natanānanda. *Cidvallī.* Commentary on *Kāmakalāvilāsa.* In [Puṇyānandanātha] *Kāmakalā-Vilasa with the Commentary of Natanānandanātha.* Edited by Sadāshiva Mishra. Translated by Arthur Avalon. In *Tantrik Texts,* vol. 10.

Edited by Arthur Avalon. Calcutta: Āgamānusandhāna Samiti Sanskrit Press Depository, 1922.

Netra Tantram with Commentary by Kshemarāja. Edited by Madhusudan Kaul Shāstrī. Kashmir Series of Texts and Studies, no. 46. Bombay: Tatva Vivechaka Press, 1926.

Nirvana Tantra. In *Tantrasangraha, Part II*.

Nityāṣodaśikārṇava with Two Commentaries: Ṛjuvimarśinī by Śīvānanda & Artharatnāvalī by Vidyānanda. Edited by Vrajavallabha Dviveda. In *Yoga-Tantra-Granthamālā*, vol. 1. Edited by Baladeva Upādhyāya. Varanasi: Varanaseya Sanskrit Vishvavidyalaya, 1968.

Padārthacandrikā. Commentary on the *Saundaryalaharī*. In *Saundaryalaharī* (Tiruchirapalli).

Padoux, André. *Vāc: The Concept of the Word in Selected Hindu Tantras*. Translated by Jacques Gontier. Albany: State University of New York Press, 1990.

Pañcastavī. In Appendix I of Awasthi, *Mantra Aur Mātṛkāon kā Rahasya*.

Pandey, Kanti Chandra. *Abhinavagupta: An Historical and Philosophical Study*. 2d ed., rev. & enl. Chowkhamba Sanskrit Studies, vol. 1. Varanasi: Chowkhamba Sanskrit Series Office, 1963.

Pandey, Sangam Lal. *Bhāratīya Darśana kā Sarvekṣaṇa*. Allahabad: Central Book Depot, 1981.

Pandit, B[alajin] N[ath]. *Śrī Kāśmīra Śaiva Darśana*. Jammu: Shri Ranbir Kendriya Sanskrit Vidyapitha, 1973.

Payne, Ernest A. *The Śāktas: An Introductory and Comparative Study*. New York: Garland Publishing Inc., 1979.

Potter, Karl H. comp. *Bibliography of Indian Philosophies*. American Institute of Indian Studies. Delhi: Motilal Banarsidass, 1970.

"Prādhānika Rahasya." In *Durgā Saptaśatī*. Gorakh Pur: Gita Press, n.d.

[Puṇyānanda.] *Kāmakalā-Vilasa with the Commentary of Natanānandanātha*. Edited by Sadāshiva Mishra. Translated by Arthur Avalon. In *Tantrik Texts*, vol. 10. Edited by Arthur Avalon. Calcutta: Āgamānusandhāna Samiti Sanskrit Press Depository, 1922.

Raghavan, V. *Abhinavagupta and His Works.* Varanasi: n.p., 1980.

Rāmakavi. *ḍiṇḍima Bhāṣya.* Commentary on the *Saundaryalaharī.* In *Saundaryalaharī* (Tiruchirapalli).

Rig-Veda-Samhitā: The Sacred Hymns of the Brāhmans Together with the Commentary of Sāyaṇāchārya. 4 vols. Edited by F. Max Muller. Varanasi: Chowkhamba Sanskrit Series Office, 1966.

Rudrayāmalaṃ. Edited by Yogatantra Department. In *Yogatantra-Granthamālā,* vol. 7. Edited by Bhāgīratha Prasāda Tripaṭhī. Varanasi: Sampurnananda Sanskrit Vishvavidyalaya, 1980.

Śaktisaṅgama Tantra. Edited by Rama Datta Shukla. Prayag: Kalyan Mandir Press, n.d.

Sāmbapañcāśikā. In *Tantrasaṅgraha, Part I.*

[Śaṅkarācārya?] *Saundarya-Laharī kā Hindī Anuvāda.* 3rd. ed. Translation and commentary by Viṣṇutīrtha. Rishikesh: Yogaśrī Pīṭha, 1970.

———. *Saundarya-Laharī (The Ocean of Beauty) of Śrī Śaṃkara-Bhagavatpāda.* 3rd. ed. Translation and commentary by S. Subrahmanya Sastri and T. R. Srinivasa Ayyangar. Adyar: Theosophical Publishing House, 1965.

———. *Saundarya-Laharī of Śrī Śaṃkarācārya with Commentaries: Saubhāgyavardhanī of Kaivalyāśrama, Lakṣmīdharā of Lakṣmīdharācārya, Aruṇāmodinī of Kamesvarasūrin.* Foreword by G. P. Ramaswami Aiyar. Translation and notes by R. Anantakṛṣṇa Śāstri and Karrā Rāmamūrthy Gāru. Madras: Ganesh & Co., 1957.

———. *Saundaryalaharī of Śrī Śaṅkara Bhagavatpādācārya with Commentaries (in Sanskrit): Lakṣmīdharā, Saubhāgyavardhanī, Aruṇāmodinī, Ānandagirīyā, Tātparyadīpinī, Padārthacandrikā, ḍiṇḍima Bhāṣya, Gopālasundarī and Ānandalaharī Tīkā.* Edited by A. Kuppuswami. Published with financial assistance from the Ministry of Education and Social Welfare, Govt. of India. Tiruchirapalli: A. Kuppuswami, 1976.

———. *Saundaryalaharī of Śrī Śaṅkarācārya with the Commentary of Lakṣmīdhara: Bhāvanopaniṣat with the Commentary of Bhāskararāya and Devī Pañcastavi.* 4th rev. ed. Critically edited by N. S. Venkatanathacharya. Oriental Research Institute Series, 114. Mysore: Oriental Research Institute, 1969.

———. *The Saundaryalaharī or Flood of Beauty: Traditionally Ascribed to Śaṅkarācārya.* Translated, edited, and presented in photographs by W. Norman Brown. Cambridge: Harvard University Press, 1958.

Sarasvatīrahasya Upaniṣad. In *Upaniṣat-Saṁgrahaḥ.*

Saraswathi, Gīrvāṇendra. *Prapañcha Sārasāra Saṅgraḥa of Gīrvāṇendra Saraswathi,* Part 1. Edited by K. S. Subramania Sastry. Tanjore Sarasvati Mahal Series, no. 98. Tanjore: Shri S. Gopalan, 1962.

Śarman, Acyutānanda. *Ānandalaharī Ṭīkā (Vyākhyā).* Microfilm, VT 396(c). India Office Library, London. Calcutta: n.p., 1885.

Sastri, Gaurinath. *The Philosophy of Word and Meaning: Some Indian Approaches with Special Reference to the Philosophy of Bhartṛhari.* Calcutta Sanskrit College Research Series, no. 5, Studies, no. 2. Calcutta: Sanskrit College, 1959.

Shankaranarayan, S. *The Ten Great Cosmic Powers: Daśa Mahāvidyās.* 2d ed. Pondicherry: Dipti Publications, 1975.

Sharma, Motilal. "Daśa Mahāvidyā." In *Kalyāṇa: Śakti Aṅka.* Gorakh Pur: Gita Press, Saṃvat, 1991.

Siṃha, Rājdeva Nandana. *Śākta Pramoda.* Bombay: Khemarāja Śrīkṛṣṇadāsa, Śrī Veṅkaṭeśvara Steam Press, 1973.

Singh, Jaideva. *Abhinavagupta: A Trident of Wisdom.* Albany: State University of New York Press, 1989.

———. *Pratyabhijñāhṛdayam*. Delhi: Motilal Banarsidass, 1963.

———. *Śiva Sūtras*. Delhi: Motilal Banarsidass, 1979.

———. *Spanda Kārikās*. Delhi: Motilal Banarsidass, 1980.

Sinha, Jadunath. *Shakta Monism: The Cult of Shakti*. Calcutta: Sinha Publishing House, 1966.

Sircar, D. C. *The Śākta Pīṭhas*. 2d rev. ed. Delhi: Motilal Banarsidass, 1973.

Śiva Sūtras: The Yoga of Supreme Identity: Text of the Sūtras and the Commentary Vimarśinī by Kṣemarāja. Translated with introduction and notes by Jaideva Singh. Delhi: Motilal Banarsidass, 1979.

Śīvānanda. *Ṛjuvimarśinī*. Commentary on *Nityāṣoḍaśikārṇava*. In *Nityāṣodaśikārṇava*.

———. *Saubhāgyahṛdayastotra*. In the Appendix of *Nityāṣodaśikārṇava*.

——— *Subhagodaya*. In the Appendix of *Nityāṣodaśikārṇava*.

———. *Subhagodayavāsanā*. In the Appendix of *Nityāṣodaśikārṇava*.

Śrīmaddevībhāgavatam Mahāpurāṇa. Edited by Rāmatej Pāṇḍeyena. Kashi: Paṇḍit-Pustakālaya, n.d.

Śrīvidyācakravartin. *Sampradāyaprakāśinī*. In *The Poetic Light: Kāvyaprakāśa of Mammaṭa*.

Subhagodaya. In the Appendix of *Nityāṣodaśikārṇava*.

Subhagodayavāsanā. In the Appendix of *Nityāṣodaśikārṇava*.

Śvetāśvatara Upaniṣad. In *Upaniṣat-Saṁgrahaḥ*.

Swacchanda-Tantra with Commentary by Kshemarāja. Edited with notes by Madhusudan Kaul Shāstrī. Kashmir Series of Texts and Studies, no. 31. Bombay: Nirnaya-Sagar Press, 1921.

Taittirīya Upaniṣad. In *Upaniṣat-Saṁgrahaḥ*.

The Tantrāloka of Abhinavagupta with the Commentary of

Rājānaka Jayaratha. Allahabad: Luzon & Co., 1981.

Tantrarāja Tantra: A Short Analysis. Translated by John Woodroffe. Preface by Shuddhānanda Bhārati. 3rd. ed. Madras: Ganesh & Co., 1971.

Tantrasaṅgraha, Part I: Virūpākṣapañcāśikā, Sambapāñcāśikā, & Tripurāmahimnastotra with Commentaries, Spandapradīpikā, Anubhavasūtra & Vātulaśuddhākhyatantra. Edited by Gopinatha Kaviraja. In *Yogatantra-Granthamālā*, vol. 3. Edited by Badarinath Shukla. Varanasi: Varanaseya Sanskrit Vishvavidyalaya, 1970.

Tantrasangraha, Part II: Nirvanatantra, Todalatantra, Kamadhenu Tantra, Fetkarinitantra, Jnanasankalinitantra & Devikalottarāgama with Commentary of Niranjana Siddha. Edited by Gopinatha Kaviraja. In *Yogatantra-Granthamala*, vol 4. Edited by Badarinath Shukla. Varanasi: Varanaseya Sanskrit Vishvavidyalaya, 1970.

Tantrasaṅgraha, Part III. Edited by Rāmaprasāda Tripāṭhī. In *Yogatantra-Granthamālā*, vol. 6. Edited by Bhāgīratha Prasāda Tripathī. Varanasi: Sampurnanand Sanskrit Vishvavidyalaya, 1979.

Tarkālaṅkāra, Jagadīśa. *Ānandalaharīvyākhyā*. India Office Library, London. Sanskrit MS 2623 ff.58, Eggling 2623: I:O: 659, n.d.

Todalatantra. In *Tantrasangraha, Part II*.

Tripurāmahimnastotra with Commentaries. In *Tantrasangraha, Part II*.

Tṛpurā Rahasya (Jñāna-Khaṅda): Edited with the 'Jñānaprabhā' Hindi Commentary. Edited by Sanātanadeva. Kashi Sanskrit Series, 176. Varanasi: Chowkhamba Sanskrit Series Office, 1967.

Tripurā Rahasya: Māhātmya Khandam, with Hindi Translation. Gurumandal Series, no. 28. Calcutta: Gurumandal Granthamala, 1970.

Tripurā Upaniṣad. In *Upaniṣat-Saṁgrahaḥ*.

Ui, H[akuju]. *Vaiśeṣika Philosophy According to the Daśapadārtha-Śāstra: Chinese Text with Introduction, Translation and Notes.* 2d ed. Edited by F. W. Thomas. Chowkhamba Sanskrit Series, vol. 22. Varanasi: Chowkhamba Sanskrit Series Office, 1962.

Upādhyāya, Baladeva. *Bhāratīya Darśana: An Authentic and Comprehensive Exposition of the Doctrines of the Different Schools of the Indian Philosophy—Vedic and Tāntric.* 2d ed. Foreword by Gopīnātha Kavirāja. Varanasi: Chaukhambha Orientalia, 1979.

———. *Bhāratīya Dharma Aur Darshana: An Authoritative Treatise on the Fundamentals of Indian Religion, Philosophy and Culture.* Varanasi: Chaukhambha Orientalia, 1977.

Upaniṣat-Saṁgrahaḥ: Containing 188 Upaniṣads. Edited with Sanskrit introduction by J. L. Shastri. Delhi: Motilal Banarsidass, 1970.

Vaidya, Mādhava. *Tātparyadīpinī.* Commentary on the *Saundaryalaharī.* In *Saundaryalaharī* (Tiruchirapalli).

Vātulaśuddhākhya Tantra. In *Tantrasaṅgraha, Part I.*

Vidyānanda. *Artharatnāvalī.* Commentary on *Nityāṣoḍaśikārṇava.* In *Nityāṣodaśikārṇava.*

Vidyāraṇya. *Śrīvidyārṇava Tantra.* Edited by Bhadrashil Sharma. Prayag: Kalyāṇa Mandir Press, 2023 Vikrama Saṃvat.

Virūpākṣapañcāśikā. In *Tantrasaṅgraha, Part I.*

Woodroffe, John. *Principles of Tantra: The Tantra-Tattva of Śrīyukta Śiva Candra Vidyārṇava Bhattacārya Mahodaya*, part 1. 5th ed. Madras: Ganesh & Co., 1978.

———. *Tantrarāja Tantra: A Short Analysis.* Preface by Shuddhānanda Bhārati. 3rd. ed. Madras: Ganesh & Co., 1971.

Yogakuṇḍalī Upaniṣad. In *Upaniṣat-Saṁgrahaḥ.*

Yoginī Hṛdaya with Commentaries: Dīpikā of Amṛtānanda and Setubandha of Bhāskara Rāya. 2d ed. In *Sarasvatī Bhavana Granthamālā*, vol. 7. Edited by Kshetresachandra Chattopadhyaya. Varanasi: Varanaseya Sanskrit Vishvavidyalaya, 1963.

About the Author

Pandit Rajmani Tigunait, Ph.D., is a disciple of Sri Swami Rama. Since 1980 he has been the spiritual director of the Himalayan International Institute, which his master founded in 1971. He is a scholar of Sanskrit and the ancient scriptures. A specialist in Vedic and tantric studies, Pandit Tigunait holds two Ph.D.'s, one from the University of Allahbad in India and the other from the University of Pennsylvania in the United States.

In addition to studying and practicing under the guidance of Swami Rama, he has been teaching meditation and spirituality in the U.S. and abroad for the past two decades. Pandit Tigunait is a regular contributor to *Yoga International* magazine and is the author of *Swami Rama of the Himalayas: His Life and Mission; From Death to Birth: Understanding Karma and Reincarnation; The Power of Mantra and the Myster of Initiation; Inner Quest: The Path of Spiritual Unfoldment; Śakti Sādhanā: Steps to Samādhi; The Tradition of the Himalayan Masters; Yoga on War and Peace;* and *Seven Systems of Indian Philosophy.*

Main building of the international headquarters, Honesdale, Pa., USA

The Himalayan Institute

FOUNDED IN 1971 BY SWAMI RAMA, the Himalayan Institute has been dedicated to helping people grow physically, mentally, and spiritually by combining the best knowledge of both the East and the West. Institute programs emphasize holistic health, yoga, and meditation, but the Institute is much more than its programs.

Our international headquarters is located on a beautiful 400-acre campus in the rolling hills of the Pocono Mountains of northeastern Pennsylvania. The atmosphere here is one to foster growth, increased inner awareness, and calm. Our grounds provide a wonderfully peaceful and healthy setting for our seminars and extended programs. Students from around the world join us here to attend programs in such diverse areas as hatha yoga, meditation, stress reduction, Ayurveda, nutrition, Eastern philosophy, psychology, and other subjects. Whether the programs are for weekend meditation retreats, week-long seminars on spirituality, months-long residential programs, or holistic health services, the attempt here is to provide an environment of gentle inner progress. We invite you to join with us in the ongoing process of personal growth and development.

The Institute is a nonprofit organization. Your membership in the Institute helps to support its programs. Please call or write for information on becoming a member.

Institute Programs, Services, and Facilities

All Institute programs share an emphasis on conscious holistic living and personal self-development. You may enjoy any of a number of diverse programs, including:

- Special weekend or extended seminars to learn skills and techniques for increasing your ability to be healthy and enjoy life
- Meditation retreats and advanced meditation and philosophical instruction
- Vegetarian cooking and nutritional training
- Hatha yoga and exercise workshops
- Residential programs for self-development
- The Institute's Center for Health and Healing, which offers holistic health services and Ayurvedic Rejuvenation Programs.

The Institute publishes a *Quarterly Guide to Programs and Other Offerings,* which is free within the USA. To request a copy, or for further information, call 800-822-4547 or 717-253-5551, fax 717-253-9078, email bqinfo@himalayan-institute.org, or write the Himalayan Institute, RR 1 Box 400, Honesdale, PA 18431-9706 USA.

Visit our Web site at www.himalayaninstitute.org.

The main building of the hospital, outside Dehra Dun

The Himalayan Institute Charitable Hospital

A major aspect of the Institute's work around the world is its support of a comprehensive Medical City in the Garhwal region of the foothills of the Himalayas. A bold vision to bring medical services to millions of people (most of whom are poor) who have little or no healthcare in northern India began modestly in 1989 with an outpatient program in Uttar Pradesh.

Today that vision has grown to include a large state-of-the-art hospital located between Dehra Dun and Rishikesh; a Medical College and nursing school; a combined therapy program that joins the best of modern medicine with the time-tested wisdom of traditional methods of healthcare; a rural development program that has adopted more than 150 villages; and housing facilities for staff, students, and patients' families.

The project was conceived, designed, and led by Swami Rama, who was a native of this part of India. He always envisioned joining the best knowledge of the East and West. And that is what is occurring at this medical facility, 125 miles north of New Delhi.

Guided by the Himalayan Institute Hospital Trust, the hospital, medical city, and rural development program are considered models of healthcare for the whole of India and for medically underserved people worldwide.

Construction, expansion, and the fund-raising necessary to accomplish it all continue. The hospital is now one of the best-equipped in India, and attention is turning to building primary and secondary satellite health centers throughout the mountainous regions where travel is difficult, especially for those in need of immediate medical attention. Future plans include a college of dentistry, a college of pharmacy, and research facilities to study Ayurveda, homeopathy, and yoga therapies.

We welcome donations to help with this and other projects. If you would like further information, please call our international headquarters in Honesdale, PA at 800-822-4547 or 717-253-5551, email bmcinfo@himalayaninstitute.org, fax 717-253-9078, or write RR 1 Box 400, Honesdale, PA 18431-9706 USA.

The Himalayan Institute Press

The Himalayan Institute Press has long been regarded as "The Resource for Holistic Living." We publish dozens of titles, as well as audio and video tapes, that offer practical methods for harmonious living and inner balance. Our approach addresses the whole person—body, mind, and spirit—integrating the latest scientific knowledge with ancient healing and self-development techniques.

As such, we offer a wide array of titles on physical and psychological health and well-being, spiritual growth through meditation and other yogic practices, and the means to stay inspired through reading sacred scriptures and ancient philosophical teachings.

Our sidelines include the Japa Kit for meditation practice, the original Neti™ Pot, the ideal tool for sinus and allergy sufferers, and the Breath Pillow,™ a unique tool for learning health-supportive breathing—the diaphragmatic breath.

Subscriptions are available to a bimonthly magazine, *Yoga International,* which offers thought-provoking articles on all aspects of meditation and yoga, including yoga's sister science, Ayurveda.

For a free catalog call 800-822-4547 or 717-253-5551, email hibooks@himalayaninstitute.org, fax 717-251-7812, or write the Himalayan Institute Press, RR 1 Box 405, Honesdale, PA 18431-9709, USA.

Visit our Web site at www.himalayaninstitute.org.